AF519444

Recent Trends in World Tourism

Edited by

Ramesh Chandra

AKANSHA PUBLISHING HOUSE
NEW DELHI - 110 002 (INDIA)

AKANSHA PUBLISHING HOUSE
4649/21-B, Ansari Road,
Daryaganj, New Delhi - 110 002
Phones: 23263193, 9811582579
E-mail: ektabooks@yahoo.com

Recent Trends in World Tourism

© Reserved

First Published, 2006
Reprint 2018
ISBN 81-8370-037-3

PRINTED IN INDIA

Published by M.P. Misra for Akansha Publishing House, New Delhi - 110 002 and Printed at Tarun Offset Press, Delhi

Contents

Preface

Though tourism can be ascribed to wanderlust of man since very beginning, it has emerged as an industry in modern times having vast potential contribution to national income. With the passage of time, 'Tourism' today is used as an important instrument for the economic and social development of a nation. The governments are even politically involved in tourism promotion and development, as it creates national integration and international understanding. It also generates huge employment opportunities and earns a lot of foreign currency.

Travel and tourism infrastructure requires an extensive investment of both public and private sectors to finance the preliminary planning, development stages and fixed assets. Due to the huge investments, travel and tourism industry is also known as 'capital-intensive industry.' Since, tourism is a capital intensive industry, it needs huge finance in comparison to other industries. Finance is required for various purposes viz., to establish a new tour company, construction of hotels, parks and so on. The supply of finance largely depends on the financing systems which vary from country to country depending on the level of tourism development and promotion. Obviously, tourism had to compete with other industries for loans from the financial institutions and tourism projects are not sound financially to raise finance from the open market.

To assess the recent trends in tourism, we have compiled here twelve articles, analysing relevant vital issues in pros and cons.

The future of World Tourism; Tourism and modern information techniques; Christian challenges to mass tourism in 21st century; Travel with a mission; Tourism promotion strategies; Management tools and techniques; Tourism in developing world; Community based E-tourism; Tourism: continuity and change; and World Tourism Organization etc. are the major themes given elaborate treatment in this book. Besides these, most vital information, glossary of relevant terms and an exhaustive reference bibliography are appended which are added features of this book.

The book is substantially devised on the information derived from secondary sources—e.g. books, reports, abstracts, monographs, journals, magazines, etc. there is no claim of originality. In fact, all credit ought go to the original contributors—learned scholars and seasoned professionals. The Editor owes a sense of indebtedness to all those great men of letters for drawing upon their views and works. Simultaneously, he is grateful to different libraries and personnel therein for making available the requisite material. Last but not the least, he is thankful to the publishers for bringing out the book superbly within very short period.

—***Editor***

1

The Future of World Tourism

> Nobody can really guarantee the future. The best we can do is size up the chances, calculate the risk involved, estimate our ability to deal with them, and then make our plans with confidence.
>
> —*Henry Ford II*

The World Tourism Organisation predicts 21st century tourism will be the antidote to high-tech living. WTO Secretary General Francesco Frangialli discusses their new report Tourism: 2020 Vision. The year 2020 will see the penetration of technology into all aspects of life. It will become possible to live one's days without exposure to other people, according to WTO's latest look into the future. But this bleak prognosis has a silver lining for the tourism sector. People in the high-tech future will crave the human touch and tourism will be the principal means to achieve this. Tourism companies that manage to provide "high-touch" products will prosper.

Upscale, luxury services that pamper and spoil their customers have a bright future in the upcoming century. But WTO's report also predicts good prospects for low-budget destinations and packages. Self-catering holiday facilities, for example, which offer plenty of opportunities for socializing among families and friends. Opportunities abound at both ends of the spectrum and there will be plenty of them.

As per prediction of WTO's study Tourism: 2020 Vision 1.5 billion tourists will be visiting foreign countries annually by the year 2020, spending more that US$2 trillion or US$5 billion every day. These forecasts represent nearly three times more international tourists than the 663 million recorded in 1999 and nearly five times more tourism spending, which last year topped US$ 453 billion. Tourist arrivals are predicted to grow by an average 4.3 per cent a year over the next two decades, while receipts from international tourism will climb by 6.7 per cent a year.

To factor in domestic tourism, WTO multiplies arrivals by 10 and quadruples receipts, which brings us to the grand totals of 16 billion tourists spending US$8 trillion in 2020.

Tourism in the 21st century will not only be the world's biggest industry, it will be the largest by far that the world has ever seen. Along with its phenomenal growthand size, the tourism industry will also have to take on more responsibility for its extensive impacts. Not only its economic impact, but also its impact on the environment, on societies and on cultural sites, all of which will be increasingly scrutinized by governments, consumer groups and the travelling public.

We hope that Tourism: 2020 Vision will be more than a useful marketing tool, that ft will act as a warning signal for destinations-helping them recognise the need to 'prepare for the pressures of growth. WTO is advising destinations to implement long-term, strategic planning and to strengthen the partnerships, both strategically and at the operational level, between the public and private sectors.

Tourism: 2020 Vision indicates that tourists of the 21st century will be travelling further afield on their holidays, often to China and even to outer space. The percentage of long-haul travel is predicted to increase from 18 per cent in 1995 to 24 per cent by 2020.

Tourism companies looking to cash in on this booming sector are advised to look towards Asia. China will be the world's number one destination by the year 2020 and it will also become the fourth most important generating market. Currently it does not even figure among the world's top twenty generating countries. Other destinations predicted to make great strides in the tourism industry are Russia, Hong Kong, Thailand, Singapore, Indonesia and South Africa.

Short pleasure voyages to outer space will become a reality by 2004 or 2005, according to the study carried out by WTO Statistics Chief Enzo Paci in consultation with 85 governments and 50 tourism visionaries.

It is expected space trips will last up to four days and cost on average US$100,000. NASA, the US space agency, has recently surveyed the travel industry for interest in space tourism and some US companies are already taking reservations and deposits from private citizens hoping to become the first tourists in outer space. But while some travellers may be suiting up for space voyages, the vast majority of the world's population will never leave their own countries, not even by the year 2020.

The study concludes that only 7 per cent of the world's population will be travelling internationally by the year 2020, up from 3.5 per cent in 1996-but still just the tip of the iceberg.

European Trends

"Tourism: 2020 Vision" predicts that Europe will remain by far the leading inbound tourism region as well as the main generator of international tourists. International arrivals in Europe will reach 717 million by 2020 ? more than twice as many as last year.

Overall, tourism to Europe is predicted to grow more slowly than the world average; at a rate of 3.1 per cent annually, though some countries will fare better than others. Central and Eastern European countries will become the new motor for Europe, feeding and being fed by other European and long-haul generating markets. Tourism to Central and Eastern Europe will grow by 4.8 per cent a year and the former Soviet Bloc countries will surpass 200 million arrivals by 2016-a doubling in just 15 years.

The Eastern Mediterranean countries of Cyprus, Turkey and Israel are also expected to show good growth of 4.6 per cent a year. Tourism to the United Kingdom is forecast to grow by 4 per cent annually, just under the world average. Reflecting world patterns and increasing air travel, Europeans will be taking trips more frequently and further from home. Total outbound travel from European countries is predicted to reach 771 million trips a year by 2010, again more than twice as many as last year.

Tourism Megatrends for the 21 Century

- Globalization versus Localization
- Electronic technology will become all powerful in influencing destination choice and distribution.
- Fast track travel—emphasis will be placed on facilitation and the speeding up of the travel process.
- Customers will "call the shots" through technology such as CD ROM atlases, Internet inspection of hotels and other facilities, brokers offering discounted rooms of Websites, last minute e-mail low fares, etc.
- Polarisation of tourist tastes: The comfort-based and the adventure-oriented.
- The tourist "shrinking world" more tourists to off-the-beaten track places and the advent of near space tourism.
- Destination as a "fashion accessory".
- Targeted product market development (especially

theme based) oriented to one or a combination of the three Es—entertainment, excitement and education.

— More destination focus on image as a requisite for diversification and expansion of drawing power.

— Everyone chasing the Asian tourist.

— Growing impact of consumer led campaigns for sustainable tourism development and "fair trade" in tourism.

— Conflict socio-environmental consciousness versus the urge for travel consumption.

Long-haul travel to countries outside of Europe will grow by 6.1 per cent a year in the upcoming decades to reach 15 per cent of all trips taken by Europeans or 115,600,000 departures. Long-haul currently accounts for 12 per cent of European outbound travel or about 42 million trips a year.

Since the typical European tourist who spends his holiday at the beach will be more frequently choosing Asian or Caribbean resorts. European beach destinations are advised to orientate their product development and marketing increasingly to new tourist sources, especially Japan, the newly industrialised countries of Asia and the Americas.

Mature European destinations will have continually to strive to seek product and market differentiation to avoid a tired or stale image in major generating markets.

While growth of the tourism industry will be unstoppable in the 21st century, increased benefits cannot be taken for granted. Competition among destinations will also become increasingly fierce.

The study Tourism: 2020 Vision outlines a series of 12 megatrends that will shape the sector and offers advice on how to better compete. No destination or tourism operator can afford to sit back and wait for more tourists to arrive. They have to be won and there will be winners and losers. To be a winner, there are a number of imperatives:

1. Development focused on quality and sustainability.
2. Value-for-money.
3. Full utilisation of information technology to identify and communicate effectively with market segments and niches.

Product development and marketing will need to match each other more closely, based on the main travel motivators of the 21st century. Tourism: 2020 vision calls these motivating factors the Three E's—Entertainment, Excitement and Education.

The study also highlights the importance of image in a tourists' selection of a holiday destination in the future. While an image of safety and security is already an important deciding factor for tourists, holiday makers of the 21st century will be looking for places with a trendy image.

As 2020 Vision points out, the next century will mark the emergence the tourism destinations as 'a fashion accessory'. The choice of holiday destination will help define the identity of the traveller and, in an increasingly homogeneous world, set him apart from the hordes of other tourists.

Boutique destinations and space agencies beware! You are on the threshold of meeting the 21st century tourist.

Tourism is the world's largest industry, with over 10 per cent of GDP globally directly related to tourism activities. Rising standards of living in the countries of the North, declining long-haul travel costs, increasing holiday entitlements, changing demographics and strong consumer demand for exotic international travel have resulted in significant tourism growth to developing countries. Tourism is the principal export for one third of developing countries. Tourism brings relatively powerful consumers to Southern countries, potentially an important market for local entrepreneurs and an engine for local sustainable economic development. There is no reliable data on domestic tourism but it is growing rapidly in South America and in China and South East Asia; it represents a very significant economic opportunity for many local communities.

Multilateral and bilateral aid agencies are wary of involving themselves in the tourism sector. In 1969 the World Bank created a Tourism Projects Department recognising that in the Mediterranean and Adriatic countries, and in Mexico, tourism had been a significant generator of foreign exchange and of direct and indirect employment. Internationally in the late nineteen sixties, there was considerable concern about high rates of unemployment and the ability of developing countries to service debt. Tourism sector studies were completed in some 31 countries and tourism staff regularly participated in World Bank macro-economic missions their reports focussed on the potential for growth in tax revenues, foreign exchange earnings and direct and indirect employment effects. The primary emphasis was on national economic impact. By 1978 when the World Bank closed its Tourism Projects Department the Bank had provided loans and credits for 18 projects in 14 countries and it was the major source of funds and technical assistance for tourism development. The Bank withdrew from tourism development for a range of reasons amongst which were anxieties about the role of the Bank in funding projects to develop luxury hotels designed to attract wealthy travellers from the developed countries. This strategy was seen as inconsistent with new policy objectives which prioritised the bottom 40 per cent, the Bank's priorities were shifting towards the poor, a group which was gaining relatively little from tourism development. There was a growing literature that focussed on the negative economic, social and cultural impacts of unmanaged tourism on local communities. The fuel crises of the nineteen seventies also undermined some of the forecasts that had been made for the strength of the market and the Bank withdrew from the sector in parallel with most other multilateral and bilateral agencies.

Tourism is the world's largest industry with an enormous potential for further growth. While the bulk of tourist arrivals are still in industrial states, developing countries are also increasingly sharing in the tourism boom. But do the poor in these countries also benefit? The international agencies followed a macro-economic tourism agenda in the nineteen seventies and eighties focussing on tax and foreign exchange revenues at the national level, major hotel and resort development, international promotion and national and regional master planning all attracted funding. In the nineties the adoption of the new poverty elimination target of halving the number of people living on less than 1 US$ per day by 2015 has refocused development assistance on pro-poor growth. Multilateral and bilateral aid agency agendas are shifting towards a microeconomic focus on local sustainable economic growth strategies which benefit local communities, and in particular those below the poverty threshold. With poverty elimination now at the heart of decision-making about international develop aid, the potential for using tourism to generate pro-poor economic growth is being reassessed.

Since the mid-1980s, interest in 'Green' tourism, ecotourism and community tourism has grown rapidly among tour operators, policymakers, advocates and researchers. All of these focus on the need to ensure that tourism does not erode the environmental and cultural base on which it depends. The emphasis has been on minimising social, cultural and environmental impacts;

rather than on positively affecting the livelihoods of the poor.

Potential of Pro-poor Tourism

There are a number of reasons to look again at tourism and to assess its potential to generate pro-poor growth. 80 per cent of the world's poor live in just 12 countries and tourism is significant or growing in all but one of them. Tourism is a very large sector, it is growing rapidly, and there is some evidence that it is relatively labour intensive. The consumer travels to the destination, creating additional-local-opportunities for the sale of additional goods and services ranging from local pottery to a guided walk. Tourism can be used to diversify local economies, it can often be developed in remote and marginal areas with few other diversification or export opportunities. These areas often attract tourists because of their high landscape, cultural and wildlife values. These natural resources and the local culture are amongst the few assets of the poor.

Pro-poor tourism generates net benefits for the poor. It can be defined as forms of tourism where the benefits to the poor are greater than costs which tourism brings them. Economic costs and benefits are clearly important, but social, environmental and cultural costs and benefits, also need to be taken into account. Pro-poor tourism aims to expand opportunities for those living on less than 1US$ per day. Whilst it will also need to be sustainable preserving local culture, minimising environmental impacts, it will be driven by the poverty agenda. Community-based tourism seeks to promote initiatives by local communities or individuals within them, much has been learnt from these projects. Maximising the poverty elimination effect requires that the emphasis is placed on involving those people who are living on less than 1US$ per day and creating economic opportunities for them. Not all community tourism is pro-poor in this sense.

Assessing the livelihood impacts of tourism is not simply a matter of counting jobs or wage income. Participatory poverty assessments demonstrate great variety in the priorities of the poor and factors affecting livelihood security and sustainability. Tourism can affect many of these, positively and negatively, often indirectly. It is important to assess these impacts and their distribution. Tourism can generate four different types of local cash income generally involving different categories of people:

- wages from formal employment;
- earnings from selling goods, services/or casual labour (e.g. food, crafts, building materials, guide services);
- and profits arising from locally-owned enterprises;
- income: this may include profits from a community run enterprise, dividends from a private sector partnership and land rental paid by an investor.

Waged employment can be sufficient to lift a household from insecure to secure. But it may only be available to a minority, and not to the poor. Casual earnings per person may be very small, but much more widely spread and may be enough, for instance, to cover school fees for one or more children. Work as a tourist guide, although casual, is often of high status and relatively well paid. There are relatively few examples of successful and sustainable collective income from tourism. Examples from Kenya, Namibia and Zimbabwe illustrate that it can match wage income in scale and that in principle it can benefit all residents, although it can be difficult to manage.

Negative economic impacts include inflation, dominance by outsiders in land markets and in-migration which erodes economic opportunities for the local poor. Impacts differ between men and women. Women can be the first to suffer from loss of natural resources (e.g. access to fuel-wood) and cultural/sexual exploitation, but may benefit most from physical infrastructure improvements (e.g. piped water or a grinding mill) where this is a by-product of tourism.

Tourism: Positive Development Impacts

On the positive side, tourism can generate funds for investment in health, education and other assets, provide infrastructure, stimulate development of social capital, strengthen sustainable management of natural resources, and create a demand for improved assets (especially education). On the negative side, tourism can reduce local access to natural resources, draw heavily upon local infrastructure, and disrupt social networks.

Tourism affects the livelihoods of the poor by changing their access to assets. In several cases, tourism's impact on people's access to natural resources or physical infrastructure has been identified as the most important benefit or concern. For example, the Ngwesi lodge in Kenya was developed by members of the Ngwesi group ranch (a registered group of around 500 pastoral households with collective tenure rights over their land). A recent participatory assessment of livelihood impacts revealed that impacts on natural capital, particularly grazing resources, and access to physical infrastructure are more important to most members than the nearly 50 new jobs. The wildlife/wilderness area around the lodge provides emergency drought grazing. The lodge's physical presence, radio, and vehicle help to keep others out and provide emergency access to a hospital, which was previously lacking.

However, there are more numerous examples where local residents lose access to local natural resources. A comparative study by Shah and Gupta provides a range of examples. On Boracay Island in the Philippines, one quarter of the island has been bought by outside corporations, generating a crisis in water supply and only limited infrastructure benefits for residents. Similarly in Ball,

Indonesia, prime agricultural land and water supplies have been diverted for large hotels and golf courses while at Pangandaran (Java, Indonesia) village beach land, traditionally used for grazing, repairing boats and nets, and festivals, was sold to entrepreneurs for a 5-star hotel.

Cultural Impacts of Tourism

Local residents often highlight the way tourism affects other livelihood goals whether positively or negatively- such as cultural pride, a sense of control, good health, and reduced vulnerability. Socio-cultural intrusion by tourists is often cited as a negative impact. Certainly sexual exploitation particularly affects the poorest women, girls and young men. The poor themselves may view other types of cultural change as positive. Tourism can also increase the value attributed to minority cultures by national policy-makers. Overall, the cultural impacts of tourism are hard to disentangle from wider processes of development.

The overall balance of positive and negative livelihood impacts will vary enormously between situations, among people and over time, and particularly in the extent to which local priorities are able to influence the planning process. The application of a 'sustainable livelihoods framework' is essential to developing pro-poor approaches. The distribution of livelihood impacts has to be considered. The poor are far from being a homogenous group. The positive and negative impacts of tourism will inevitably be distributed unevenly among poor groups, reflecting different patterns of assets, activities, opportunities and choices. The most substantial benefits, particularly jobs, may be concentrated among few. Net benefits are likely to be smallest, or negative, for the poorest. A recent review, by Shah & Gupta, of two dozen case studies in Asia indicates economic gains for all sections of the community, but with those already better off gaining most.

Despite innumerable case studies of tourism development, there is relatively little assessment of practical experience in strategies to make tourism more pro-poor. Nevertheless, lessons can be drawn from a wealth of small initiatives (many from 'community tourism' or 'conservation and development' programmes), supplemented by expanding knowledge on 'pro-poor growth strategies', several policy implications clearly emerge.

1. Put poverty issues on the tourism agenda

A first step is to recognise that enhancing the poverty impacts of tourism is different from commercial, environmental, or ethical concerns. PPT can be incorporated as an additional objective, but this requires pro-active and strategic intervention. There may well be trade-offs to make for example between attracting all-inclusive operators and maximising informal sector opportunities, or between faster growth through outside investment, and slower growth building on local capacity. These trade-offs need to be addressed.

2. Enhance economic opportunities and a wide range of impacts

Two approaches need to be combined:

- Expand poor people's economic participation by addressing the barriers they face, and maximising a wide range of employment, self-employment and informal sector opportunities;
- incorporate wider concerns of the poor into decision-making. Reducing competition for natural resources, minimising trade-offs with other livelihood activities, using tourism to create physical infrastructure that benefits the poor and addressing cultural disruption will often be particularly important.

3. A multi-level approach

Pro-poor interventions can and should be taken at three different levels:

- this is where pro-active practical partnerships can be developed between operators, residents, NGOs, and local authorities, to maximise benefits;
- national policy level—policy reform may be needed on a range of tourism issues (planning, licensing, training) and non-tourism issues (land tenure, business incentives, infrastructure, land-use planning);
- international level—to encourage responsible consumer and business behaviour, and to enhance commercial codes of conduct.

Fig. Traditional cloth design is blended with modern fashion styles in this tourist shop in Accra, Ghana. The sale of local textiles offers additional income to the poor.

4. Work through partnerships, including business and tourists

National and local governments, private enterprises, industry associations, NGOs, community organisations, consumers, and donors all have a role to play. It is particularly important to engage businesses, and to ensure that initiatives are commercially realistic and integrated into mainstream operations. Private operators will not be able to devote substantial time and resources to developing pro-poor actions. NGOs and donors can help in reducing the transaction costs of changing commercial practice-for example, facilitating the training, organisation, and communication that would enable businesses to use more local suppliers. Changing the attitudes of tourists (at both international and national levels) is also essential if pro-poor tourism is to be commercially viable and sustainable.

5. *Incorporate pro-poor tourism approaches into mainstream tourism*

Pro-poor tourism should not just be pursued in niche markets (such as eco-tourism or community tourism). It is even more important that mass tourism is developed in ways that benefit the poor. It is also important to assess which tourism segments are particularly relevant to the poor. Domestic tourists are likely to be important customers.

6. *Reform decision-making systems*

It is impossible to prescribe exactly how each tourism enterprise should develop in ways that best fit with livelihoods. The most important principle is to enhance the participation of the poor. Three different ways of doing this can be identified:

- Strengthen rights at local level (e.g. tenure over tourism assets), so that local people have market power and make their own decisions over developments.
- Develop more participatory planning.
- Use planning gain and other incentives to encourage private investors to enhance local benefits. These approaches require implementation capacity among governmental and nongovernmental institutions within the destination, and require a supportive national policy framework.

It is time to reconsider the role of tourism in contributing to pro-poor development. Tourism should be judged against other possible strategies and where it offers the best opportunities for pro-poor growth, or where it can make a useful contribution by increasing the diversity of opportunities for the poor, tourism it should be considered. However, careful and effective local management will be essential if it is to contribute to meeting poverty targets and if tourism dependency is to be avoided.

2

Tourism and Modern Information Techniques

> Don't keep forever on the public road, going only where other have gone. Leave the beaten path occasionally and dive into the woods. You will be certain to find something you have never seen before. It will be a little thing but do not ignore it. Follow it up, explore around it, one discovery will lead to another and before you know it, you will have something really worth thinking about.
>
> —*Alexander Graham Bell.*

"In many ways and for many purposes, printed matter-books, newspapers and wallpapers will always be the best and the cheapest form of communication. But now electronics has given us tools that can perform miracles impossible to the printed word and which, of course, can reach millions who are unable to read. The newest and most powerful of these communication devices depend upon pace technology, a fact that is not generally recognised." What Arthur C. Clarke had said almost two and half decades ago may seem to be a history as so much has been done in so little a time that one really wonders about the various changes that have taken place since then. In fact there has been a revolution in the various techniques in the field of information. The electronics have performed miracles in the last decade.

Today we find ourselves in the middle of a new era, an

era of information revolution. New techniques of data processings, mainly transmission of data and telecommunication, have already formed a new field of activity characterised by an enormous potential for growth. These developments have greatly facilitated rational management of the business world. Telecommunication devices are in use today in almost all fields of economy. Be it in industry, agriculture, medicine, travel or any other field these telecommunication devices are extensively used for the benefit of both the industry as well as the consumer. In this information revolution the new means of public telecommunication such as telex, telecopy or videotex have given a very tough competition to pioneer public communication means like newspapers, magazines, etc. At the same time, however, the new communication-means also offer great possibilities for improvement, rationalisation and the expansion of the existing facilities for data collection and transmission.

New Information Techniques

The modern mass media techniques are as follows:

- Satellite Television
- Cable Television
- Videotex (in the framework of transmissions from individual television stations)

Since the above means ate very widespread ad they are very important. However, because of their wider coverage and their technical methods of transmission, they have one shortcoming. The short coming is that they cannot be directed to one specific person. In addition the person receiving the information is only partially informed. The receiver of the information also cannot start a dialogue or communicate. On the other hand, unlike the mass media, the following means give the possibility of direct transmission of information:

(a) Telecopy

Telecopy provides the possibility of exchanging photocopies through a data network. Information in the form of either written document or technical drawing is remote copied. This means that two facilities for copying are connected. One at the sender's end and the other at the receiver's end. Transmission time is only a few minutes.

(b) Videotex

Videotex occupies a special Position among the "new media". It plays a key role in the link between telecommunication and the computer sciences. It's advantages lie in the possibility it provides for linking computers, and also in its interactive dialogue capabilities. Using videotex, information and communication systems can be converted into interactive systems capable of communicating with one another. In fact, videotex is a multipurpose instrument with multiplicity of uses.

(c) Teletex

Teletex is an improvement over telex and has in fact developed from it The receiver for teletex is an electronic "typewriter, which can send electronically enriched "letters" to owners of Ordinary telex equipment. The transmission of message time is usually shorter in comparison with time taken with telex. Besides, it is also possible to transmit more office typewriter symbols. A normal electronic typewriter can be used as a receiver for teletex.

It serves as:

(i) an instrument for data processing
(ii) an information medium
(iii) an organisational aid
(iv) a communication system, and
(v) a marketing instrument.

This relatively new service connects various forms of use of the above-mentioned facilities and at the same time offers some other possibilities. To operate the service, a television set with a decoder and telephone is necessary without which the service cannot operate. In Europe, nearly all the households have television sets and a telephone and with the help of videotex. Separate households can be reached in large areas. Members of German BTX service as well as Members of France Telecom Service can now obtain all kinds of information from external computers or use data bank all through their television sets. In many other countries in Europe, USA, etc., similar systems are in use. The use of videotex (VTX) is prevalent today in many fields. In addition to its use in the field of business because it allows fast message transmission, fast and inexpensive data collection and up-to-date information which are crucial for advertising, the system is also used by specialised groups of users for collecting orders in the field. It is also used in the field of tourism as a one-way system, for receiving bookings. Because of its low unit costs, it is used extensively mainly in connection with personal computers. It has been found that videotex (VTX) is the most advantageous means of communication, taking into account its low cost and the wider range of its application.

(d) Telefax

Infact, Telebox is an electronic post office box system. Each member of the system has his or her "post office box" in the computer, where other members can leave their message. The owner of each box can electronically contact the others. All the above means discussed permit the exchange of information electronically through a data "network". The exchange of information between the members with the assistance of electronic transmission is very fast. The data are also available in written form in printouts. "Network" is a system of transmission linking facilities for automatic data processing. In this way different computers are connected, permitting data exchange and processing over long distances. Telecommunication is possible only when there is such a network available. Telephone is the simplest and the best known network. In addition there is also a separate clear data network for the exchange of data which works digitally. In this way a high transmission speed is achieved and there is a very low ratio of errors during transmission. There are different types of networks which can be used for telecommunication purposes either separately or combined. Text on the screen is provided by telephone network or any other network. Communication with other members or computers in any place by anyone can be achieved by combining the telephone network with additional facilities provided. The new communication techniques discussed above are extensively used today by a large number of enterprises as well as individuals. In tourism, in addition to travel agents, tour operators, hoteliers, airlines, travel journalists, etc. use these techniques. Journalists who especially travel extensively use the following facilities: (i) telecopy (for sending previously prepared texts as originals); (ii) teletex (for collecting and sending texts); and (iii) data banks (for collecting information).

The use of telecommunication techniques offers basic facilities and advantages in the following areas of work:

(i) collection of information
(ii) processing of information, and
(iii) transmission of information.

The data bank is like a "master book" in which mass of books, newspapers, and materials from different meetings and all kinds of published work are stored. All the relevant information can be collected in no time by means of electronic data bank Collecting the same information from a book and a visit to a library would be time consuming and rather expensive. The journalist seeking information on any subject for an article on tourism can order the articles which are of interest to him, though the record room of his own editorial office, or directly through the data bank and these are recorded on the screen. He can also acquire a article through a directly connected printing machine. In this way, in a matter of minutes, he can finish his search and the collection of data for his article. A lot of time and expenditure is saved.

Processing of Information. Information processing is an original and most crucial part of a journalist's work. A journalist has to evaluate collected information, combine the same with his new ideas and summaries the same in the compact from of an article. As can be done only to a limited extent by means of telecommunication devices. For collecting data, the personal computer can offer, new applications without much difficulty, a journalist can process articles collected with the help of electronics. The wordings of an article or the get-up can be changed as often as a journalist desires and it can be transmitted easily.

Transmission of Information. When the article is prepared on the basis of collected data, the same is to be transmitted to the editorial office or directly to the printers in their office. Journalist can do this personally by a telephone call or in a written form. But the quickest and simplest method is to transmit the information with the assistance of telecommunication devices. If the article is written in the normal way on a typewriter, then it can reach the editorial office in no time if the journalist uses telecopy facilities. The process of writing can be speeded up if the article-is written using a personal computer as this will not require additional printing. The article then can be transmitted directly to the computer available in the printing office.

Use of Computer Technology

The computer technology has made its entry in the field of tourism in a big way. In fact, computers are in use in some way or other in various branches of tourism since the early sixties. Be it a travel agency, hotels, airlines or recently the railways, computers have played a key role in making the task of providers of travel services an easy affair. Not only this, through home terminals, computers, is undertaking among other Jobs the planning of vacations for an individual and his family. Let us first of all understand the meaning of a computer.

Computer. A computer is a managerial tool capable of processing large amounts of data rapidly. A computer can perform arithmetic functions (addition, subtraction, division, and multiplication) and logical operations (sorting and ranking and assembling) in a fraction of a second. It dispenses results in a large variety of formats. The computers are capable of repeating programmed instructions almost endlessly without error, and maintaining a vast data base of stored information. The computer can be put too great number of uses in the day-to-day activities of human endeavor. In the travel industry, computers are extensively used today and they perform innumerable functions. The principal users of computers are: (a) Airlines, (b) Hotels (c) Travel Agents, and (d) Railways.

Computers in Airlines. The sudden growth about thirty years ago in the global travel meant a huge pressure on the existing handling of air traffic, especially the passenger traffic for the airlines. It was then that need was felt to computerise passenger reservation systems in major airlines. Growth patterns in passenger traffic had begun to indicate that handling reservations manually could not be sustained long without affecting the efficiency in the customer service. It was in the early 1960s, that IBM took the initiative and developed a computerised reservation system known as

Programmed Airlines Reservation System, PARS. The system was not developed for or with any one airline. It was designed as an all-purpose software package that would fit the requirements of any domestic airline. The system was designed around IBM's new hardware range system 360, which was later to revolutionise the entire computer industry. Continental Airline was the first United States Airlines to use, the PARS System in the year 1967. Most major US airlines followed and used the system making PARS, a most successful software product of the time. It was an achievement for the IBM. The system was later expanded to meet the needs of several other airlines outside the United States of America resulting in the creation of International Programmed Airlines Reservation System, IPARS. Initially this system was a joint venture between IBM and British Overseas Airways Corporation, BOAC, and aimed at adapting PARS to the needs of airlines that had mainly international operations.

In the following years many airlines adopted the system. The international package became almost as much of a standard as PARS. Although many airlines modified the system extensively, PARS was at the base of most international airlines system. By the late 1960s, however, it became obvious that the system was too costly for smaller international airlines. These airlines developed their own IBM oriented reservation systems in early 1970s. The system developed was known as CPARS (C for Compact). This system was followed by a system known as Univac Standard Airline System, USAS. With the passing of the years more and more systems developed incorporating more functions to enable the airlines to have more transactions and instructions. The popularity of any system to a large extent also depends its coverage and online reservation network. The number of terminals which a system has is also an important consideration. The more the terminals a system has, the larger will be the online reservation network. The number of reservation transactions carried out by a system in a given time is yet another important aspect to be considered by an airline before using a system. To sum up the following main aspects are important to make a system perfect and universally acceptable:

— Number of reservation transaction to be handled
— Data links with other airlines
— Number of terminals
— Information processing capacity
— Data volume capacity.

And of late a major advance has been made, in the airline reservation system in West Germany. A computer system capable of carrying out as many as 1000 reservation transactions every second, involving data links with 28 airlines, a host of car hire agencies and hotels and about 20,000 travel agencies in Europe alone has been set up at Erding in the Southern part of Germany. The system known as "Amadeus", has been developed jointly at a cost of DM 350 million by four airlines, Air France, Iberia, SAS and Lufthansa. The information processing capacity of the mainframe IBM and Unisys computers installed at Erding, the world's largest computer center, involves a data volume equivalent to a library of 3,50,000 books.

Computer in Cargo. Most of the airlines are now using computers for cargo handling operations as well. The handling of cargo shipments on ground is a costly affair and the cost has been increasing over the year. Almost 50 per cent of the handling of cargo, shipment reflects the cost of manual information processing. Freight rate increases have not kept pace with cost increases, so airlines had either to accept reduced margins or take steps to reduce overheads. Computerisation of cargo has helped reduce costs as this speeds up the handling of information related to consignments and also reduces the time the cargo spends on the ground. The pioneer in cargo computerisation was Alitalia, whose PO 4-cargo system was adopted and modified by many major airlines, such as Swissair, TWA and British Airways. Univac's USA has a fully developed cargo module. Almost all major airlines in the world have now adopted one or another system of cargo computerisation. To sum up, computerisation in airlines has the following major advantages.

— high profile applications like reservations
— applications of departure, control and cargo
— accounting & budgeting,
— forecasting and planning
— engineering management
— revenue accounting
— fare construction and fare quotations
— ticket printing
— crew scheduling
— crew management; and
— yield optimisation

In addition to the above; airlines have several other advantages from the use of computers. Each airline is developing its own system to suit its requirements. In addition to the airlines, the computer industry itself has also benefited a lot with the introduction of computerisation in the airlines. The computer industry in general has directed considerable attention to the lucrative airline market and has reaped the profits. Hardware manufacturers saw the potential and produced special airlines terminals to meet their needs.

SITA. The role of SITA, 'Societe International de Tele Communications Aeronautiques' in airlines automation has been very crucial. Automation is the key to achieving a higher level of productivity in any industry, especially in the airlines industry and automation of airline functions will continue with more emphasis being put towards achieving short term benefits. SITA is responsible for providing Data Processing Services. In fact, SITA is the major supplier of information handling services for the airline industry. SITA's aims are to foster efficient telecommunications, data processing and transmission means for all categories of information required in the operation of air transport enterprises with the specific aim of promoting safe and regular air transport in all countries. There has always been a continued high growth of demand for the services offered by SITA. SITA provides data processing services in the following areas.

— Passenger Reservations
— Departure Control
— Meteorological Data
— Volcanic Ash Reports
— Credit Authorisation and Document Verification
— Baggage Tracing (BAGTRAQ)
— Share Cargo Service
— Shared Flight Operations Data Base
— Flight Planning
— Baggage Handling and management Service
— Common Customs Interface System
— Fuel Management
— Airline Schedules and Flight Availability Data Base
— IATA Passenger Tariff Conference Support

From the above, it is observed that SITA is providing a valuable service to the airlines. Almost all the information required in the operation of air transport in the world is being provided to the airlines industry. The range of services offered by SITA is very extensive and new services are being added as and when these are required.

Computers in Hotels. The computer technology has entered the hotel industry in a big way. A hotel's most crucial internal resource is information and with the use of computers the information is available in a way that saves labour and ultimately increases the profits. Although computers in the hotel industry started being used as far back as in the late 1960s, it was only in the 1970s that the technological advances in the computer technology made possible the right combination of compactness and versatility for different sizes of hotels. The lower cost encouraged many individual hotels to install the system. Today computers are installed in large numbers and are widely accepted in the hotel industry. One of the most important factors for its large scale acceptance in the industry has been its reliability. The computer system has been found to be very reliable in the dissemination of the right kind of information at a push of the button. Hotel Industry today is a major market for the computer manufacturers and the software vendors. It has been increasingly realised that the hotel computer systems achieve better internal and external control and, through the use of analysis methods, provide the opportunity to improve the overall profitability of the unit. Like in the airlines, the computers offer substantial advantages for reservation systems in terms of speed and accuracy. The errors are almost negligible.

Application Areas. Hotel systems all over the world have traditionally been divided into the following two main areas: Front Office Application Areas and Back Office Application Areas.

Front Office Application Areas incorporate the following: Reservations; Registration; Guest accounting; Night auditing; and Communication operations (telephones, telex, fax

Back Office Application Areas incorporate the following: Financial management; Inventory control systems accounts;

Profit/loss accounts; General ledger; and Credit card verifications.

The computer system streamlines the functioning of all the above areas in a hotel set-up. It helps in the smooth functioning of the hotel, better guest relations, increased efficiency of staff and the overall profitability of the hotel. The key to successful operation of a hotel lies in the information system with the introduction of computers in the hotel the information system has become more accurate and efficient. The guest has an access to the required information with push button convenience. Since the computer is used as a communication medium, there is better coordination between various departments. The computer has relieved the staff of many routine jobs enabling them to devote more time and attention to the needs of the guests. The computers have made guest accounting systems more sophisticated and reliable. It automatically collects and calculates agents receipts and payments and consolidates and verifies credit card payments and cash controls. The sales outlets like restaurants automatically record the guest's expenditure at the point of sale, while direct electronic links to the telephone system in the guest rooms can monitor guest calls for instant charging to their accounts. The computers have eliminated cumbersome accounting machines often seen at the cashier's desk giving a front office system a modern and sophisticated look, resulting in greater guest satisfaction and adding to the prestige of a hotel. Back office systems have a large number of areas having great potential for cost control where computers are used to a great advantage for the hotel. With the use of computers, management can, monitor the progress of individual restaurants and other sales outlets against targets and budgets which may be set for various items. Daily reports on inventory usage become available by way of organising input from each center collected at regular intervals throughout the day.

Computers in Travel Agency. As compared to the airlines and hotels, travel agents have rather been slow to computerise their operations. It was in the year 1983 Thomson Holidays first used computers. With the success of Thomson's Top (Thomson Open-line Programme) in introducing reservations via Prestel several more big tour operators introduced similar systems to sell their 1984 summer programmes. A Prestel set allows travel agents to make reservations with as many principals as agree to it. The videotex technology which allows tour operators to open reservations through Prestel sets is applied to airlines through British Telecom's Skytrack. Today there are several airlines whose reservations are now open to Skytrack. Skytrack, an automated airline reservations system, enables travel agents to make booking on hundreds of world's airlines, using a standard Prestel television set and a keyboard. Prestel is being used for the basics required in the travel industry finding out airline schedules and fares, making reservations and getting information on a tour operator's holiday packages. The advantage of the system over travel books and brochures is that information is automatically updated and only flights or packages that are available are shown. Today many new systems have been developed which are being used by the travel agents and tour operators the world over. The advantages which the use of computers has given to agents are far more than the investments made in installing and using a system. Such advantages as knowing the availability of airline and railway reservations, hotel accommodation, amendments and cancellations, processing of documents such tickets, processing, account and management information etc., immediately just by pushing a button has proved to be a boom to the travel industry.

Computer Terminals. Modern day business traveller is increasingly getting used to have a computer in his hotel room. In fact, many such business travellers in countries like USA, Belgium, Holland, France, Germany, Japan, Canada and many other countries are enquiring before booking a room as to whether guest rooms where they are planning to stay have an in room computer terminal. The computer has thus entered the guest room of many hotels in the west and has become the latest novelty of a luxury hotel. A number of individual hotels as well as hotel chains have introduced in-room terminals that are hooked by television and telephone into a data system that includes official airline guides, news agencies, stock market agencies, weather bureaus, shopping services, travel, club, entertainment guide, electronic games and even job listing features.

Access to the computer terminal is gained by the guest by way of punching a credit card number which is charged for their time at the terminals on sliding rates roughly equivalent to those for long distance telephone calls. Computer systems in hotels have, in fact, revolutionised the hotel information systems resulting in ever increasing satisfaction for the guests and profitability for the management.

Videotex System. Videotex system has been a great help to travel agents and tour Operators in their functioning. The system invented by British Telecom is a way of providing computerised information without expense of supplying a computer terminal. All that is required is a telephone line and a standard colour television receiver with an adapter to link it to a keyboard and a decoder. Videotex provides efficient, low cost information and reservation facilities which allows direct communications between agents and principals throughout the industry. Information is transmitted quickly and accurately via ordinary telephone lines to be visually displayed on a television type screen. At the touch of a button it displays information on holiday packages, airfares, accommodations, cruises, car rentals, insurance, and many other travel-related services. Videotex system provides the following services to the travel agents/ four operators:

— fast and efficient means of obtaining accurate, up-to-date information on every aspect of the travel industry with excellent visual capacity
— direct access to the information supplied by industry principals, thereby speeding up transactions and increasing both the efficiency of selling and the quality of customer service.
— information on new product developments, fare changes, special offers and any other information put into the system
— display of tour itineraries, graphic illustrations of hotels, resorts and tourist attractions by selling staff.

Other videotex system benefits to users include:

— key word: immediate access to a specific piece of information
— increased sales: more sale conversations due to immediate access of information
— increased productivity: more efficient customers servicing
— cost efficient: reduced costs due to greater efficiency of communication
— up-to-date information: continued access to an entire library of travel-related information

The various systems in operation in travel agencies and tour operating companies have made a world of difference in their operations. In addition to the supply of immediate instant information the systems are also designed to supply printouts of itineraries, ticket vouchers, flight manifests, confirmations and a host of other relevant documents for both the customers as well as principals.

Computers in Railways. Railway systems in Europe and some other countries have now been using computers extensively. In countries like France, Germany and Belgium, to name a few, computers have been in use for over a decade. The most important use of computers in railways, however, is in the area of ticket reservation. The information regarding availability of seats is now available instantly in various networks. In addition to the use of computers by railway retail agents, travel agents and tour operators, these are also being used directly by the railway systems. Railway systems use the computers for route planning, engineering, accounting, inventory planning and control, purchase and a host of other functions. The most remarkable use of computer in railways has, however, been made by France. The metro system in Paris is one of the best in the world. France has been making great advances in the technology in its metro system. The latest technological marvel has been achieved beneath the surface of the earth through a concrete cylinder. No one on board is at the controls because there are no controls on board. Instead the sleek good-looking aluminium and steel train is being guided by a computer from a distant command center. Moving at 100 kilometers an hour the train suddenly stops as soon as bright lights appear ahead. Glass doors slide open and the passengers step on an immaculate platform awash in filtered daylight tastefully decorated with mosaics and sculptures. The train is the remarkable VAL (Vehicle Automatique Leger) the most ultra-modern futuristic subway system in the world inaugurated in the year 1983 in the northern French city of Lillee. Built by the French high technology giant Matra, the 20 mile network has almost been completed linking Lille to the nearby cities.. This is considered to be the most advanced automatic subway line in the world. VAL is distinguished from most conventional subway systems by its compact size, speed and computerised operating system. Each tar is only 6.75 feet wide and 42.6

feet long as compared to 8 feet by 49.2 feet for a Paris metro car. Each-train with two cars carries normal capacity load of 124 passengers in clean, well-lighted comfort. The system is operated from a remarkable control complex on the outskirts of Lille city. Two rows of television screens from an electronic tableau of the entire system. Four operators can call up images on the video monitors from 250 cameras installed in stations, tunnels and garages. The systems' computer is programmed to run the trains at a rate of one train every minute during peak hours and every five minutes at other times.

The computer is linked to about 200 microprocessors located in the stations and on board the trains. In case of any mishap or accident, VAL operators can stop a train, slow it or make any of the over 2,000 possible electronic commands. The trains are equipped with telephones that enable passengers to report any crimes and summon the system's 20 member security force. The driverless system is almost foolproof as is claimed. Indeed, during one of the trial runs, a pigeon alighted on an elevated section of the line, tripping automatic detectors and stopping a train for only ten seconds before its onboard computer ascertained that it was safe to proceed. Railway systems, however, may be able to indulge in such luxuries for a very long time. .

3

Christian Challenges to Mass Tourism in the 21st Century

Christianity has not been tried and found wanting; it has been found difficult and not tried.

—*G.K. Chesterton*

And whether it be a rich church
Or a poor church anywhere.
Truly it is a great church
If God is worshipped there.

—*Author Unknown*

For the Church to develop relevant and more creative pastoral initiatives in the area of tourism as we draw closer to the 21st Century requires a fundamentally new approach on our part.

This new approach requires firstly a fuller understanding of complexity of modern day mass tourism. We need to examine the web of intricate interconnectedness of all aspects of life today. Tourism has always been associated with the activity of the movement of people, but today it has become one of the most organised industries in society today that involves huge sums of money and utilisation of human and natural resources. This phenomenon often termed mass global tourism brings physical, cultural, economic and social changes to many aspects of society today. Its impetus for rapid and extensive expansion is not just the penchant and desire for people to reach out to other persons and cultures and to look for adventure but the fact that this growing industry it is one of the biggest "Dollar-Earners".

Mass Tourism today is in the context of Globalisation. Globalisation is the emergence of a new "borderless world". Trade liberalisation and the onslaught of information technology that makes the movement of capital and information, labour and goods truly make the world one. Available data shows that although globalisation has accelerated the creation of wealth, it benefits the wealthy. Rich countries are becoming richer while poorer countries are becoming poorer. In 1965, the poorest 20% people in the world had a 2.3% share of the global income and the richest 20% had a 70% share. In 1995, the poorest 20% shared just a 1.4% of the global income while the share of the 20% richest had increased to 85%. Furthermore, just 385 billionaires have a combined income equivalent to that of 2.5 billion people: and in the last 10 years the number of hungry people has increased from 500 to 840 million. Mass Tourism today has to be placed in the context of Mass Poverty in the Third World. Mass tourism has one face in the world of the poor and another in the world of the rich.

Secondly, we as Church need to be clear about our *Vision and Pastoral Orientations* in the area of tourism. Our Vision is born out of the awareness of the situations of the grief and sorrow in the world of today. These move the People of God to recognise the need to respond with our joy and create situations of hope. We have been challenged to offer radical alternatives to society today founded on our faith as a People of God and in Jesus Christ. We cannot be satisfied with superficial responses to social problems but to work for the building of the Kingdom of God in a holistic way through our work and our lives as Church.

To bring more humane conditions to life and to act

justly and with compassion begins with a clear option for new values of community and solidarity. This is only possible with Dialogue and Conversion. It has to be a process and a methodology that touches the core of human values. The foundations of this methodology began with the inauguration of the Federation of Asian Bishops' conferences in 1970. Since then we have attempted to journey as a People of God in Asia. This has been a pilgrimage of dialogue and discovery with the Lord and with each other to live more fully the teachings of the Second Vatican Council. This journey has brought to our experience a Vision of *"A New Way of Being Church"* that challenges us to Listen to what the Lord is inviting us to as Church through the "Signs of the Times

Thirdly, as a result of a deeper understanding of a holistic Vision we will be able to promote a sustainable and humane tourism. This is a process of transformation that begins with the implementation of programmes and activities that affect peoples' lives today. New possibilities are only possible with a new heart and new mind according to the ways of Jesus in our time and situations.

We therefore in this paper will Look at the World of Tourism, Listen to what the Lord is teaching us through the "signs of the times" and the official teachings of the Church, so that we will be able to Respond with Love.

I. Mass Tourism in the context of Globalisation

Tourism is a "sunrise" industry worldwide. It provided employment for about 212 million people in 1995, and the figure is expected to increase to 338 million in the next 10 years At the same time, the gross revenue of the tourism sector has reached US$3.4 trillion in and is expected to more than double by the year 2005, to US$ 7.2 trillion. The share of the Asia-Pacific region is US$804 billion. The region is only third in ranking behind Western Europe at US$1.5 trillion and North America at US$956 billion. In the world today 1 out of every 9 person is in tourism and that amounts to 278 million in 1996. 17% of world tourism comes to East Asia and the Pacific. Tourism grows 23% faster than the world economy. Between 1995-1997 travel and tourism grew 50 per cent faster than world employment and 60% of all international air travel was related to tourism.

We note some of the characteristics and issues related to mass tourism in Asia today:

1. In evaluating the role and impact of the tourism industry we need to take into account both the level of socio-economic development and the importance of tourism as a "Key-Player" in the national development plans. If tourism is a priority the governments should make higher allocations for tourism development compared to other sectors. Very often it is an option between tourism related infrastructure development and promotion and the production of basic goods, provision for education and health or development of the agricultural sector etc. In some countries in Asia, Governments give priority to the building of Golf Courses for the tourists and investors by taking away rice fields of the fanning communities. We cannot therefore look at the development of the tourism industry in the Third World without taking a look at the choices that need to be made and the consequences on the people.
2. The rapid growth of the tourism industry in Asia is related to what we term the "Fast-Track Growth Oriented Development". The recent financial crisis in Asia has shown very clearly the fragile nature of our economies and especially the tourism industry. The recent haze in South-East Asia kept away thousands of tourists from their destinations and

the earnings of people have dropped drastically. We have noted in the past eight months the chaos in the financial markets, the rise of unemployment and the direct impact it has on the poor and marginalised. The crash of the property market, for example, in Thailand has serious consequences for the tourism industry and the workers. It is clear that mass tourism as the means to boost the economy and alleviate the poverty of the people is being questioned and challenged.

3. The technological advancements in communications and transport and the incredible improvements in information technology and use the mass media have made tourism the fastest growing industry today. What people see on the television screen, they want to experience in reality. They don't mind working longer hours to be given the opportunity to enter into another cultural world. They don't mind getting into debts ("Fly First, Pay Later" Schemes) to enjoy for the moment. There is the danger that it can become a status symbol or self-gratification due to the highly competitive advertising industry.

4. Tourism, understood in its full context is for the formation of one humanity, able to fully experience the gifts of God given to the whole of humanity. But current experiences show that much is to be desired when little respect is paid to the cultural heritage of the people and basic needs of the people are neglected. Development has to respect the rights of other persons and communities. Tourism can be an opportunity to enter into the world of the "others" but not trampling on their "flower gardens"

5. The lack of proper provision of alternative forms of employment and inability to reduce poverty in the rural areas often boosts tourism as a viable

alternative. The opening of territories owned and occupied by indigenous peoples, farmers, fishing communities have resulted in the forced eviction of communities and the loss of cultural identifies. Burial grounds and sacred sites have been converted in luxury resorts and golf courses. Cultures are commercialised for entertainment for the sake of profit and in the name of development.

6. The instant nature of mass tourism, moves people from one part of the world or a continent to another but often ensure only a superficial encounter with the mere externals of world of nature and culture. Such an experience in a purely artificial environment can result in a lack of sensitivity. Commodification of "culture and nature", denies the deeper aspects of ones life and sharing the more humanising aspects of the culture from which one comes from. Examples can be cited in various countries, where family life has disintegrated; marriages are broken and threatened by the promotion of sex tourism. The influence on youth and high school students is devastating. Lured by opportunities to earn easy money Within a few late evening hours, they have lost interest in studies, games and other usual pastimes. They are immersed in the life of restaurants, shacks, beach-umbrella renting, vehicle-hiring and as masseurs, quite a number in drug peddling, prostitute soliciting including children, and finally falling into the web of drug-taking and prostitution. H1V carriers and full-blown AIDS have

We are aware that the tourism industry is a key economic institution in every single part of the world and is proposed as the panacea for underdevelopment of the Third World today. We cannot deny the role of the mass media and the communication networks in bring new information to prospective tourists looking for an escape from the drudgery of modern day life in a highly competitive and consumerist society. Highly marketed mass tourism entails higher financial costs for the traveler and become an exclusive privilege of the few in the developed and developing countries.

8. It is very debatable if the type of mass tourism that is being promoted in Asia today is for the integral development of the nation and people. Economic growth does not necessarily mean total human development, the creation of equitable structures and justice. The evils of drug abuse and prostitution cannot be the price one has to pay for economic growth and development.

Thus we have attempted to point out that tourism cannot be driven by only the market forces and solely motivated by profit. We need to look for alternatives that will bring new dimensions to humanity and to the world of nature.

II. Discernment in view of our Vision of "A New Way of Being Church"

Our involvement as Church is to be founded on our Vision of Church in **Asia**, born out of the living out of the Second Vatican Council in the context of Asia. The Federation of Asian Bishops' Conferences has articulated this vision of "*A New Way of Being Church*" as the journey of the People of God in Asia called to the service of the Gospel of Life in the context of Asia. This vision has to find expression in our mission of evangelisation in Asia by being leaven, salt and light in the societies that we live and word. It is this vision that serves to make our process of Looking at Life and Responding with Love more meaningful.

For us "From the dynamic forces at work within Asian

realities a basic vision of life emerges. In the living heritage of cultures and religious traditions of Asia we discern values and their expressions in symbols, stories and art forms, that embody a vision of life; while we are critically aware of the distortions that have entered into these traditions. In these cultural and religious traditions we also discover the responses to life given by past generations of Asian peoples, which in turn become sources for our contemporary response.

We Asians are searching not simply for a meaning of life but for life itself. We are striving and struggling for life because it is a task and a challenge. But life is a gift too, a mystery, because our efforts to achieve it are far too short of the ultimate value of life. We speak of life as a *becoming*- a growing into, a journeying to life and to the source of life.

So what might this vision be?

In the rich diversity of ancient Asian cultures and faiths is a vision of unity in diversity, a communion of life among diverse peoples. In this context we seek to become persons of dialogue. Ours is a vision of holistic life, life that is achieved and entrusted to every person and every community of persons, regardless of gender, creed or culture class or colour. It is the fruit of integral development, the authentic development of the whole person and of every person.

We envision a life with integrity and dignity, a life of compassion for the multitudes, especially for the poor and needy. It is a life of solidarity with every form of life and of sensitive care for all the earth. It is thus a life that unites us Asians among ourselves and with the whole of creation into one community life.

For us Life is to live with integrity and dignity in peace and justice, in freedom and participation, in mutuality and complementarity. It is to live in simplicity and friendship.

At the heart of our vision of life is the Asian reverential sense of mystery and of the sacred, a spirituality that regards life as sacred and discovers the Transcendent and its gifts even in mundane affairs, in tragedy or victory, in brokenness or wholeness. This deep interiority draws people to experience harmony and inner peace and infuses ethics into all of creation". Noteworthy among them are the growing consciousness regarding human dignity and empowerment of the poor, the growing voices of groups and peoples for humanised development, and the cries of marginalised groups for participatory and democratic governance. We dwelt on the movements for the protection of the environment and ecosystem linked to justice, and the solidarity of committed groups and peoples especially in the struggle for the rights of women, children, especially the girl child, and those of indigenous peoples. Truly remarkable is the increasing number of young peoples moving towards solidarity and community, and seeking a deeper spirituality. We are consoled by efforts of many groups to foster dialogue with people of other faith". (VI Plenary Assembly 1995 No. 10)

It is therefore this Integral Vision that has enabled us to articulate some basic principles that should be the foundation of our involvement and participation in the world of tourism.

Our Path towards a Humanising and Sustainable Tourism in Asia

1. Our focus on the "Most Affected"

The negative side effects of tourism development can be avoided or minimised greatly through a holistic and integrated approach towards development. Tourism developers pay little attention of the wishes and desires of the local communities as well as the physical environment. We as Church need to be more conscious of the cultural and religious values of the people and look for way to protect them. Their well being and interest should not be overlooked. We need to listen to their side of the story. It is by knowing their lives and situations more fully that we will be able to help them to confront some of these problems. We thus need to be more sensitive to their hopes and aspirations and examine concrete ways in which to work with persons and communities so that they can have an impact on society general and the environment and ecology as well. Thus Pastoral ministry for tourism begins with some form of dialogue with the "disadvantaged" and "small people" resulting in negotiations and advocacy with the policy makers, in order to redress the negative impact of tourism on their lives.

2. Our Dialogue with the "World of Tourism"

It is as a result of our participation and involvemsnt in the lives of people affected negatively by tourism that will enable us to be familiar with the views and perspectives of the poor. It is then that we can enter into dialogue with the Government and agencies involved in the tourism industry. We listen to them and evaluate the criteria they employ to make plans in the area of economics and social development, environmental protection etc. It is in the context of this process of active involvement through dialogue, participation and advocacy that the Church can find both long term, holistic and lasting solutions to the problems related to mass global tourism. We need to know enough of this phenomenon to be able to address the various new problems that are arising, or to make these new opportunities of encounters of peoples and cultures, religions and traditions to promote a more harmonious and just world for all people?

3. *Our Readiness to Journey and Dialogue with the Marginalised*

It is not just knowing about their lives but entering into a process of dialogue with them. Our experiences have shown that the best way to lessen the negative impact of mass global tourism is to begin with positive actions at the micro-local levels. Our journey and struggle with the people has given us new insights into tourism so that we can come up with more creative ways to overcome some of the problems. What is truly new is not in concepts and words but in concrete lived experiences. Thus we can see that the process of globalisation of tourism can be arrested at the local level by new actions of behalf of justice and equitable structures. It is our responsibility to evaluate the impact tourism of on the lives of the people of Asia and promote the involvement and participation of the Church without reservations. This dialogue helps us to educate the members of the Church to a greater commitment. In our experiences it has been clear that to create greater awareness in the Church has to be through the communication of the heart. We need to share the stories of the people and what has feelings of hurt and discouragement have been felt and how they through the living out of their faith were able to experience the hope and joy that comes with lives lived in love and service.

4. *Implementing "Deeds that Transform"*

If our involvement is to be true it has to affect the lives of people and transform the situations that they live in. Thus new Pastoral Ministries are the result of a long process of "Dialogue-Discernment" resulting in Deeds that Transform. We cannot run away from the fact that our reflections on various aspects of life have to inevitably lead us to expressions of our Christian faith in our lives. Whatever touches our lives and that of human persons leads us to experience our faith in a new and renewed way.

Our diverse experiences in the pastoral ministry of tourism in Asia and the other continents has been the basis for continuing the search make our responses ever more relevant and meaningful. It is the light of the Gospel as enunciated in the Social Teachings of the Church that will have to influence our economic and social perspectives when it comes to formulating a new agenda in matters related to tourism.

III. Pastoral Orientations and our Pastoral Responses

The basic thrust of the Church is to promote the positive effects of tourism and reduce the negative aspects. It has been pointed out that we need to take a broader and holistic perspective of the real issues related to modern day mass tourism. This perspective has to be one that does not view tourism as only the means to promote a solely "Growth-Oriented Development" but one where the positive aspects of tourism are enhanced to ensure that tourism is Sustainable, Person and Community-Centred and Environmentally Friendly.

There are therefore some basic principles that we would not as central to our task in promoting new pastoral ministries in the area of tourism.

1. Community-Based Approaches

In order for this to be possible, there has to be greater importance given to the role of the local community and government in the planning, implementation, monitoring and evaluation of all tourist related projects. It is through this participation of the community that will help the local people to strengthen their current standard of living and to ensure that other social and cultural situations are given vital importance. It is essential that the rate of growth of the industry is determined by the authorities in consultation with the people and in dialogue with all those who are interested in developing the tourism industry.

This will go a long way in ensuring the economic criteria namely profit does not become the sole criteria for determining the success of a tourist destination. The local population will be part of the labour force and thus strengthen the local economy. This has been our experiences in many of the programmes and projects in various parts of India, in Thailand, Malaysia, the Philippines, Sri Lanka and Indonesia. Various examples can be cited of local communities that have campaigned against the violation of their rights by education and awareness campaigns both at local and national levels.

2. Need for Exchange and Networking

A greater and more effective exchange of information among people engaged in the tourism industry ensures the emergence of more healthy forms of tourism and the eradication of effects that negatively affect the lives of the local people. Sustainability seems to call for local solutions to problems. Bio-diversity and fragile Eco- systems can only be protected by a firm commitment to look for holistic solutions to modern day tourism. The information network created among the various countries in Asia both through the Ecumenical Coalition on Third World Tourism and other networks have had much impact on the work of the local communities. It has helped to control the global forces, especially in the area of child prostitution and trafficking of women.

3. Inter-religious and Ecumenical Collaboration

Response of the Church in Asia in the area of tourism resulted in more and more programmes involving other Christians and people of other faiths in Asia. This is the result of greater involvement of the laity, both in their professions and in their everyday lives. This is what will make our contribution to be at the service of a more humanising life for all our peoples. The vast majority of the people of Asia have very few opportunities to travel beyond the borders of our country. Those privileged have to be helped to enter into a meaningful and enriching experience with their neighbours. The people they visit have to be with respect and with justice and being sensitive to their plight, the cultures and to ensure harmony and goodwill. We need to learn to walk on the sacred grounds of other religions and traditions.

4. Priority for Projects with the Poor

In the context of mass tourism with its numerous dehumanising effects, it is a loud and clear call on the part of the Church today to respond with love and compassion to those who are victims of mass tourism. Our awareness that it does not matter who has caused hurt but the need to remedy the pain and the sorrow, the suffering and the humiliation is what has to move us to look into the well being of these vulnerable people. We need to get close enough to the "context" in which these people "survive" more that live. The Church as a sign of hope has not only to be voice to bring comfort to these persons and communities but also speak with truth on behalf of justice, when the forces and institutions in society, continue to bring misery through damage to dignity and personhood. We believe that this process of "Dialogue of Life" is also the process of evangelisation. We through our words, deeds and witness bring to reality the Kingdom of God and Gospel of Jesus becomes visible among the people whom we live and work. When the Church gives new meaning to the lives of the downtrodden we become to them the Good News of the Gospel of Jesus. In the context of the crisis in our societies and the challenges posed by mass tourism we cannot remain neutral and indifferent.

5. Pastoral Care for Tourism-Education and Awareness

Pastoral Care for those engaged in tourism, has also to mean caring for those who have to face the harsh consequences of the negative effects of mass tourism as well as those who visit other lands. A process of awareness and education seems central to making tourism a humanising phenomenon. The vigilance over policy makers and business corporations seems central to make tourism a meaningful encounter of peoples and their cultures and to protect the environment. It is therefore in the context of this our integral and holistic vision that we need new and creative responses each in the context of our countries and local situations.

Conclusion

Thus, we can conclude that whatever involvement the Church has in promoting a more just and equitable tourism from our experiences begin with involvement with those who are living in the world of tourism, especially the workers and the host countries. It is this involvement either in the form of offering direct services to them or educating them about their rights and responsibilities that enables us to work progressively to bring more just and humane dimensions to their lives and situations. We need to be at their service to ensure that the rights of the visitors and those of the visited are protected. This is only possible if we engender a deep respect for others. We need exploit or oppress, deprive people of their freedom to enjoy the goods. We can share this with all peoples and the whole of humanity. Our Vision of tourism should be to ensure that whole human family has an opportunity to live life to the full. This for us Christians is possible by bringing of the values of the Gospel to every strata of society and to its workings. This for us is an integral aspect of our evangelising mission and thus the real challenge for all those who are involved in the world of tourism.

4

Travel with a Mission

Our most valuable possessions are those which can be shared without lessening—those which, when shared, multiply. Our least valuable possessions, on the other hand, are those which, when dividend, are diminished.

—*William H. Danforth*

In a conventional sense the whole concept of tourism—the programme or organisation related to journeying from place to place as holiday, for pleasure or excursion—is undoubtedly a product of modernity brought about by better means of transportation as well as accumulated or surplus resources (e.g. time and money). Although the Bible has so many accounts about people moving around, traveling or migrating to different places, these journeys were done by the early people mainly because of duty or necessity (very often, they had no other choice), not in pursuit of pleasure. Hence, none of the travels in biblical or ancient times would in any way resemble the concept of tourism that we have today. But we will try to reflect on tourism with the hope that something can be gleaned from Jesus teachings as we try to deal with such a modern phenomenon.

Travel according to the Bible Dictionary

In the *Harper Collins Bible Dictionary,* the closest entry to the word 'travel' (there is none on tour, tourist, or tourism) is "Trade and Transportation," which deals with the movement and exchange of goods and services that make up commerce Trade in the olden times had to do with occupation in general, and with commercial trading in particular. It was part of domestic as well as international activities and relations. At times it was seen as a royal enterprise for purposes of diplomacy or profit. At times it was blamed for the waning faithfulness of concerned believers. For most common people, it was seen as a means of survival. It was also seen as something that brought wealth and, hence, as something that could breed violence and corruption. There was a clear connection between transportation and trade though it was difficult to pinpoint which came first. "People probably moved to follow food supplies as hunters and gatherers or moved to safe quarters or to a more dependable water supply before they had the means of accumulating surplus goods with which to begin trade" But the domestication of plants and animals, which is the beginning of agriculture, laid the foundation of cities that soon brought about the series of technological developments in human society. And so we can surmise that travel slowly evolved from the basic purpose of survival and trade in the olden times into today's more pleasure-seeking journey that has come to be termed tourism.

Travel According to Jesus

During Jesus' ministry, travel meant doing the required Sabbath journey to Jerusalem especially for the religious festivals prescribed by the Jewish law. It also meant his going to the wilderness for what we now call retreat, and to the villages for teaching and preaching, healing and exorcism. Then it also referred to his sending out the disciples to do the same. After Jesus, the disciples, later called apostles, also went about sharing the good news. Among those apostles, Paul is probably the one who traveled very widely to share the gospel. It is very clear that travel therefore had a mission; travel was for a mission.

I would like to lift some passages from Scripture that talk about this whole notion of travel. It would be interesting to see any parallels between what was taught in these passages and what is happening today with this phenomenon that we call tourism.

In Luke 10:1-11 Jesus is depicted as sending out his seventy (-two) disciples to carry out his ministry of healing, teaching, preaching and exorcism. It is clear that pleasure was not on the agenda of such a travel. Hence, it was not tourism as we call it today. But let us see how Jesus prepared the 70 or 72 for the mission trip. I will put the biblical passage in one column and write on another column the parallel teaching, advice or warning to would-be tourists that we often hear or say today.

- There is a *warning of opposition* — the metaphor of lambs in the midst of wolves. This warning might be seen in the context of the growing opposition to all that Jesus and his community of followers stood for.
- There is an instruction on *what to take or really not to take* — no purse, bag, or sandals. This seems to recall the earlier instruction to the Twelve (Luke 9: 3) to take nothing (no staff, no bag, no bread, no money, no extra tunic). This must be seen in the context of the belief in the schatdlogical imminence.
- There is an instruction *not to greet anyone along the way*. Seen in view of 2 Kings 4:29 and Psalms 129: 6-8, it seems to underscore the need for urgency and singleness of purpose.
- There are instructions on *how to receive hospitality*, which seem to be an expansion of Luke 9:4 where the command was for the Twelve to stay wherever they were received. Implicit in the command was the need to remove all social barriers as disciples

were to be received and fed in Gentile homes. The instruction not to 'move about from house to house' was probably to prevent them from seeking better quarters or seeking to prolong their stay, which would not be in keeping with the urgency of their mission.

- There are three instructions on the *conduct of the mission* in each village: (a) eat what is provided, (b) heal the sick; and (c) announce the reign of God. The three constitute the creation of community through table fellowship, the care of physical needs, and the proclamation of the gospel. All these were instructions on how to respond to a positive reception.
- *Response to rejection,* however, involves shaking off dust from their feet, which is a traditional act of repudiation. It was also a declaration that the rejection of the message did nothing to threaten the truth of God's reign coming near.

It is very clear that travel according to Jesus was for a mission — a mission in service to the reign of God. Hence, it was characterized by the threat of danger, opposition, and rejection and by a sense of urgency and haste. But it was also centered on the building of a new community through table fellowship, healing of the sick, and proclamation of the reign of God — a community that heeded the gospel demands. What does Jesus' commission to the early disciples have to say to us today? Is there anything from that ancient piece of advice to the early missionary travelers for us who are still traveling around today? Can tourism be something that is mission-filled?

We are not suggesting of course that the traditional motive of Christian mission — i.e., to proselytize people so that they will all embrace the Christian faith and join the church — should be the agenda of tourism. Far from that! We already know how such a motive has caused so much havoc in communities with their own well-established religions and forms of spirituality. We also know that such a concept of mission often falls short of Christ's own mission which is to bring abundant life for all, especially to those who have been deprived an (John 10:10). Today's tourism is without any purpose at all because there is definitely a purpose for every type of tourism — whether it is leisure-tourism, reverse tourism, eco-tourism, or other alternative forms of tourism.

According to *The New Interpreter's Bible, Jesus'* commission sets ten principles for the early disciples, missionary travel. Once again, I will put these 10 principles in one column and on another column I will raise what I think could be the possible parallelisms for today's mission traveler.

After Jesus, one of the later disciples-turned-apostles who traveled widely is Paul. The book of Acts provides a kind of summary of such travels while the letters written by Paul to the churches in various places he had been to or places he was planning to visit reflect the many relationships that he had made through his mission-filled travels. Definitely, Paul's travels as an apostle to the gentiles were the result of his response to the commission of Jesus. It is true that he was forced to leave some places and hide elsewhere because of growing opposition. But all these were because of his zeal for the gospel. It would be too long to describe all these travels but it might just suffice our purpose if we can put together some of practices. Paul brought greetings from where he came to the people he met. In a sense, he brought people (or congregations), friends and acquaintances in touch with each other through those greetings. Aside from preaching and teaching about Jesus' gift of salvation, he often got involved in local issues and tried to help solve the community's problems. Then he tried to link one place with another, thereby building solidarity among people in their sufferings and concerns.

A concrete example of this was his bringing gifts for people in need in the places he visited and his raising or soliciting funds from wealthier places to help the poorer ones that he visited.

Mission-Filled Tourism Today

The present day s tourism is a result of the evolution of human society, i.e. from its primitive food-hunting stage to modernity. While in ancient time people moved around in search of food and water, today, most people travel as tourists because of surplus time and money and because of advanced transportation and communication facilities. However, much of what goes on as tourism today, even that which has been so conveniently labeled as eco-tourism, has been found to cause so much havoc to local people — i.e. the indigenous people and their culture, the natural environment or ecology. Our use of easier/faster transportation facilities and comfortable hotels has also been proved to ensure our participation, often unconscious participation, in the enlarging hole of the ozone layer, and consequently, the worsening of the global warming — an ongoing ecological destruction that until now is so difficult to counter. Our shopping sprees at places where goods are sold so cheap are also a sure contribution to the market economy that has only enriched the already rich companies (often of foreign origin) at the expense of small-time local workers. This is not to say however that only when we travel outside our country do we get to participate in such a lopsided economy. After all, globalisation has made it possible for us to enjoy many cheap goods that have been made in Third World or developing countries where labor is so cheap, thus, ensuring more profit to the multinational corporations. Furthermore, we may not be the types who go to the Red Light areas as "customers" except probably as "exposurists" (as we say in the Philippines), but these are definitely the places that surely breed and have been bred by tourism. We know that where there are tourists, there also are a number of women and young children being sold into prostitution to whet the appetite of visitors with some dollars.

Tourism today is a giant phenomenon that involves all of us, whether we like it or not. For sure, it is not something that we can be rid of so easily, if at all. But maybe, we can help transform it by transforming its spirit. Maybe we can begin to re-think and evaluate the motive of tourism today. Maybe we can help evolve a sense of mission or vision in tourism that is more people-friendly and ecology-friendly. And through this way. We can indeed begin to change the spirit of tourism from perversion to pilgrimage and from self-centered satisfaction to solidarity with the other.

5

Tourism Promotion Strategies

> For fifteen hundred years the great wall of China stood unconquered. On day, by the gate, a guard was drunk, and a simple, harmless-looking shepherd came along and engaged him in conversation, corrupted and bribed him. The guard left the gate a moment, it was thrown back and hordes of barbarians poured in. They could not overcome China by bringing force against the wall, but they gained entrance through one man who was weak.
>
> —*Dr. Norman Vincent Peale*

The human capital is an important determinant of a region's economic well-being. Policy makers must choose between developing human capital within or attracting it, elsewhere they may do both. The region should be awakened to the vast benefit from attracting retirees, a best suitable form of regional competition for people.

Since regions are there which seeks to attract outsiders simply due to significant depopulation. Almost all villages population has threatens their viability. Therefore, resident attraction policies are essential to develop land, settle homes, and provide kids for schools. This use of incentives is predicted on attracting modern pioneers with the means to buy a house, invest, pay taxes, or stand a business. Areas losing population need specific actions to reverse this decline. Target specific industries with the lure of a low-tax environment advertise nationally. New companies will attract newcomers and retain the old ones.

Obviously, there are some areas with high growth. These need anti-growth sentiments of residents. In these areas population growth forced to produce presumed benefit of more job, higher income, and lower taxes. On the contrary, the dynamics of growth produced rising taxes for infrastructure and schools, traffic congestion, and population that in many senses detracts from quality of life, technical and scientific job opportunities. The whole region of central Himalayas is facing growing labour shortages and cultural crises, if it modifies its immigration policies by introducing foreign workers. Thus, immigration policies affect a nation's foreign and domestic policies. It has a significant impact on how the region markets itself.

Laws have been enacted excluding certain population segments from full participation in their civic, social and economic life based on race, ethnicity, political beliefs, religion, physical or mental condition and economic means. Vagrancy and loitering laws, literacy tests for voting, residency requirements for welfare, and tresspass laws are but a few of devices, used in some countries to discourage people from living in a place, or forcing out those, who are unwanted.

The region should be proactive for residents who meet certain characteristics and profiles due to the following reasons:

- Demand for skilled workers due to labour shortage.
- This region has a vastly expanding retirement market whose spending exceeds the costs of the area and local services consumed.
- The wage gap is growing between college graduates and the less educated.

Policy Toward Residents

In addition to attract tourists, businesses and investors, people attraction is likely to become an even more important aspect in regional competition. Attracting people is a complex and complicated business in a democratic society just as the national immigration policies have changed to reflect global competition for the skilled, talented and wealthy, so the region should enter the contest in competing for residents. The region should attract certain groups and by same token, discourage other groups. The targeted groups typically may include professionals, investors, the wealthy, young families, retirees and those with specific skills such as physicians. At the same time low-income families, the houseless, criminal types, and illegal immigrant should be discouraged.

Policies need to be developed whose purpose is to attract, exclude, encourage or discourage, and market/de-market geopolitical areas to certain public or identifiable groups. At the national-state level, the issue is immigration policy: whom to admit, on what basis, and for what period of time. At the state level, the issues largely involve taxes, spending, and regulatory considerations. Most regions and areas share the proceeding responsibilities with states, but have direct responsibility for land use zoning, building codes, health, and safety standards.

The government actions, the policies and the programmes are rarely neutral regarding people's attraction. They have impacts and consequences, which usually benefit some population segments more than others.

People's Attraction

Due to the conquest or slavery or feudal system, most of the nations were frequently directed at exporting cheap labour or populating new markets. Demography is the statistical study of human population. In the information stage, demographics provide regions with valuable date to affect the flow of people and resources. This area is concerned about famine and unemployment. It is slow growth population region. Population is essential to economic progress-jobs, economies of scales and rising standard of living. No region without a substantial population can hope for lasting global influence. The region should be strategically positioned on its ability to attract human and physical capital both nationally and globally. Singapore, for example, aims to be the 'brain capital of Southeast Asia'. It advertises around the world for professionals, with the objective of building Singapore's future to its ability to export expensive services to the rest of Asia. India seeks to persuade expatriates currently employed abroad to return home for high paying jobs. Growth in population in a region occurs from notional increases in birth rate and less death rates, slow migration from cities, migration from other cities, and migration from abroad.

Senior Citizens

The region vary in the groups it can and wants to attract. It may reach out for retirees, skilled professionals, high income earners and in some cases, unskilled workers. In targeting a retired population segment, the region should take a lead. With the aging of the region, competition for elderly residents should increase. Medium household income peaks for householders aged 50-65. The region should target the elderly—income, to networth, high consumption, and often low service demands. Retirement migration boosts spending and broadens the tax base—a new growth industry for small areas. Few years back many rural areas became hot retirement areas as migration of old people increased. Rural areas and villages grow faster than urban areas. These hot spots are mostly located near the city areas, frequently areas of scenic beauty and recreation, revitalising communities and expanding business and employment opportunities. Cold-climate, out of the way places are sought by retirees. The region should place advertisements throughout the nation for retirees. Areas could be promoted with retirement development which includes sports, trekking, golf, tennis courts and similar other facilities.

The region shall have to struggle with various combination of anti-tax, anti-development and anti-growth sentiments. The region seeks growth restrictions through environmental laws governing land use, zoning, and housing, court-approved extraction and development fees from developers for infrastructure and public services.

There are other areas of the region which are neither growing nor shrinking, and although desiring growth, realistically must learn to live with very limited growth prospects. These places are experiencing slow growth and are likely to do so in future because the only two sources of growth — natural increase and in-migration has diminished. Slow growth, no growth, and growth loss is resulting in economic stagnation. Some areas may try an economic transition to more stable industries as these possess well-trained labour force, and have advantage of good location. They have good prospects of remaining healthy in the absence of significant population growth. With rural migration to these areas depleted and attraction of immigrants from places elsewhere limited, their tasks are largely to attract and retain skilled labour.

Remarkably, a wide difference exists among various areas in their effort to increase, decrease or stabilise their resident populations. Retirees generally seek places offering recreation activities where they can pursue hobbies such as writing, handicrafts, painting, etc. They can be attracted by medical care facilities, have health care, and various forms of service transportation such as special buses, etc. Some businesses, may greatly benefit from the aging population and are willing to help a place attract retirees. These businesses are oriented to the home, health care, leisure, counselling, education, managing finances and slowing the aging process. A growing retiree population brings with it a demand for certain services which a place can both market to and help develop. A warm or cool climate and picturesque surroundings are not the only factors in attracting retirees. The area or region should make organised efforts to contact thousands of military service people who retire in much larger numbers. Many of them seek opportunities for second careers (the average retiree is in his forties, following twenty years of service) and locations near military bases so they can utilise discount retailers and medical facilities. Like other affluent retirees, ex-soldiers should be sought because they are typically well-educated and in good health, having higher than average disposable income and become involved in civic projects.

Many organisations are leaders in seeking ex-military personnel for key jobs. There should be a second career's office in this region. The areas containing college or universities should make itself attractive to the elderly and plan suitable retirement communities. The quality of life in these communities is directly associated with university life and resources. Their increased attractiveness to senior citizens has a downside to students, as property values rise. Another recent trend over the last several years is for Himalayan retirees to return to their native areas or village, where the cost of living is low and extended care is available at modest prices.

Other Life Style Groups

One of the major factor of people attraction is the increased inability of the population. In the information age, people are able to define where they live to work rather than where they work to live. Now the world thinks of an office less city, a new era of electronic cottage industries with more people employed at home, as independent contractors than at centralised work stations. The exodus from planes to hills as a place of residence and work is a phenomenon in many countries. The marketing challenge for the region is how to accommodate these technological and life-style trend to slow the exodus and retain certain segments of urban dwellers. The urban areas of the region seek to capture a share of the city to city migration of professional, attract new urban migrants and bring certain sub-urbanities back in to the urban areas.

The region should accommodate to a nation of movers. The vast majority of moves are within the region. Very few movers migrate to other areas. Job change is the main driving force of a region. People change jobs and also careers. To attract and retain a mobile population, the region must learn to market various individual life-styles. Demographics and life-style proliferation have led to an entire language characterising attitudes and behaviours. Changes in household size and income are critical, to area marketing. Life-styles are associated with, but not necessarily determined by household size and income. In order to attract or retain people by skills, income, or other characteristics, the region must also accommodate the life-style needs of these population segments. Most of big cities have things of big-city-life such as sport, art, shopping, etc., without many problems. This region could market itself as an alternative to the big-city hustle-all the benefit, and none of the costs. Quality-of-life factors such as air, natural beauty, recreational facilities and cultural and social amenities can be valuable assets in attracting people. Small hidden areas could be discovered by pursuing micro-marketing strategies. Urban areas are defenseless in this competition. The attractiveness of urban life compared to Himalayan region for young and old is a real phenomena which the urbans are learning to adjust.

In some areas, revitalisation may occur when more affluent new comers buy and refurnish homes in run-down areas and upgradation occur when low and moderate residents rehabilitate deteriorated neighbourhood themselves. In some other areas an entirely new residential colony has been built on the edge of the urban areas. These edge areas are the culmination of a generation of individual value decisions about the best ways to live, to work, to play and about how to create-home. These edge urban areas contain all the functions of a urban areas offers with shopping halls as the equivalent of village square. They are new and growing phenomenon, a new area between urban and traditional villages.

As natural, Consumers prefer to live in those communities that best satisfy their preferences. But people find it difficult to and risky to move even when their community has become unattractive and other communities appear more attractive. In addition, they may feel unwelcome and even discouraged from moving into certain communities. This region will have to develop suitable policies to attract, retain or discourage certain people from moving. Exclusionary, discriminatory and unnecessary regulations constitute formidable barriers to affordable housing. Tax and regulatory structure—no income tax, no inheritance tax, and tax bankrupter laws in some countries are highly geared to the elderly, while relatively low education expenditures are not particularly attractive to a young family looking for the best public education for their children. Areas like Nainital, Mussoorie, Dehradun, etc., are attractive to young upper-income families because of their fine public system. A region's attractiveness is influenced by its bundle of public services and taxes that must be levied to provide these services. The region should decide how much to spend on building a good public school system providing services to its senior citizens and providing welfare payments to its indigent population. However, it must be borne in mind that too many immigrant and welfare viewpoints may consume region's benefits and the income producing middle class may move to lower-cost areas. The middle classes are leaving Himalayas regions and villages, in their prime earning years.

The producers are being replaced by people who receive more in state service than they pay in taxes. A stage may develop that the region may seek to cut back its welfare programmes drastically and discourage needy migrants from locating there. The larger they provided service bundle the higher the taxes. When those population groups that provide the bulk of the taxes receive disproportionately less of the benefits, many young middle-class families relocate from urban to the sub-urban where they get proportional benefits.

Nearly all the places in this Himalayan region are friendly, warm and welcoming to out of area dewellers. The informal fabric of the area—its places of worship, civic and fraternal groups, social clubs, educational and business organisations—all go a long way towards shaping the region's real hospitality norms. Therefore, in seeking to attract a certain segment of residents to the region, how the area is to develop, nurture and mobilise these resources is as important in resident attraction as formal policies to be laid down for the entire region.

The influx of immigrant and the conflict between environmental concerns and employment concerns and employment opportunities, is bound to collide when the government seek to attract certain groups and avoid others. The caste composition of the Himalayan region has changed dramatically in the past. Such changes are not uniformly distributed by areas throughout the region. The changing race and class composition of the areas is raising the question of whose responsibility it is to pay for the homeless, the unskilled, the education of children, and other economic and social costs. One way to solve the problem of unskilled immigrants and the homeless is to attract industrial businesses that can employ them. The more environmentally conscious an area, the more such policies work against attracting low-income populations, blue coloured manufacturing, and affordable housing. The region should decide how it wishes to attract, retain, or otherwise, accept. The problem of identity crisis involves values, traditions, and ethnical concerns. Therefore, the people attraction business is unlikely to produce a common consensual basis for action. It may be highly divisive and openly conflictual for this region.

6

Tourism: Management Tools and Techniques

It is the social obligation of management in make certain that its executives are functioning at peak performance, both physically and psychologically. To keep top men from spinning, management must see that executives, should: receive periodic medical checkups; receive periodic psychological evaluation; be given an adequate number of assistants of proper ability; have their time pressures reduced through improved selling; be given training in leadership.

—*Dr. Stanley G. Duesky*

Marketing

Ecotourism has been described as 'a complex phenomenon, involving integration of many actors including tourists, resident peoples, suppliers, and managers and multiple functions'. Moreover, these actors, or stakeholders, are engaged in a symbiotic relationship revolving around the idea of tourism as a means of economic development and as a means of promoting conservation of natural resources. If the ecotourism industry is to be developed more fully, and sustained for future generations, it will be necessary to understand the connections between conservation and tourism. In the 1987 report of the World Commission on Environment and Development, Our Common Future, it was suggested that problems of the environment and development could be solved if planning and decision making in those two spheres could be linked with cooperation between the tourism industry and government. As such this chapter intends to propose a model of planning, development and management of ecotourism that maximizes the opportunity to solicit input from the various stakeholders groups who could potentially be affected by management decisions.

Lessard described a 'General Framework for Integrated Ecological Assessments' in which they argued that Managers are faced more and more with the need to make decisions involving complex cultural, social, economic and environmental issues' and must adapt management strategies and goals to fluid situations. Ecotourism management is an undertaking of such complexity. According to Lessard, this involves 'a continuing process of action-based planning, assessment, monitoring, research and adjustment with the objective of improving implementation and achieving desired goals and outcomes. Fennell and Eagles (1990) described a framework for understanding and integrating conservation and visitor use. They suggested that tour companies, government agencies, remote communities and visitors could all prosper through cooperation and suitable planning. Within their conceptualisation, the resource tour (i.e. tourism to see a specific resource) is identified as the central focus of ecotourism, influenced by both the service industry and the visitor. While some ecotourists seek their own experiences, many avail themselves of the infrastructure and assistance provided by tour operators, guides and/ or interpreters. The natural settings that ecotourists desire are typically owned and managed by governments through institutions such as resource management agencies responsible for managing public parks and wildlife refuges. The framework further amplifies the interrelationship between community development and resource conservation.

Marketing is essential to create visitor desire for the

destination and can occur at the international, national and local level. The policies created by visitor management ultimately affect the visitors' experience by controlling allowable activities and proscribing others. Finally, the ecotourists' attitudes will be affected by the positive and/ or negative experiences during their visit, which may in turn affect their cognitive assessment of their tour. This cognitive assessment will aid in the determination of whether or not to revisit the destination, and will also influence the decisions of others to travel to that destination. Fennell and Eagles 1990 concluded that successful ecotourism ventures are dependent upon the 'complicated integration of public policy and private enterprise'.

Another framework for understanding and integrating conservation and visitor use is the ecotourism opportunity spectrum (ECOS) developed by Boyd and Butler (1996). ECOS incorporates concepts from the recreational opportunity spectrum and the tourism opportunity spectrum (Butler and Waldbrook, 1991) and was developed to give ecotourism destination management a similar conceptual framework with which to guide decision making. The eight components included in the ECOS framework are: (i) accessibility; (ii) relationship between ecotourism and other resource uses; (iii) attractions offered; (iv) existing tourism infrastructure; (v) level of user skill and knowledge required; (vi) level of social interaction; (vii) degree of acceptance of impacts and control over level of use; and (viii) type of management necessary to ensure long-term sustainability of the destination's resources.

In order to identify the viability of potential ecotourism offerings, the first seven components are assessed on scales ranging from eco-specialist to eco-generalist, with a midpoint of intermediate. An eco-specialist is a tourist requiring minimal infrastructure, having little impact, and generally participating as an individual or in a small group immersed in the local natural and cultural environment. On the other extreme, eco-generalists require a tourism infrastructure in order to be comfortable, have more impact, and usually participate in larger groups. These two poles are comparable to the hard-soft continuum, where the eco-specialist is the same as the hard ecotourist, and the eco-generalist equates to the soft ecotourist.

With the use of the ECOS, potential opportunities for ecotourism may be identified by management. Further, according to Boyd and Butler, if the ECOS can aid tourism marketers in 'attracting and maintaining the desired and appropriate type of ecotourist to a destination, then it could reduce the pressure on the area which a set of undifferentiated users would exert'.

While each of these models is instructive, they do not address the broad nature of ecotourism beyond the ecotour, nor acknowledge the diverse set of organisations and stakeholders that are the hallmark of the ecotourism industry.

Ecotourism Organisations

The ecotourism industry comprises organisations that run the gamut from governmental agencies to non-government organisations,(NGOs) and private enterprises. Stakeholders in this process refer to these organisations, as well as local residents. Also included are interest groups that may benefit from or be affected in some way by the outcome of ecotourism development in a community, even if they themselves are not directly participating in the ecotourism sector. This organisational diversity complicates the challenge of ecotourism management, often leading to fragmentation of efforts, a high potential for conflict, and an overall lack of synergy and focus. Even among governmental agencies. the responsibility for managing ecotourism is rarely consolidated under a single department. The management of wildlife, forests, water and other natural resources, for example, is typically assigned to a single, agency the managing wildlife is assigned to state wild life agencies). In contrast, responsibility for developing and managing tourism most often falls under the purview of departments of commerce, economic development, or similar organisations. Coordination between these agencies is often sporadic at best. In many ways, ecotourism suffers from the problem of 'everybody's business is nobody's business'.

Moreover, ecotourism has suffered historically from fragmentation of efforts among the different strata of organisations whose missions and policies affect the ecotourism industry (i.e. governmental, NGOs and private enterprises). For example, governmental agencies have regulatory power, as well as responsibilities for management of natural resources and economic development. In similar fashion, NGOs have traditionally reflected the more singular orientation of their affiliates in government. Long a stalwart of protection of critical ecosystems through land acquisition, The Nature Conservancy's stated mission, for example, is 'to preserve plants, animals and natural communities that represent the diversity of life on earth by protecting the lands and waters they need to survive.' For their part, private enterprises traditionally have been the 'front line' of suppliers of ecotourism products and services. They benefit economically from the provision of ecotourism goods and services and are the catalyst of economic development within the community. Whereas governmental and nongovernmental organisations have been primarily oriented toward management and protection of resources, private businesses historically have been profit oriented. After all businesses that do not make a profit do not stay in business long.

However, a blurring of the historical distinctions between these organisations is beginning to occur, manifest in programmes related to the concept of ecotourism. An excellent example of this is The Nature Conservancy's Ecotourism Programme. This provides 'technical assistance to their international partners in order to better harness the potential of ecotourism as a conservation tool that contributes to the long-term protection of biodiversity and the natural resources upon which it is based' (Ecotourism Society, 2000). Additionally, private enterprises aspiring to capitalise on societal interest in the environment and recreational travel can no longer fail to recognise their dependency on the natural resource base, nor acknowledge the importance of resource protection and sustainability. Conversely, natural resource management agencies cannot afford to ignore the recreational use of natural and cultural resources. Although arguably still in its infancy, the recent movement by these agencies into the human dimension arena is encouraging, and moves governmental agencies further in line with the common purpose of ecotourism. Many resource management agencies, particularly state wildlife agencies, have begun to develop active human dimensions research programmes, develop positions specifically related to human dimension management, or revise their missions to include the provision of recreation and tourism opportunities. Illustrative of this evolution, in the past decade, is the Virginia Department of Game and Inland Fisheries' initiative to become more aggressive in conducting research with external stakeholders and to hire a 'human dimension specialist' to coordinate these efforts. Further, their mission statement was revised to include the provision of outdoor recreation opportunities

> To manage Virginia's wildlife and inland fish-to maintain optimum populations of all species to serve the needs of the Common wealth; to provide opportunity for all to enjoy wildlife, inland fish, boating and related outdoor recreation; to promote safety for persons and property in connection with boating, hunting and fishing.

Even the longstanding distinction between profit-oriented private enterprise and then on-profit-oriented governmental and nongovernmental entities is being eroded.

Many public agencies and NGOs are now actively promoting and delivering ecotourism programmes, tours and events, for a profit. Whether the motivation is economic or stewardship, organisational missions and strategies are beginning to coalesce around the idea of ecotourism, capitalising on public interest in the environment. Therefore, the need for collaboration, cooperation and synergy among this multitude is as obvious as it will be challenging. In the past, economics have often run counter to protection and preservation interests. But ecotourism, perhaps for the first time, provides a feasible mechanism to align economic incentives with stewardship of the environment. It is at this interface, between the resource systems and human systems, that ecotourism exist and have the potential to flourish.

Management Information System

The information necessary to successfully develop and manage a sustainable ecotourism industry is vast. Information needs range from advancing the knowledge of ecology and the tolerance of natural resources to human use, and the market segmentation of ecotourists. Research of interest to the ecotourism industry is regularly conducted by seemingly disparate organisations. For example, resource management agencies typically conduct research on wildlife populations, forests, and wilderness and other common resources of interest to ecotourism managers. Inventories of natural resources, as well as cultural and historical resources, are commonly conducted by public agencies, including universities. The environmental impacts of development and the tolerance of resources to increasing human encroachment are assessed and mitigated through environmental Impact Assessment. Most of this research is undertaken for the purpose of protecting biodiversity, and promoting the preservation and sustainability of our natural and cultural heritage. Unfortunately, even though it has relevance, this research often has not been translated into the context of ecotourism, nor the results disseminated widely.

On the human side, private businesses and tourism-oriented corporations have great knowledge of their customers: their likes, dislikes, motivations and constraints. Chambers of commerce and economic development authorities invest large sums in gathering intelligence on which to base business and development decisions. Attitudinal surveys, needs assessments and social impact assessments have traditionally been the domain of marketers and social scientists, and are only beginning to find their way into natural resource management organisations. The melding of both natural and social science into comprehensive ecotourism research, therefore, is a relatively recent phenomenon. What is needed is a better mechanism for increasing the number of organisations involved in the collaborative conceptualisation of ecotourism research, thus increasing the views of more stakeholders in the planning process, and providing better way's of disseminating the results throughout the industry. The management information system described in our integrated systems model advocates broadening the number and types of organisations involved in ecotourism planning. This multi-organisational approach to eco-tourism planning-research has the advantage of being more cost-effective, as well as increasing the efficiency of information dissemination. However, gathering intelligence is only the first step in planning ecotourism projects. Involving stakeholders in the ensuing decision-making process is as important to the success of projects as gathering good intelligence.

Although resource systems and human systems planning are depicted in this model as two separate components, this does not suggest that they function independently. Information is transferred between the two. Failure to include information related to stakeholders' preferences and opinions cannot be ignored. Using the information gleaned from the management information system, ecotourism decision makers can begin the process of planning policies, programmes and development of ecotourism experiences. From this, consensus related to plans may emerge. Important actors in the management decision process are the stakeholders groups referred to earlier. Stakeholder participation in the ecotourism management planning process is critical to its success. Stakeholder participation refers to the opportunity for stakeholders to take part in the process of ecotourism development. If governmental bodies are to manage resources for future generations, then it is critical that such organisations gain the support for this approach to ecotourism development from the beginning. Stakeholders such as commercial operators may perceive no harm in attracting unlimited numbers of visitors to the resource each year. Resource planners on the other hand, are likely to espouse another view, considering their mission statement. Resource planners, cognizant of the social and environmental impacts that too many visitors will have on the resource and ultimately contribute to its demise, will have an opinion that may be in opposition to that of some commercial operators. Community residents may have another opinion. Stakeholders have a variety of opportunities or times during which they can participate in the process, including the planning stage, during implementation and evaluation, and in the distribution of benefits. Participation in the planning process includes such tasks as problem identification, formulating alternatives, activity planning, and resource allocation. Participants may also manage or co-manage ecotourism projects, hence stakeholders receive economic, social, cultural and/or other benefits from the project either alone or together.

Paul (1987) suggests these four levels of stakeholder participation: (i) information sharing; (ii) consultation; (iii) decision making; and (iv) initiating action. Information sharing refers to the exchange of information between stakeholders in order to facilitate action. For example, plans to expand a beach front hotel should be shared with the stakeholders who may be impacted, negatively or positively, by the expansion. Failure to do so will only encourage the development of negative rumors and result in opposition to the project. In the next phase, consultation, stakeholders are not only informed but also consulted on essential issues during the planning process. Stakeholder groups may possess the type of information needed by an agency to make timely and accurate decisions. The third level, decision making, involves stakeholders in making decisions about the ecotourism project. In these situations, stakeholders are equal partners. When stakeholders take the initiative in terms of actions and decisions related to the ecotourism project, they themselves begin the process. There are many advantages to incorporating stakeholders in ecotourism projects. One advantage lies with the early warning system that they bring to the table. Stakeholders may provide information that, if suppressed or inaccessible, could otherwise cause conflict. Because stakeholder involvement fosters better planning and decision making, conflicts are brought out earlier and have a greater chance of being resolved. In addition, inclusion of stakeholders would provide opportunities for these participants to become aware of the benefits of the project, and to be more likely to provide support for the project. If stakeholders understand an ecotourism project, they are more likely to become proactive and involved with the project. Their inclusion also provides some aspect of legitimisation to the ecotourism project, especially if they represent a diverse array of interests. Additional benefits, such as cost sharing and the protection of' cultural norms, may accrue to the ecotourism project.

Ecotourism Development

It is important to consider the development of ecotourism

products/ experiences in the context of policy. Essential to the development of sustainable ecotourism is consideration of each of the impacts that a management decision may have on the resource's ability to deliver the experience the ecotourist seeks. Several aspects of ecotourism development must be considered together, as follows.

Objectives of Ecotourism

Management decisions regarding ecotourism projects and related issues will result in the need to establish specific, measurable project objectives, just as the missions of the various organisations will vary with respect to its approach to ecotourism management, the objectives formulated for projects will also be somewhat different. Competing objectives result in conflict during implementation. Therefore, care must be taken to be cognizant of the opinions among the various stakeholder groups regarding objectives. Project objectives assist managers in guiding development. Objectives should be couched in terms that are measurable, results-oriented, and time dependent. They should address the concepts of effectiveness, efficiency and equity and form the bases of project evaluation.

Product Experience

Ecotourism destinations can produce a broad range of experiences. They range from wildlife watching, to mountain biking, river rafting experiences and other activities that incorporate an adventure or cultural component. However, these activities are only the means by which ecotourists satisfy their needs. Research has shown that ecotourists are often motivated by the desire to escape or to relax, to see nature, and to participate in nature experiences as a means of socialising with friends. If managers concentrate on activities rather than the benefits visitors seek, the experience may be less than satisfactory to the visitor. When experiences do not fulfill ecotourists needs, then the ecotourist is likely not to return. Failure to manage the benefits associated with the. ecotourist's experience can also result in conflict among ecotourists. Mistakes of this nature will ultimately result in product or even destination failure. Ecotourism managers are also asked to manage interactions between ecotourists and the resource.

Vickerman (1988) stated that wildland fauna are particularly impacted by tourist development. Interaction with wildlife is often the critical aspect of the ecotourism experience. To that end, some tour operators provide regular feeding of wildlife such that they will appear and perform at the correct time, thus performing for tourists. But, while this may facilitate the ease with which visitors view wildlife, in most cases, feeding wildlife is frowned upon. These practices may actually do harm to wildlife, thus violating the premise of protecting the resource. Therefore, a common dilemma facing management of ecotourism destinations is how to minimise environmental damage and provide visitors with a memorable tourist experience, while affording local communities benefits from the process. A management tool that can aid in this process is the use of visitor codes. Visitor codes, also termed visitor guidelines or codes of conduct, put in writing principles that a destination would like their patrons to follow, it is believed that with the proper use of well-formulated visitor codes, incorporated within an overall management strategy, the impacts of visitors on natural environments can be reduced.

Several ecotourism destinations, including, Belize. Madagascar and Nepal, have already instituted visitor codes. The countryside Commission in England was one of the initial organisations to employ the use of a code of ethics for visitors more than 20 years ago. This code advises visitors to take their refuse home with them, help keep water clean and protect wildlife; plants and trees. The International Association of Antarctic Tour Operators has a code of ethics for visitors to the Antarctic which cites the need to dispose of waste materials properly, and informs visitors not to leave footprints in fragile environments or encroach upon the habitat of seabirds and animals in protected areas. It is hoped that this initiative will decrease the environmental damage caused by ship borne tourism to Antarctica.

Ecotourism managers may also utilise the temporal and or spatial zoning as a means of protecting resources and the ecotourism experience. The number of visits may be limited or restricted. For example, back-country visitation is restricted in areas of Yellowstone and other national parks when the danger of bear-human encounters is high. Man-made structures, such as viewing stands and boardwalks, may be employed to restrict foot traffic in wetlands or other fragile ecosystems to protect the resource from too many ecotourists and their activities.

Distribution of Products/Experiences

In the past, many environments were protected from ecotourists because they were inaccessible, or due to the high cost of accessing the site. This, however, is no longer the case with most natural areas. The introduction of low cost airfares, new, lightweight backcountry equipment, and other lower participation costs have removed these barriers for many, thus increasing access to the pristine environment. This aspect of ecotourism planning refers to the ecotourists' access to the tourism product/experience. First, the destination must be accessible. How difficult is it for ecotourists to arrive at the destination? What are the destination's hours of operation and seasons? Additionally, decisions related to the use of tour wholesalers, tour brokers, travel agents or other travel intermediaries are made at this time. Selection of partners to distribute ecotourism experiences is critical to the effectiveness of ecotourism development.

Ecotourism destinations must ensure that all members of their distribution network share the same code of ethics for ecotourists. Recently, conflict between tour dive ships and those interested in protecting the resource has occurred. Although dive captains are supposed to instruct their divers not to touch coral reefs, many divers still do so as dive captains watch. Selection of dive ships in which to issue permits becomes an issue of distribution and protection of the ecotourism resource.

Price

Price is one of the four major variables that the ecotourism manager controls. Price is important because it affects 'profitability'. Guided by an organisation's objectives and mission statement, ecotourism managers must develop a set of pricing objectives and policies to guide their pricing decisions These policies should spell out how flexible prices are, at what levels they will be set, and who shall receive discounts. Ecotourists exchange money and non-monetary costs for the benefits they expect to receive from the ecotourism experience. Monetary costs refer to user fees, admission charges, rates, fines, or fees. Monetary costs can also be attributed to the costs associated with travelling to the resource, or with the cost to obtain the equipment necessary to participate. Non-monetary costs include time, opportunity and effort costs.

Not all ecotourism agencies will charge for the experience. The decision to charge or not to charge often depends upon the costs associated with collecting the fees. In some cases it will cost more to collect the fees than the fees collected. Prices are usually charged if ecotourism agencies wish to recover costs or part of the costs from the tourists. Fees can also be charged to motivate the tourist to become aware of the value of the resource. In other instances, fees are charged to motivate resource managers. User fees can also be charged for admission to Protected areas. However, agencies must determine their pricing objectives prior to determining the price to charge.

These pricing objectives must be consistent with the agency's objectives. Prices may be charged to generate revenue, or for efficiency, equity or income redistribution, to reduce demand to place it in balance with the area's existing carrying capacity, or to increase the carrying capacity. Efficiency is concerned with getting the most out of a given set of resources. Equity means that the price should be fair. Income redistribution refers to the use of subsidies to assist tourists in the use of the resource.

Ecotourist managers must next decide which proportion of their costs they wish to recover. They can recover all fixed and variable costs, a proportion of fixed or variable costs, only fixed costs or only the variable costs. The key factor for ecotourism agencies to decide in setting the price is to discover what it costs them to deliver the experience. Next they must decide how much of their costs they wish to recover and why. Another consideration in using a price to recover agency costs is the life cycle stage of the experience. New eco-tourism destinations may be expensive because access is limited, the costs are high, or because the destination may wish to communicate a value image using price. During the growth stage of the experience the pricing strategy may differ. The price charged to ecotourists could be used to cater certain types of tourists, or to keep visitation levels within manageable parameters. Increasing the price of the experience during peak seasons can also deter some ecotourists for the same reason. Charging the price serves to distribute demand for the experience across other seasons. Prices may be lowered to reflect lower costs, or they may be increased or they may stay the same. During declining popularity ecotourism managers may decide to lower the price so that they cover the minimum costs. The price to charge for the ecotourism experience may be restated as the cost of the experience to stakeholders.

What will it cost stakeholders if the ecotourists do not come and what will it cost if the ecotourists do come?

Communications

Ecotourism destinations must develop communications programmes that portray the destination's desired image. The ecotourist destination may include the following components:

- Advertising
- Personal selling
- Public relation
- Incentives.

Advertising refers to all paid forms of communication from print to broadcast. Personal selling are the act of personal communication-between individuals and/or groups. Public relations are those activities the destination engages in as a corporate citizen. For example, ecotourist destinations may sponsor a children's nature photography contest as a means of raising the level of awareness about the ecotourism experience.

Evaluation

Perhaps the most important component of the process is evaluation. Ecotourism managers must evaluate the effectiveness of all of their programmes and policies. Feedback from tourists' evaluation of their experiences can give destination managers the information necessary to change, modify, or delete existing programmes or policies. Problems associated with communication, pricing, products/experiences or distribution can only be addressed if ecotourism managers are aware of the problems. Information needed by ecotourism managers can be obtained from internal and external records held by the agency. Internal records are the data that the organisation already has, such as guestrecords, permits, revenue generated, etc. To answer questions for which the agency does not have the information will require the agency to obtain the data. They may conduct research to answer the questions, or they may use outside sources, government documents for example, to answer the questions. Additionally ecotourism managers will not be able to assess the agency's progress toward their goals if they are not evaluated.

Ecotourism managers may be interested in the efficiency with which a programme operates. Are the current visitor codes working? On, the other hand ecotourism managers may wish to know about equity. Equity refers to fair allocation of resources, when decisions are made. This attempts to address the issue of balance and who wins and who loses as the consequence of a decision. For example, how does the development of an ecotourism resort affect the residents of the community?

Agencies interested in ecotourism are multifaceted, and as such operate under many conflicting mandates at times. Thus there is likely to be 'conflict between the stakeholders in the management process. The ideas presented in this chapter offer a process consisting of management tools focused on an integrated approach to decision making. Adoption of this integrated model offers several advantages. Using the model presented in this lesson, assessments conducted at appropriate scope can provide more relevant and cost-effective information for decision making than some limited perspectives. A quality assessment can provide a synthesis of relationships of human and natural resources. Better experience development can be achieved by focusing on the needs and wants of the ecotourist and balancing this with the resources and capabilities of the agency. From human systems planning, stakeholders can learn about the social and economic issues facing ecotourism planners.

7

Elements of Modern Tourism Planning

> A man would have no pleasure in discovering all the beauties of the universe, even in heaven itself, unless he had a partner to whom he might communicate his joys.
>
> —*Cicero*

The creation of powerful images of the region is one of the important parts of regional development. What comes to mind when you hear of hills, Himalayas, Uttaranchal, Uttrakhand, Garhwal, Kumaon, Arunachal, Sikkim, Nepal, Bhutan, Himachal, Jammu and Kashmir, Ladakh. Drive to hills, and high-rise mountains, valleys, rivers, natural beauty, adverse climate and beautiful environment, high hills and unpolluted water comforts you. Highlanders evoke warmth, friendliness, and neighbourliness, are hardworking and honest people. The area will have to reposition its image — trying to attract new industry, finding ways to attract tourists and make them spend-money in the area and try to keep the best of the education for students. The regional image is a critical determinant of the way citizen and business responds to area. The whole region must try to manage its image.

Regional Image

The Himalayan image is comprised of beliefs, ideas and impressions that people have of the region. Basically, the image represents a simplification of a large number of associations and pieces of information connected with the region. They are a product of the mind trying to process and 'classify' huge amount of data about the region. An image is more than a simple belief, is a whole set of beliefs about regions, such as picturesque land, beautiful natural scenery, pleasant climate, and wonderful valleys. People may have different attitude towards a region because each one of them may have different attitude toward different element which create an image. Thus, an image is a more personal perception of a region that can carry from person to person.

Strategic image management of the region is an ongoing process of researching a region's image among its audiences, segmenting and targeting its specific image and its demographic audiences, positioning the region's benefits to support an existing image or create a new image, and communicating those benefits to the target audiences. The regional images are identifiable and change overtime. Cne must be able to track and influence the image held by different target audiences. Formally, an image sticks in the public mind for a long time, even after it looses its vitality. A place image may change more rapidly as the media or word of mouth spread vital news stories about the region. Thus image management for a region is an ongoing process of researching image changes and trving to understand their dynamics.

Measurement of Regional Image

To access the Himalayan image, let us proceed by following two important steps: *First,* to select a target audience. *Second,* to measure the target audience's perception along relevant attributes.

While selecting the target audience segments, all must have common characteristics, trait, interests and perceptions. There may be varied audiences interested in living, visiting, or working in the region and each one of them may hold different images. Some of these audiences are given below:

New Residents

New residents may be welcomed if they bring in good score into the region.

Visitors

The number of tourists and visitors should be increased and study the image the visitors have of this region.

Factories

Small and medium type of factories and industries be encouraged to the region and find out what the prospective management knows and think about the place.

Corporate Headquarters and Offices

Major companies could be approached and attracted to the region to open their offices, therefore, understand the opinions of location specialists and company leaders.

Entrepreneurs

Attract entrepreneurs and small businesses and understand how the prospects view the place as a community to live and work.

Investors

Real estate developers and other financiers who have confidence in the region's future be attracted so as to get generous loans and investments.

Foreign Purchasers

Convince the foreign buyers that the region's products and services are of high quality. The region is so vast and varied that die image of the places may be different in each group of audience. Tourist perceptions differ, depending on their interests, similarly, the perceptions of manufacturers differ depending on the type of industry such as software or heavy-duty industries. While targeting specific audience groups one should avoid the problem of unstable or inconsistent images. Researchers should identify characteristics that maximise discrimination among groups holding different images. These characteristics include the following:

- Objective measures: demographic, geographic
- Complex measures: social class, family life-cycle, life-style, etc.
- Behavioural measures: buying decision, usage etc.
- Informal measures: personality, need sought benefits, etc.

Within the country, the Himalayan's image has one of the low industrial potential, and industrial backwardness. This image kept the Himalayan region out of the running for major manufacturing projects. The area needs to assess its specific strengths and opportunities it offers. One of the Himalayas greatest strength is its natural beauty. It boasts of sunshine, snow, beautiful natural scenery, forests, valleys, mountains, wildlife, green environment, and pleasant climate. The area has to search the best of industries suitable for the area.

The analysis of character segment is of vital importance. They should have following characteristics:

- Mutually exclusive: The various identical segment should not overlap.
- Exhaustive: Every potential target member should be included in some segment.
- Measurable: The degree to which the size, purchasing power, and profile of the resulting segment can be readily measured.

— Accessible: The degree to which the resulting segments can be used, effectively reached and served.
— Substantial: The degree to which the resulting segments are large enough to be work pursuing.
— Differently responsive: The segment is useful one it responds differently from the other segments to various amounts, types, and timing of marketing strategy.

For example, we want to advertise high potential prospects for skiing at Auli, by sending direct mail. We will have to characterise the people who would be interested in skiing, know whether they have discretionary income to respond positively, access their addresses, ascertain that a sufficient number of them exist, and project that a sufficient number of them will open their mail and respond positively. Now, the audience is segmented by relevant criteria and group of interest need to be selected. Identify the attributes of a particular target audience user to profile a place. For example, a study of tourists who returned repeatedly to a small hill resort area revealed the following attributes:

— Availability of facilities
— Scenic beauty
— Opportunity for rest and recreation
— Suitable accommodation
— Pleasant attitude of people.

Hidden Image

Different approaches could be used for measuring image such as:

— Familiarity-favourability measurement
— Semantic differential, and
— Evaluative maps.

In applying familiarity-favourability measurement approach, the first step is to establish how familiar the target audience is with the region and how favourable members feel towards it. To establish familiarity respondents may be asked to check one of the following:

— Never heard of
— Heard of
— Know a little bit
— Know a fair amount
— Know very well.

The result will indicate the audience's awareness of the region. Those respondents who have some familiarity with the region, may he asked to describe how favourable they feel towards it by checking one of the following:

— Very unfavourable
— Some what unfavourable
— Indifferent
— Some what favourable
— Very favourable.

The next step to it is to research the content of region's image by the most population semantic differential tool. It involves the following steps:-

Step I - Develop a Set of Relevant Dimensions

The researcher should ask people of the region to identify the dimensions they would use in thinking about the place. He may question people such as, what things do you think of when you consider a vacation? The answer could be weather, recreational opportunities, historical interest, cost and so on. Turn each of these answers into a bipolar scale, with adjectival exercises at each end. The scales can be rendered as five or seven point scales.

Step II - Reduce the Set of Relevant Dimensions

This will avoid respondent's fatigue in having to rate several vacation sites. The researchers showed remove redundant scales and add little information.

Step III - Administer the Instrument to a Sample of Respondents

Ask the respondent to rate one area at a time. The bipolar adjectives should be arranged so as not to load all of the negative adjectives on one side. After the results are in, the scale can be rearranged to display all the positive adjectives on one side for convenience of interpretation.

Step IV - Average the Results

The respondents perception are averaged on each scale. When the average are connected, they represent the average image that the audience has of the place.

Step V - Check on the Image Variance

As each image profile is a line of means, it does not reveal how variable the image actually is. If the variance is high the image does not mean much and further audience segmentation is necessary.

An example of a set of bipolar scales, which could be used to measure the image of this region. The line connecting the means shows the image that a particular group of respondents had of the Himalayan region.

Use of Evaluative Maps

Another measure of how people view an area is to inventory their visual impressions. Interview the area residents and collect their impressions and feelings about different areas of the region. The evaluative map reflecting how Himalayan residents view their area. The label represent words that are collected when residents are asked about the different parts of the area. The heading show how the residents evaluated different areas from most liked to the least liked.

All residents and visitors dislike the appearance of chaotic and downtown districts, paths and edges. They like the looks of new, spacious land mark areas, vegetated areas, and that with view of rivers, valleys, green maintains and hills. If the region or area does nothing, it will continue to lose population and will not attract tourists. Exploring all the opportunities, the region should act with vigour to capitalise its longstanding image problem. Gradually, the region may transform its subsequent negatives, into attractions. Icon marketing is another strategy for correcting a negative image of the region. Circle the image of the whole Himalayan region, which, until recently, struck people as vast, scattered region, grim shortages of food and products, citizen living in *kachcha* houses, lack of transportation. The overall impression is one of darkness and inaccessibility—a place that few people wanted to visit. New styles outstanding icons could enter and use their personality to help reshape the public image of this region. Even a single person, well positioned in understanding the demands of the region, can influence and reshape public perception of a place. Visit to foreign countries, personal interviews with international TV personalities, toast with great humour, and mixing with foreigners on a street, give positive impression of the region. The strategy may work best when the issues are less dramatic and the audiences are not troubled by political or economic problems.

Image improvement is one of the panaceas or a quick fix for regional problems. But in most of the cases it will not work, if the region does not start to correct its deep seated problems. A place may be a mixture of poverty, drink, and violence. It may earn its reputation and attract government grants to rehabilitate tenement and public places. Various political forces cooperate. There may be change of attitude in the people that run the area. New jobs are created and the attitude starts improving. People begin to police themselves, encourage innovation and change, and monitor their own political, economic and educational institution. The regions image makers may tie together the changing realities of the area. Glossy purchases demonstrating the region's transformation, visually and in words could be prepared. Articles in newspapers and magazines indicate the arrival of a new giant and a new image will be set.

Designing an Area Image

After understanding the image of the area, deliberate on what image can be build up of the region. A desired image may include words such as boring housewives, fictional oranges, leechies, fruit, etc. Each response has some justification. For an image to be effective it must fulfill the following criteria:

— Validity: Promote an image which is not too far from reality.

— Believable: A proposed image may be valid but it may not be readily believable. If we claim that Garhwal is more beautiful than Kumaon, while it may be true, people may not be ready to believe it. Therefore, it must first claim that Garhwal is beautiful as Kumaon and later on increase the claim.

— Simple: If the area disseminates too many images of itself, it may lead to confusion.

— Appeal: The image must suggest why people want to live there, visit, invest and so forth. *1* love Himalayas', 1 love Garhwal', I love Kumaon' has more positive content in suggesting that there are things to love about these areas.

— Distinctive: The image works best when is different from other common themes. Don't overuse the words such as friendly places "Place that works', Wonder Himalayas', etc.

Communicating an Image

You may use *three* tools to implement an effective image of the region.

— Slogans, themes, and positions
— Visual symbols, and
— Events and deeds.

Slogans, Themes and Positions

Develop a suitable slogan to unify, a specific campaign. Slogan may be carried over many campaigns. The slogan should be a short catchall phrase that embodies an overall vision of the area. The slogan are useful in generating enthusiasm momentum and fresh ideas.

A good slogan provides a platform from which the regional image can be further amplified. The tourists feel quickly about sporting the beautiful scenery. The area, therefore, should provide echo tourism, a form of seeing and not disturbing.

The image must also be backed by real performance. Image positioning is another tool for communication. The region should be positioned in the national and international levels as an area for certain type of activity or as a viable alternative location/ attraction to another place that may have a stranger or more well established position. The challenge of image positioning is to develop an image that communicates benefits and unique attributes that make the area standout among other areas.

Image position should be supported by reality of the region. There must be message as well as the product. If we want tourist image positioning of the region, there must be tourist infrastructure—road, hotels, etc.

Visual Symbols

Many landmark sites of the area may permanently be etched in the public mind by visual symbols, for example, the Taj Mahal (India), the Great Wall (China), the Eiffel Tower (Paris), the Big Ben (London), the Red Square (Moscow) and the Astrodome (Houston). When used well, these visual symbols appear on official stationary, brochure, billboard, and other places.

A visual image needs to be reinforce as an image argument. If the visual is inconsistent with the slogan, themes, or positions, it undermines the area's credibility. It will be a mistake to represent Himalayan region as only rural wonder land featuring tourist brochures as never ending collage of hills, streams, and thatched houses and cottages. This will project the region as brutal and dangerous. The region need a more believable visual image strategy than pastoral greenery, and might emphasise its wide range of natural attractions. Following *four* visual image strategies could be used for this region:

The Diverse Visual

Treat the viewers to a wide range of visual images about the region. The aim is to dispel the nation that the region has a single character. Photographer of tourist attraction, abstract paintings, land mark, and pages devoted to local artist, will reflect the overall visual effect of versatility and completeness.

The Humorous Visual

In the humorous strategy, the visual treats the region in witty style. This strategy is when dealing with a negative aspect of the region'. The visual may tell the story of the region as, it is redeveloping, it is a short trip destination, and it is a region that trusts itself enough to parody itself.

The Denying Visual

Another way to handle a negative image of the region is to overwhelm the target audience with positive images, some of which subtly deny the negative aspects. There are many areas in the region where ignoring the obvious is risky.

The Consistent Visual

When the area possess a positive image, it is easier to assemble strong visuals. A visual image of high-tech park may spoil the deeply rooted and carefully developed historic image of the region. The far better strategy is to pursue an education image, students and new residents. The accompanying visual would work well together.

Events and Deeds: Generally, image campaign takes the form of catchy slogans, advertisement, and video. However, events and deeds are also the best method to communicate. In image, the events could be bold, or they can be on the quite side, subtly influencing an audience overtime use of events and deed could be made for communicating the image of the region.

Correcting a Negative Image of the Region

When any part of Himalayas suffers earthquake, or experiences any natural or external calamities, there can be tremendous wave of negative publicity. Similarly, when an area has a poor economy, humid climate, or repressive leadership, it has to address the problem of its negative image.

In all the above cases the best option is to admit to the problem and turn the negative into positive. The whole Himalayan region lived with the reputation of being cold weather region, from which one should flee the extreme winter that begins in October-November and persists till March-April, is the most negative aspect of this region.

These winter problems migrated many people from this area. How to deal with this problem? Himalayas could aggressively promote its winters. Not only the region promotes the tourist attractions and winter events and also feature downtown walk ways that could shield residents from the winter. The region could sponsor its winter carnivals. Some areas could be marketed as short trip destinations by hosting a yearlong celebration of great calamities. Activities such as rock concerts, screening of earthquake films, etc., will make people to visit the area for the event and interest in the region could be maintained.

Promoting and Distributing Image and Messages

There are challenges involved in distributing and promoting strong and coherent image of this region, immediately, following question arise regarding the distribution of image of this region:

— Who is the target audience?
— What are the tools available?
— What major advertising media channels are available?
— What are the respective characteristics of these advertising media channels?
— What criteria should be used in choosing specific advertising vehicles?
— How should the advertising messages be timed?
— How can the mix be developed?
— How can the communication results be evaluated?
— How can conflicting media resources and messages be handled?

The region has to develop a story about itself, which needs to be told consistently and well. The image of the region should evoke a picture of many lakes, good skiing, a healthy climate and beautiful natural scenery. The region could attract many tourists to its lakes, fishing and other inexpensive activities it could draw tourists and businesses. It must operate a very efficient regional marketing mechanism. The promoters include state tourism, commissioners, various cities and regions, hotels, motels, restaurant, tourist attraction, universities, colleges, sport teams, and cultural attractions. It must have a high profile phone numbers that reaches a large number of potential visitors. It must operate clean attractive tourist centers along with its road providing information, regional maps, hotels and motels, and advice on where to find the best of tourist attraction. The region should have its own chamber of commerce, tourist bureau, and business attraction efforts. Each area should invest in tourist advertising specially to promote summer vacations. The whole region should develop promotional plans, publish and distribute newspapers and brochures, describing its attractions and accommodations. Fishing, water sports, summer camps, country/tillage fairs, local products, etc., could be promoted. The resorts and hotels should actively promote their properties as well as the area. Ads could be run is different areas and locations seeking to attract tourists. Promote the virtues of living in the Himalayas. Hotel chains could run regional advertisements for summer time vacation. Restaurants should acquire regional reputation.

Industries should create favourable impressions of the region though their products. Pure water, natural beauty, etc., could be promoted. Articles could be published and distributed — advising restaurant owners to become friendly. Tourists be advised where to go for entertainment and how to keep the kids engaged on a rainy day. Thus, the region could achieve a virtual integration of its image distribution system.

Target Audience

The *first,* step before choosing messages and media is

to classify the target audience. Does the tourist traffic in the region want to attract young singles, young married, families or retired people. Each potential target calls for different messages and media. Should the tourist traffic rely on ads or feature articles? Should the message be placed in magazines, or news letters?

The *second* step is to visualise the target behaviour that is wanted from the target audience that message may be to spend four-five days on hill, or to visit in the summer than in the winter.

It is also necessary to determine the target buyer's stage of readiness to undertake the target behaviour. A tourist seeking a summer vacation may hold one of the several mind-sets regarding the region as destination:

— Knows nothing about Himalayan region
— Has some awareness of Himalayan region
— Would like to go to Himalayan region
— Intend to go to Himalayan region.

A media strategy could be different for each group. It may be in the form of television sports, or an incentive of discount campaign.

Influence Tools

The broad influence tools to promote the Himalayas to target markets are: advertising, direct marketing, sales promotion, public relations, personal selling, and other tools for example, films, television, shows, popular music, team sports, bout games, T-shirts, caps and posters.

Advertising Media Channels

There are hundred of newspapers, magazines, radio stations and television station. The first step in selection, calls for allocating the advertising budget to the major advertising media channels. Examine each channel as regards it capacity to deliver frequency, and impact the major media channels include television, radio, magazines, newspapers, bill boards, direct mail, telephone and brochures. Less conventional media channels are audiotapes, videotapes, faxes, interactive videos, trade mission, travel winters' convention, welcome centers, and consulates.

Choose the media channels by counselling the following variables:

— Target audience media habits
— Pro, duct or service
— Message
— Cost.

On the basis of media characteristic, allocate the given budget to the various media channels.

Evaluation of Media Results

The next step is to choose the specific media vehicles within each media category that could produce the desired response in the most cost-effective way. Suppose we want to advertise skiing adventures of Auli to young male adults. We should consider the category of male-oriented magazines. Examine circulation and, cost information for different sizes, colour options, ad positions, and number of insertions. Evaluate the different magazines or quantitative characteristic such as credibility, prestige, availability of geographical or occupation, edition, reproduction, quality, editorial climate, lead times and psychological impact. Make a final judgement as to which specific vehicles will deliver the best reach, frequency, and impact for money. Calculate the cost per thousand persons a particulars vehicle reaches. The budget heavily shapes media choices. The budget can be set by arbitrarily allocating a certain amount of money or percentage of sales to be spent. The budget is influence by how much should be spend to attract visitor and tourist. To invest little money can be worse than investing no money. A certain minimum level of investment is required to create initial interest in the region. Higher level of investment produce a high level of audience response. If the message is seen too frequently, most people stop noticing it and other become irritated.

Media Timing

Audience size and interest in the Himalayan region vary at different times of the year. Don't advertise when there is little interest. Spend bulk of advertising budget when natural interest in a place increases and peaks. Consider three possible patterns—burst advertising, continues advertising, and intermittent advertising. Shorter the audience memory, the more continuous the advertising should be.

Evaluation of Media Results

Evaluation research help to locate possible weak points in the communication implementation process. Did the message reach to the right people? Did they understand the message or find it credible and persuasive? Did it reach them frequently enough or at the right time? Should more have been spent? Evaluate the communication effects and sales effects of advertising. Measurement efforts are designed to answer three basic question:

- What response was obtained?
- Were the objectives meet, and
- What changes are recommended?

A well-designed set of evaluation procedures enables the message and the media to be constantly improved.

Conflicting Media Sources and Messages

The region may spent million of rupees advertising for tourists, residents or factories only to find controlled communication overwhelming the formal messages. Informal impression tend to offset and negate the more formally controlled impression. The planners should reinforce planned impressions with less formal ones and stage events. The best of all possible words occurs when informal and formal impressions merge to reinforce the image. The region should showcase only its positive features. It should like to hide from view the backward areas, homeless people, indelicate treatment of minorities and other unflattering impression. This degree of media control is unavailable. The region is driven by unplanned and often unwelcome events.

In the swirl of real events, unplanned events can heat or destroy entire economy overnight. We may present a services of commercials and advertisement stressing safety and friendliness, strongly highlighting programmes where tourist spend time in the homes of native people. The paid campaign may be overwhelmed by media reports of tourist robberies and beatings. Many tourists may return dissatisfied because when they wonder the tourist paths, they may encounter threatening situations and neighbourhood that may seem less than safe.

The region may also suffer a further cruel blow hit by devastating natural calamities. Tourists may find their treatment by the government during calamity less than satisfactory. The tourist reaction could be like *1* will never go to Himalayan region' — 'never again'. These remarks and negative impression may linger indefinitely and ultimately undo all the good words and deed built up meticulously over the years. In these natural calamities the region need to demonstrate compassion and efficiency. A spokesperson could explain the problems and the relief work being undertaken one-sided and unanswered story, could be very harmful in the region's interest.

What to do about negative impression? We suggest *three* possibilities:

— 'Ignore them', act as if it does not exist and it will go away.

- 'Counter attack' by swiftly sending out a counter message.
- 'Solve the problem' that gives rise to the negative impressions.

Which response is the best, depend on how serious is the negative impression, how widespread it is and how to remedial it. If the damage is not serious, if public knowledge is very limited, and if it is easily remedied, it is best to ignore the negative impression. If the damage is not serious but is widely known, and easily remedial, it may pay to counter attack. If the situation is very serious and widely known and not easily remedial, it is best to work towards a long-term response rather than ignore the situation or counter attack. A particular event may occur leading to a negative development. One course would be to ignore the event. The second course is to use the event as catalyst for redevelopment and further improvement.

A coordinated media and public relation campaign need to support the strategy to tell the new Himalayan regional story. The event should serve as an opportunity for the region to plan the area's redefinition. The area has fair warning. As one strategy, the chairman of district board, leading business people and residents should take a media training course in which they could become proficient at extolling the virtues of the area.

8

Regional Developmental Planning Techniques

> He who every morning plans the transactions of the day, and follows that plan, carries a thread that will guide him through the labyrinth of the most busy life. The orderly arrangement of his time is like a ray of light which darts itself through all his occupations. But where no plan is laid, where the disposal of time is surrendered merely to the chance of incidents, all things lie huddled together in one chaos, which admits of neither distribution nor review.
>
> —*Victor Hugo*

Today we find the growing plight of many villages, towns and areas of a region. Why the plight of this particular region? Is it victim of powerful global forces and sea changes that no amount of planning could have averted? Or is the region partly the cause in failing to plan its future better?

A region must do a better job of managing its future. Regional threats need to be recognised. Community development programmes, rural and urban planning and designing, and economic development approaches need to be introduced to design a better future. Special attention be placed in providing the area's situation, identifying the area's strengths/weaknesses, opportunities/threats, and main issues, setting a vision, objectives and goals, defining effective strategies for accomplishing these goals, developing appropriate actions, and implementing and controlling plan.

The region fails to anticipate changes, and may simply resist changes. It requires to do a job of forecasting and planning for the future. Basically, there are *two* questions to answers:

- What planning approaches could be used to guide regional development?
- How to improve the planning results by using strategic planning procedures?

Let us discuss the following *five* time honoured approaches to regional development:

- Community development
- Rural and urban design
- Rural and urban planning
- Economic development
- Strategic developmental planning

Community Development

Community development could help to create a quality environment for the people. Good schools, strong neighbourhoods, increased public safety, and adequate health facilities affect the quality of the region. The basic community development philosophy should be based on the idea of community participation and citizen improvement. The region should develop strong neighbourhood organisations and invest its limited resource in improving basic services for its citizens. Its major infrastructural elements—education, health, public safety, housing, and transportation needs to be improved.

The region will succeed in developing more livability and a better quality of life. It will be easier to attract new businesses and retain the existing businesses.

The community development alone cannot serve as a complete solution for improving the whole region's viability and attractiveness. Much of the area of the region lacks the required resources to make the levels of investment.

There is always a tug of war between neighbourhoods and organisations as to which are more deserving of community redevelopment findings. The community development approach suffers from inside-out thinking instead of outside-in thinking. It plans community's future without paying attention to the turbulence reshaping the national and world economy. No systematic attempt is made to figure out how to fit the community competitively into its village, district, regional, state, national and global setting. It is assumed that if a village is a 'good product' people will want to live there.

Rural and Urban Design

The professional designers, both rural and urban, share the assumption of community development professionals/ that a place must be pleasant to live in. More emphasis should be laid on architecture—open spaces and land use, street layout and traffic flow, cleanliness and environmental quality. Peoples attitudes and behaviour are strongly influenced by the quality of their physical environment which in turn are improved attitudes and behaviour. The designers should be active in small villages, towns and communities whose streets and buildings are neglected. These need face lifting and, broad schemes are needed to put a prettier face on the villages and towns. Ecological/ environmental consideration should be incorporated in thinking and planning. Ecological consequences of greater density and high rise living on traffic congestion and parking, air pollution, city space and so on, need to be assessed. Similarly, aesthetics and quality of life need to be emphasised. The designers should make an inside-outside perspective on village development. They should seek to make the village a place more habitable and attractive.

Rural and Urban Area Planning

Every district has rural planning commission at government level, stepped in land use, zoning density concerns, and traffic control. The commission should evaluate the projects proposed by developers and various government agencies. The commission should evaluate the cost/benefit impact of competing proposals and recommend the best investments. In some cases the commission may initiate projects and proposals on their own. They may take responsibility for evaluating the community's economic base and proposing new industries to attract the community. They may propose long-term plan for improving the village and town's infrastructure and attractiveness.

Economic Development

Economic growth refers to more output which means more jobs for people, and related impacts such as congestion and pollution. Economic development suggests more output but with a different kind of output than produced before. It includes new industries, more productive use of resources, and greater innovation. Economic development professionals focus largely on helping a village enhance its competitiveness. They analyse area, strength and weaknesses, opportunities and threats. Their task it to determine how the local community best fits a changing regional, national and global context. Every village and area needs a business core and related support industries to earn the money to pay for the goods and services they import. Urban community development agencies and economic development agencies need to be established. Economic development agencies should help to determine the best industries to target, recommend improvements in infrastructure and zoning, and help plan specific development programmes to attract the target industries. Economic development is the best process through which community will improve its capacity to incorporate community development thinking along with economic growth and develop-economically, educationally, socially and culturally development thinking. The village's attractiveness depends on many community factors and economic infrastructure.

Community Factors

- Quality of life
- Positive image
- Economic development capacity, and
- Physical infrastructure.

Economic Infrastructure Factors

- Accessibility technology
- Skilled, adaptable and motivated human resources
- Available financial capital.

We may also adopt a grassroots approach. A steering committee of 25-50 people and task forces involving 300-400 people could be guided to develop their own strategic plan, thereby involving strong community support.

There are various approaches to be applied to urban development and improvement, which differ in scope, approach, balance and responsiveness. A comprehensive approach incorporating perspective from community development, urban design and urban planning, along with urban economic development would be most suitable. In order to succeed, villages should use the tools of businesses, because they are competing resources. They must recognise dynamic global forces that impact their local industries. They must understand that they compete with other villages and areas for tourists, conventions, educated residents, factories, corporate head quarters, and start-up firms. They must be superior or excellent in some special ways. They must be market-conscious and market driven. The infrastructure, industries, attraction and people's skills that they build today will affect their position tomorrow. If wrong industries are chosen, if wrong bets are made, these villages will nose dive into obscurity. To think like a business, villages must develop and operate a planning methodology. We must not turn to planning as a result of hard times but must adopt planning to avoid hard times.

Strategic Development Planning

During the *first stage,* the region lures businesses, plant and investment by promoting better business climate. Exploits least cost of production—cheap labour and land, low taxes, and public financing to attract new business and investment. The regional competition aimed at business attraction changes little in goals, method, rational, and promotional messages. The whole region remains unaffected by changes occurring outside. Its task is to reach buyers, discover their needs, package various incentives into a competitive deal.

The *second stage* is of target marketing instead of pursuing a single goal business attraction, it moves to multiplicity of goals-retention, start-ups, tourism, export promotion, and foreign investment. As the economy changes and competition intensifies, regions change from hit or miss approach to redefined strategies based on competitive analysis and market positioning. Regions move from mass marketing of different products to specialised marketing. More emphasis is laid on maintaining and supporting internal market and resources, the businesses industries, entrepreneurs, new products and collective resources such as universities, research forces, financial institution, etc.

In the *third stage* regions move to product development and competition niche thinking. Each region defines itself as distinctive with specific competition advantages for target industries.

Economic and Demographic Characteristics

It must start with the region's economic and demographic features such as population size and composition of sex, age, income, race, education, housing; industry structure and human resources, community health characteristics, natural resources, education and research institutions and recreational and cultural resources. This information helps in attracting different target market. It also helps to answer the following:

— What is the region's Tivability' when it comes to attracting new residents?
— What is the region's Visitability' when it comes to attracting tourists?
— What is the region's "invisibility' when it comes to attracting business and investment?

The region needs to identify other areas with which it has a close rivalry. There are three levels of competitors. A *weak* competitor is one who loses to the community most of the time. A *peer* competitor is one who wins approximately half of the time. A *superior* competitor is one who, when competing with the specific community, wins most of the time. The region has to improve its odds over its peer competitors and in the long-run catch up with its superior competitors. The challenge is to learn how the particular target buyers make their decisions. The community should know which criteria buyers are using, the important weights they assign to the different criteria, and their perceptions of how the competitors rank in the criteria.

Major Trends and Developments

Major trends and developments as well as macro development needs to be identified and assess their impact and take steps to respond these developments. Preparing for the future involves anticipating the following trends and developments likely to affect the region:

- The region will receive less direct funding from national and state resources and have to rely on generating their own funds to support basic services.
- The region will have to be more attractive to environmental forces and regulations in planning their future. They may require getting most out of existing facilities, malign public facilities and investment, fit better into natural environment, and meeting needs more creatively.
- The region will be influenced by global development and changes and therefore, must monitor and anticipate their impact on the place.
- The region will be caught between business—increase in taxes to support public services and dealing in service. Different and many productive approaches be introduced to services industry.

Regions will be seeking to define themselves as distinctive areas with specific advantages for target industries. They will develop those niche products and services that create value for target customers. They will invest in a diversified portfolios of industries while pursuing some clusters of related businesses. They will educate human resources so that the citizen can function effectively in a high-tech information society. They will invest in a well-functioning infrastructure to support a good quality of life.

Strengths and Weaknesses, Opportunities and Threats of the Region (SWOT)

The region needs to identify which of its characteristics represent a major strength, minor strength, neutral factor, minor weaknesses, or major weakness, in terms of what specific place buyers are seeking. A survey conducted to assess U.S. visitor's perception about India as a vacation destination revealed that poverty, low cleanliness standards, political instability, and quality of transport were reported weaknesses. On the other hand respondents were impressed at India's culture, history, and exoticism—all aspects attracting visitors to the country. In the short run, India can only tout its strengths. In the long-run it must try to correct its weaknesses. *(Source: Inferred by the author from Richard Boyer and David Savageau, Places Rated Almanac* (Englewood Cliffs, N.J. Prentice Hall, 1989).

Let us consider the Himalayan region. These analyses constitutes macro assessment of the region's strengths and weaknesses. A micro assessment would reveal specific strengths and weaknesses within the larger categories. It is necessary to choose the attribute of importance to each target group and assign important weight to these individual attributes. One major weakness of the region is the transportation. Minor weakness is the crime. Major strengths are climate, cost of living, health care and environment. Their analysis institutes a macro assessment of the region's strengths and weaknesses. Not all attributes are equally meaningful to different target groups that the region wants to attract. It is necessary to choose the attributes of importance to such target group and assign important weights to each individual attributes.

In cell *'A' are* important attributes where the region rates poorly and, therefore, where critical improvements are needed, hence, the region should 'concentrate here'. In cell 'B' fall important attributes where the region is already strong, hence, "keep up the good work'. In cell 'C' fall unimportant attribute, where the region is performing poorly. 'These attributes consequently are of low priority'. In cell 'D' fall unimportant attributes, where the place is performing strongly, perhaps, it is over investing in these attributes, that is 'overkill'.

The region has major strength but it does not necessarily

constitute a competitive advantage. It may not be an attribute of any importance to the target market. Competitors may have the same strength level on that attribute. The region should have greater relative strength on an attribute important to a target group. The region need not correct all its weaknesses nor push all its strengths, because some attributes are unimportant. The region should probe deeper into those strengths and weaknesses most affecting the perceptions and behaviour of target markets. The resultant analysis becomes a major basis for laying future plan.

Identify all the opportunities and threats facing the region. The strengths and weaknesses as stated above are internal to the region, opportunities and threats are external. The region's opportunity is an area for action in which a place has a fairly good chance to achieve a competitive advantage. All opportunities must be assessed according to their attractiveness and success probability. Each opportunity ends up in one of the *three* types. The best opportunities are those that are intrinsically attractive and a high success probability.

Management needs to develop plans to exploit these opportunities. The worst opportunities are those with low attractiveness and low success probability, and they should be disregarded moderate opportunities, those with either high attractiveness or success probability, but not both, should be monitored. In addition to opportunities, the region faces threats, a challenge posed by unfavourable trends or development in the environment that lead to the erosion of the region's condition. Regional planning groups need to identify various threats. Major threats are those that can seriously hurt the place and have a high probability of occurring. The region should prepare a contingency plan that spells out what steps to take before or during a major threat occurs. Minor threats are those with either high potential harm and high occurrence probability but not both, they must be watched.

In the Himalayan region we may identify strategic issues such as housing, transportation, finances, and job and business opportunities. Assemble a picture of all the major threats and opportunities. An ideal region is one that is high in major opportunities and low in major threats. A speculative region is high in both major opportunities and threats. A mature region is low in major opportunities and threats Finally, a trouble region is low in opportunities and high in threats.

Identification of Issues

Through the SWOT analysis we can carry out issue identification and management. The main issues currently faced by the region are:

— Should the region attempt to reinvigourate its varied shrinking bases or market itself as a service center?
— Should the region expand its tourism facilities and which areas need to be identified?
— Can the region improve the quality of its primary and secondary school system?

Once issues are identified, planners should appoint committees to research each issue and report its findings and recommendations. All issues involve investments and long-term commitments. All information can be publicly debated to allow community participation and hearings as well as media scrutiny. The strategic planners should work on these recommendations.

The regions require strategic regional planning process. Strategic planning does not mean budgeting or project planning or short-range planning or long-range planning. Strategic regional planning starts from the assumption that the future is largely uncertain. The community must establish information, planning, and control systems. Prepare plans and action that integrate the region's objectives and resources with its changing opportunities. Through strategic regional planning process, a region decides which industries, services and markets should be encouraged, which should be maintained, and which should be de-emphasised or even abandoned. Strategic regional planning is unlikely to succeed in sharply divided communities where consensual building mechanisms fail to work. The strategic regional planning process can work in those communities where institutions and procedures exist to make decision about a region's future. Strategic regional planning can be carried on in various ways, such as:

— A single government department can conduct strategic regional planning functions.
— Several government agencies might join forces, pool resources, divide tasks and form a joint strategic regional plan.
— Private, public committees and commissions could be formed to carryout the planning task.

The strategic regional planning process moves through *five* stages:

Regional Audit

The first task is to understand accurately what the community is like and why. It requires a systematic examination of the region's economic/demographic characteristics, sort them into competitive strengths and weaknesses and make an effort to relate them to opportunities and threats. Thus, regional audit will provide the basis for constructing a potentially attractive future for the region.

Vision and Goals

Once we arrive at a comprehensive picture of the community's situation, the planners should prioritise these projects and invest in those that fall within the regions resources constraints. Vision development calls the planners to solicit input from the citizen as to what they want their community to be like after 10 or 20 years from now. Two or three broad alternative visions could be developed and debated. Suppose we want to attract new residents, *three* scenarios or visions could be distinguished.

- — Uncurbed growth
- — Managed growth
- — Zero growth.

The *fourth* choice is to drift along rather than to adopt any vision. To be without a vision is to be without direction and motivation. Developing alternative vision goes further than distinguishing among potential growth paths. A vision should take a stand on issues, such as:

- — Which mix of industries make sense for the region
- — What land and housing pattern make sense for the region
- — What public services should be provided by local government and which should be let out to private contractors
- — How should public services be financed? How much financing should come from general tax verses user taxes.

The choice of vision is influenced by the values that citizen and government official hold. If immediate jobs and profits are highly valued, high growth is favoured. On the other hand, if preserving a way of life is valued high, one can lean toward managed or restrained growth

Once the visions are agreed, the next step is to set specific objectives and goals. Objectives and statements about what a region wants to achieve and goals add specific magnitude and timing to these objectives. In case we want 'managed growth' vision in the region, following objectives could be decided:

— Attracting high-tech industry and discouraging heavy industries.

— Discouraging the immigration of low-income residents by increasing the construction of low-cost housing.

— Improving business zoning standard and enforcement to prevent unsightly commercial strips from developing.

These objectives are directions. These need to be turned into goals to make them measurable and motivating those who are responsible, for example, the first objective, could be turned into the goal statement such as, attract four-or more high tech companies to move their regional/head quarters to this region with the aim of creating 250 job by 2,000 ! This statement provides a clear direction to those in the region in economic development office as to the expected achievement. This also becomes the basis of allocating the resources needed to accomplish their goal.

Once the vision, objectives and goals are defined, one can move into identifying and choosing strategies for accomplishing the goals. For example, to attract high-tech companies and creating jobs, there could be large number of possible strategies, such as:

(a) Attracting international personalities to the famous educational centers of the region.

(b) Establish a high-tech industrial park area offering low-cost facilities and tax advantages, and promoting through feature, articles, ads, and direct mail.

(c) Identify some national high-tech companies and induce them to move to the region.

(d) Targeting a specific set of high-tech companies and inducing them to move their offices to the region.

The Action Plan

To carry out the strategies, we require a master plan, which lists the actions that specific people must take at specific times of the year. For example, the region may call for three government officials attending the shows/ architectures to search the names of promising high-tech entrepreneurs. The action plan should list each action and next to it *four* additional components.

— Who is responsible?

— How the action is to be implemented?

— How much the action will cost? and

— Expected completion date?

Implementation and Control

Any plan is not worth anything until it is effectively implemented. It needs to be reviewed at regular interval for its progress towards its goals. For example, if the region has not managed to attract any high-tech company, the goal, strategy or action have to be considered. The region should prepare an annual report to highlight its accomplishment for the year as well as discuss its failure to achieve certain goals. The report should contain various statistical indicators describing where the region stands on its jobs, income, housing,, health, crime and public transportation in relation to where it planned to be. The report should be publicly distributed, and publicised. It could be discussed and pressure could be built on officials to sustain the drive to achieve the region's long-run objectives. The region, so far, failed to recognise threats. It reacts rather than protects. It must do better job of managing its future.

9

Tourism in Developing World

> Nature never hurries: atom by atom little by little, she achieves her work. The lesson one learns in fishing, yachting, or planting, is the manners of Nature; patience with the delays of wind and sun, delays of the seasons, bad weather, excess or lack of water.
>
> —*Ralph Waldo Emerson*

Tourists often come from particular socioeconomic layer of the population of industrialized and capital-surplus, oil-exporting countries. It requires relatively sophisticated market research to identify and analyze and profiles and preferences of these visitors.

Although in most developing countries a prosperous minority exists that is capable of undertaking domestic tourism, many inhabitants lack the income and wherewithal to travel. Accordingly, research must focus not only on measurement of domestic tourism but on ways and means of improving access of underprivileged layers of the population to holidays and travel, and on devising economical, but adequate, means of supply to achieve this aim. The need to import goods and services to supply the tourism sector and the prominent role played by nonresident (frequently transnational) enterprise and expatriate staff make evaluation of tourism's economic impact more difficult for the developing country. Scarcity of foreign exchange in many developing countries makes it a priority to measure accurately tourism's foreign exchange contribution to the economy (WTO 1980b).

The disparities of culture, attitudes, and lifestyles existing between developing countries and industrialized nations require more attention to be paid through research to tourism's sociocultural effects (WTO 1981d).

The delicate environments of many developing countries make it more urgent to undertake impact studies and research into carrying capacity to determine the optimum number of visitors a destination can receive.

Costs of tourism investment for a developing country are likely to be higher relative to the size of capital markets than in industrialized countries. Too often projects will compete for scarce investment funds. Accordingly, research needs to focus on practical and effective project appraisal techniques. If developing countries have great research needs, what are they and how should they be met? This chapter will attempt to answer that question. It therefore has both an analytical and a prescriptive aim. First, available data concerning the research efforts deployed by national tourism administrations (NTAs) of developing countries will be analyzed in broad quantitative terms, i.e., budgets and human resources. Second, suggestions will be formulate regarding developing countries tourism research needs, bearing in mind in particular the new responsibilities incumbent upon States as a result of their adherence to the principles of equal access to holiday expressed in the Manila Declaration of 1980 (WTO 1980).

Analysis of NTA budgets is not quite a precise indication of total tourism research effort ongoing in developing countries. Apart from the NTA, tourism development corporations exists in some countries as well as research and teaching establishment such as Utalii College (Kenya) or the Asian Institute for Tourism (Philippines). Also, at any time, sectorial support or technical co-operation missions to developing countries may be under way through multilateral assistance.

Workshop on Environmental Aspect of Tourism (1984), organized jointly by WTO and the United Nations Environment Programme (UNEP) at Madrid from 5 to July 1983. Madrid: WTO.

However, while the achievements of individual institutions or particular research missions should not be neglected, it will be necessary for the purposes of this analysis to disregard them since they are essentially temporary or sporadic and not concerted or permanent.

Published research budgets of developing countries, taken from the most recent edition of WTO's *Budgets of National Tourism Administrations,* were analyzed (WTO 1982c). This produced data for thirty middle-income countries (using the World Bank classification) and seven low-income countries. Under the heading of middle income, 1980 GNP ranges from $420 per capita in the case of Ghana to $5820 per capita in the case of Czechoslovakia, $4930 for Singapore, and $4380 for Greece, so the spread is quite great and a number of quite industrialized tourist-receiving countries are included (World Bank 1982). Low-income countries appeared to be under-represented which would tentatively lead to the conclusion that they do not enjoy abundant research opportunities due to constrained financial circumstances. While accepting this as a working hypothesis, an attempt was made to correct for underreporting by having recourse to a previous survey carried out in 1975 when NTAs were asked to describe their research activities in detail.

In *Budgets of National Tourism Administrations* (WTO 1982c), NTAs are asked to classify their research activities under three headings: research into tourism development, collecting and compiling tourism statistics; and drawing up plans and sectoral programmes for national tourism development. Most countries indicate that their research activities fall under all three headings.

TABLE 1: RESEARCH STAFF AND BUDGET OF MIDDLE- AND LOW-INCOME COUNTRIES-1981

Country	*GNP Per Capita 1980 in U.S.$*	*Research Budget of NTA in U.S.$ (Thousands)*	*As Percentage of Total NTA Budget*	*No. of Staff*
Middle-Income Countries				
Argentina	2390			
Bahamas	na[a]	244 (1980)	1.3	26
Bermuda	na	133	1.5	26
Brazil	2050	2594	16.0	35
Colombia	1180	273	1.5	na
Congo	900	152	25.3	5
Cyprus	na	35	1.1	9
Czechoslovakia	5820	739	0.5	32
Ecuador	1270	24	0.4	54
Ghana	420	55	0.8	11[b]
Greece	4380	3	0.01	14
Hong Kong	4240	107	1.0	15
Hungary	4180	288	3.7	8
Indonesia	430	192	0.2	42
Iran	1648	290 (1979)	0.9	20
Jamaica	1030	114	0.8	12
Kenya	420	22	1.1	na
Malaysia	1620	250	2.5	na
Morocco	900	281 (1980)	4.2	16
Papua New Guinea	780	15	3.3	5
Paraguay	1300	5	0.6	na
Peru	1285	900	4.5	na
Korea, Rep.	1520	201	0.6	32
Senegal	450	73	2.1	15
Singapore	4430	48	0.2	23
Syrian Arab Rep	1340	1500	10.8	18
Thailand	670	263	5.0	85
Venezuela	3630	1000	3.3	na
Yemen	430	24	2.9	3
Yugoslavia	2620	62	1.0	4

Country	*GNP Per Capita 1980 in U.S.$*	*Research Budget of NTA in U.S.$ (Thousands)*	*As Percentage of Total NTA Budget*	*No. of Staff*
Low-Income Countries				
Sierra Leone	280	12	1.8	3
Sri Lanka	270	4	0.1	na
United Rep. of Cameroon	670	31	1.1	15[c]
Madagascar	350			2
Togo	410			4
Burkina Faso	210			3

Source: WTO, Budget of National Tourism Administrations 1978-1981.
[a] na = not available.
[b] Includes investment staff.
[c] Includes training staff.

Taken together, the three headings comprise data gathering, data analysis, and formulating propositions of further action based on the conclusions of analysis. Before analyzing the figures some preliminary comments are necessary. The overall budgets of NTAs conventionally include the following main headings: promotion, investment, research, training, and administration. With the exception of those NTAs which invest significantly in tourist plant, "promotion" is generally the most important budgetary item. The NTA is unlikely to be alone in engaging in promotional activities. Airlines, hotels, tour operators, and regional and local tourism bodies are also active. Accordingly, in 1980, for every dollar spent by the NTA on promotion a "return" in the form of international tourist receipts of $570 was earned. Put another way, for every $100 earned in receipts, the average NTA ploughs back only 17.5 cents in promotional expenditure. Even when the existence of other tourism promotion bodies is born in mind, this is remarkable low ratio and conventional wisdom has suggested that NTAs should aim to reinvest at least 1% and preferably closer to 3% of international tourist receipts. The fact that promotional budgets are relatively small will place firmly in perspective the following conclusions about the size of NTA research budgets quoted from *Budgets of National Tourism Administrations,* 1982 edition: "Research budget ranks the lowest in NTA budgets. At times, this item is not even budgeted and rarely does it exceed 2 per cent, except in Australia (3.7 per cent in 1981), Canada (3.1 per cent in 1981), Chile (4.5 per cent in 1981), Colombia (3.3 per cent in 1980 but 1.5 per cent in 1981), Ghana (5.8 per cent in 1980 but 0.8 per cent in 1981), Italy (3.2 per cent in 1981), Malaysia (2.6 per cent and 2.5 per cent in 1980 and 1981), Morocco (4.2 per cent in 1980) Peru (4.5 per cent in 1981), Turkey (2.5 per cent in 1980) and Yemen (2.5 per cent in 1980 and 2.9 per cent in 1981). There are two exceptions, viz. Brazil, where the research budget ranges from 6 to 16 per cent and in Thailand where it exceeded 9 per cent in 1979 and 1980 (as opposed to 5 per cent in 1981)." (WTO 1982c, pp. 22-23)

It is easy to conclude on the basis of these figures that the research effort of developing countries is insufficient. But the conclusion requires amplification if it is to lead to useful recommendations. The following questions might be asked. How do developing countries' research budgets compare with those of industrialized countries? What should be the priorities? How can research assist in meeting future responsibilities? The reply to the first question seems to be that most developing countries spend much the same proportion of their total budget on research as industrialized countries but that absolute amounts spent on research by individual developing countries often exceed those of industrialized countries of comparable market size. These conclusions show research budgets of eight industrial market economics (according to World Bank classification) (World Bank 1982). Thus, among major industrialized countries whose research budgets do not exceed 2% of the total NTA budget are Finland 1.3%, Federal Republic of Germany 0.6%, Netherlands 0.9%, and Spain 1.3% (perhaps surprising given its pre-eminent tourist-receiving situation). By way of comparison, in 1981 Venezuela spent U.S. $1 million on research compared with Spain's U.S. $770 thousand; Peru spent U.S. $900,000 compared with Italy's US $667,000; Syrian Arab Republic spent U.S. $1.5 million compared with France's U.S. $176,000; and Brazil spent no less than U.S. $2.6 million compared with Federal Republic of Germany's U.S. 100,000. Naturally, these figures should be compared with caution as a number of industrialized market economies possess independent research institutions whose activities are not reflected. Before proceeding it would be well to underline that the research needs of particular countries will vary according to the degree of development of tourism. Thus, a country which is embarking on tourism development will give more emphasis to project appraisal planning. A country with a significantly developed market may be more concerned with improving market research and impact analysis. A country with an undeveloped domestic tourism market will be more concerned with way of ensuring equal access to tourism. Therefore, while the areas "Planning and Programmes," "Statistics," and "Development" should be germance to the needs of all countries, each country will need to give slightly differing emphasis to the different aspect and to vary deployment of human and financial resources accordingly.

Planning and Programmes

The planning function enable the research unit to contribute to policy formulation and avoids the danger of its activities being carried out in *vacuo*. Lately, tourism planning has become appreciably more sophisticated with the technique known as integrated planning gaining in importance. Simply defined, Integrated Planning is techniques which takes account systematically of alternative forms of development to the one being considered and of the repercussions of planning decisions in the area concerned beyond the limits of the sector being developed, in the case of tourism. Naturally, integrated planning techniques have come to be closely identified with a more immediate concern for the sociocultural impact of tourism and its impact on the natural environment. (Lawson and Baud-Bovy 1977, WTO 1978, Pearce 1981). But a key role of planning in the developing countries will be in the formulation of the immediate goals of tourism policy. These can conveniently be placed under two headings.

(a) Goals for domestic tourism,
(b) goals for intercontinental tourism, and
(c) Goals for intercontinental tourism.

It is important to confront peacemakers with these three goals since otherwise attention may focus only on international tourism at the expense of other market sectors. A close link should also exist between the tourism planning function and the overall national planning process. While this is implicit in the concept of integrated planning, it does means, for example, that regional development aims should be borne in mind when planning for tourism. This technique should frequently bring the planners of the NTA research department into contact with the formulation of overall national policy goals such as whether to develop an area for tourism or for farming. The use of an integrated approach should be especially helpful in indentifying linkages and synergy effects.

Likewise, a more intensive pattern of air transport for tourism purposes frequently improves prospects for merchandise trade. So flights to industrialized tourism-generating market may create opportunities for air-freighting high-value, perishable goods such as tropical fruit and flowers. Given high levels of unemployment in developing countries, particular emphasis in planning should be placed on the creation of small-and medium-sized, often family run, enterprises and on providing the necessary practical training opportunities. Opportunities may exist in the tourism sector itself, or in export industries such as those described above, or again in the field of import substitution, whereby goods intended for use and consumption by tourists can be produced domestically rather than brought in from abroad. A manager of a transnational hotel chain has claimed to this writer to have virtually created a local market for fruit juice served in hotels while local production of furniture and decorations for hotels (often in authentic local style) is an established feature of much tourism development.

Three specific area should receive the attention of planners: tourism supply, manpower and infrastructure. Supply planning will be concerned fundamentally with accommodation to be offered to international and domestic tourists. Work by WTO has shown (WTO 1981 a) that import content in hotel construction need not be too high, while there is an urgent need for the developing of new models of supply for domestic tourism consistent with income levels and possibilities of domestic tourists. Manpower planning should concentrate on staff numbers and skills and on identification of training needs—the last being a constant concern for most developing countries. Finally, in the field of infrastructure, the tourism planner will need to be alert to the possibilities that exist for joint use of resources. Evident possibilities are offered by projects such as construction of roads and airports or provision of water supplies which benefit not only tourists but also local populations.

Statistics

Statistics may be considered in two part: the gathering of statistics and the analysis of statistics. It is apparent from the 1975 WTO survey some research units cover both these aspects, while other are concerned only with the analyzed final results. Naturally, when a research unit is responsible for the gathering of statistics the effect upon manpower is significant. Possibly, the research unit will be responsible too for the conduct or commissioning of market research based on the need for additional information about tourists' motivations or their socioeconomic will be commissioned out-of-house with consequent budgetary appropriations being set side for this purpose. While the need for market research should not be belittled, it is evident that the undertaking of meaningful market research by a developing country may involve considerable expense since it is basically interested in the profiles and attitudes of a small segment of the population in the industrialized or energy-surplus countries often situated at considerable distances. Accordingly, given the generally lower intensive of tourist flows to the developing countries, the lesser pressures of facilitation, and the opportunity for eliciting more statistical information form tourists at both the beginning and the end of their stay, it is suggested that before market research is undertaken the possibility of obtaining additional relevant information form tourists actually visiting the country should be seriously considered. Departure surveys, connectrating on attitudes, socioeconomic profiles, and expenditure patterns, are likely to be particularly worthwhile since international tourists preparing to undertaking relatively long-distance journeys generally arrive at the point of departure in *in good time* and can be relied upon to recall fairly accurately the details of their expenditure on their trip as well as giving impressions of their stay and other matters.

It is strongly recommended that a data base be compiled covering the three sectors:

(a) Domestic tourism.
(b) Regional tourism.
(c) Long-distance intercontinental tourism (WTO 1981c).

One more possibility of keeping market research expenditure to a reasonable level was suggested at the World Tourism Conference, Manila, 1980. The Conference drew attention to the frequent duplication of effort existing in the obtention of market information on tourism and called upon WTO "to continue its efforts to facilitate the exchange of technical tourist information, specifically by considering the possibility of establishing a worldwide tourist information system... so as to increase the capacity of all countries and especially developing countries, for action and management and thus to strengthen their technological economy by means where appropriate of advanced technologies such as data tele-processing" (WTO 1980a). Finally, the possibility exists of a number of countries within the same region undertaking join market research within the generating market and sharing the expenses. In this context it may be noted that a similar policy is pursued by the industrialized countries them selves through bodies such as the European Travel Commission.

Development

The third principal area of research for which NTAs assume responsibility is that of feasibility analysis (from the economic, cultural, political, and social standpoints) of tourism development. Evidently such activity gives a useful practical orientation to the NTA research unit since it involves close contact with tourism enterprises (hotels, etc.) and with techniques for calculating the financial and other returns of the tourism sector. In the field of project appraisal two needs are strongly felt. They are, first, access to the methodology of appraisal employed by major international financing institutions (the World Bank, regional development banks, etc.), and, second, the elimination of manual calculations and the introduction of computer techniques for project analysis. As a result of this, not only can the whole process be speeded up but also a greater degree of sensitivity analysis can be conducted, aimed at identifying the fate of the project under a wide series of assumptions. In this connection, inexpensive but versatile microcomputers are becoming more widely available, while data teleprocessing through the use of terminals installed in developing countries offers the possibility of feeding input data into a central computer located, perhaps, in another continent, so as to obtain relevant output data rapidly and economically for project appraisal purposes. Interest is also being shown in the models employed by the major hotel chains for project analysis and the possibility of applying these models to projects put forward by hotel development corporations and similar semipublic bodies established within the developing countries to promote the development of tourism particularly in the regions lacking in the supply facilities (WTO, 1980b).

The study of impacts is one of the most interesting and challenging tasks facing the research unit of the NTA in any developing country. Social, cultural, and environmental as well as economic impacts should receive attention and a whole series of techniques and models must be brought to bear upon the task confronting the researchers. This may, therefore, require the use of a large number of techniques by a relatively small group of individuals comprising the research unit. Again, the need is felt for ready availability of a number of models which can be employed to analyze situations prevailing in different countries using input data compiled by the research unit. So far as economic impact models are concerned, while the development of a single universal applicable impact model is no easy task, it does appear, nonetheless, that within the next few years certain basic impact models should be available to subscribers in developing countries through the data teleprocessing network. Other areas of impact involve so many subjective factors that the use of mathematical model may not always be appropriate. Possibly the greatest area of difficulty in relation to, for example, social and cultural impact models has been that researchers coming from developed market economy or socialist countries have interacted insufficiently. Their reports, considered the work of outsiders, have (as might be expected) come to be treated somewhat at arm's length and the impact upon the planning process has not always been of significance. In talking this urgent and frequently delicate problem in the future, a greater degree of preparation would be desirable, involving both the technician and researcher, possibly from the third country, but also a counterpart from the developing country and representative of travel trade partners such as tour operators and the management of transnational hotel chains. Clearly this approach is more likely to yield results which command a consensus and can lead to timely action to reduce unfavourable impacts and strengthen favourable ones.

Research and New Responsibilities

The three main area of responsibility described above are those which, conventionally and historically, have been entrusted to research departments of national tourism administrations. Accordingly, they fulfil the classical research needs of NTAs. However, they are not a sufficient nor a complete statement of needs since they fail to reflect the dynamics of tourism research and especially the requirements which will increasingly arise as result of the new responsibilities incumbent upon States as a result of their adherence to the Manila Declaration of World Tourism of 1980. In this part of the chapter some attention will accordingly be devoted to this subject (WTO 1980a).

The Manila Declaration on World Tourism laid the foundations for a much broader conception of tourism than hitherto accepted with noteworthy emphasis being placed on social, cultural, and educational aspects of travel.

Also, the right of underprivilege layers of the population to gain access to vacations was emphasized, as was the need to give proper weight to domestic vis-a-vis international travel.

The practical effect to the Manila Declaration is to place new responsibilities before States and their tourism administrations. Some will evidently be entrusted to research departments. Possible research topics suggested by the operative paragraphs of the Manali Declaration are listed. This list is of course only indicative since the Manila Declaration is a rich source of projects and activities for the research departments of developing and, indeed, industrialized countries. Two final points might be made. A number of developing countries, particularly in Africa, are showing evident signs of frustration as they contemplate a development process which— in their view—seeks to impose alien cultures and modes of life. Development of international tourism is not free from such criticism. In such a situation, it may be asserted that those countries who opt for a sizable tourism research effort choose rightly because of the capability that a research unit possesses of operating as a "think tank" for the whole rational tourism administration. Not only figures but ideas too may be expected to flow from a properly functioning research team and some of those ideas may germinate to become the policy guidelines of tomorrow, expressing the distinctive personality of the country concerned and avoiding stereotyping.

Second, it is implicit in this chapter that other travel trade partners, such as transporters, with the national tourism administration in a coherent programme of research. The research needs of developing countries are too great for fragmentation of the research effort to be tolerable.

Choice of Personnel

Staffing an NTA research department is no easy matter

since qualified researchers are unlikely to be more readily available in a developing country than in their industrialized counterparts. Faced with scarce resources, both human and financial, what should be the response of NTA? Staff should, naturally, reflect the basic skills demanded by the three areas: planning, statistics, and analysis, which would suggest a planner, a statistician, and an economist. Better still, a combination of skills could be deployed so as to achieve a degree of multidisciplinary interaction, e.g., a planner with some sociological/cultural background, and economist with experience of financial/ project analysis, and a statistician with understanding of market research/ household techniques. As previously emphasized, communication of results is vital. So at least one member of the team should have the ability and the personality to communicate the findings of research to management and to outline their significance for policy. It is not to be expected that all relevant disciplines will be represented in a research unit. This would be uneconomical as input of certain branches of skill and knowledge will be required only on a part-time or short-term basis. Therefore, recourse will frequently be had to outside consultants, experts and firms. Here a further skill is required which may be reflected either in management or in the research team itself: the ability to buy in research, to brief consultants, and to integrate the results of their contribution into the overall research effort.

Summing Up

The research needs of the developing countries are grater than those of the industrialized countries for the following reasons: (a) distance from generating countries; (b) highly segmented markets; (c) lack of means of domestic tourists; (d) complexity of economic impact; (e) culture and lifestyle differences: (f) fragile environment; and (g) high project costs-scarce investment funds. Analysis of resources attributed in 1981 to the research departments of NT. As of both medium-and low-income countries revealed that these were low in relative in absolute terms there was some clear evidence of their being substantially higher than those of the industrialized countries (WTO 1982c). Analysis of figures published subsequently by WTO revealed that, under the effects to the world recession, there was little change in resources devoted to research during the period 1982-1984. However, due to the strength of the U.S. dollar and the weakness of the currencies of certain developing countries, especially in Latin America, the gap which had earlier been apparent between absolute resources devoted to research by industrialized and developing countries narrowed.

Functions of research departments were deduced from a detailed WTO 1975 survey (WTO/IUOTO 1975) supported by the information contained in WTO's 1981 *Budgets of National Tourism Administrations.* Needs of developing countries were seen to focus on three specific areas: planning, statistics and development. But emphasis placed on each area was seen to vary according to the stage of development of tourism in the country concerned. In planning, the value of an integrated approach was recognized. Statistics were seem to fall under two headings: gathering and analysis. The somewhat less urgent pressures of facilitation in developing countries were seem to justify the use of administrative checks for gathering statistics. Scope was seen for joint market research and a centralized data bank accessible to all less developed countries. Under development could be grouped activities of project appraisal and impact analysis. The need was seen here for developing countries to become more familiar with project appraisal methodologies employed by major financial institutions, without the results just being "handed down."

Analysis of new responsibilities was carried out by reference to the Manila Declaration of World Tourism of 1980 to which the vast majority of developing countries throughout the world have subscribed. A primary focus of this analysis was on the need for study of ways and means of ensuring more equal access to tourism and vacations. Research into possibilities of domestic travel and tourism development, focusing on small-and medium-size, often family-run, enterprises, was seen to be a key activity too (WTO 1980a and 1985).

Finally, the personnel requirements of tourism research in developing countries were analyzed. On balance, it seemed to be worthwhile to cultivate a reasonable range of specializations within the research department while recognizing that it will not be possible to include all relevant disciplines. Stress was laid on research personnel having the ability to communicate the findings of research to management and to outline their significance for policy.

REFERENCES

Burkart, A.J., and S. Medlik (1981). *Tourism Past, Present and Future,* London: Heinemann.

Lawson, F., and M. Baud-Bovy (1977), *Tourism and Recreation Development,* London: Architectural Press.

Pearce, D. (1981), *Tourist Devélopment,* London: Longman.

World Bank (1982), *World Development Report 1982.* New York: Oxford University Press.

World Tourism Organization and International Union of Official Travel Organizations (1975). *The Structure of Research Units of National Tourist Organizations,* Geneva: IUOTO unpublished report.

World Tourism Organization (1978), *Integrated Tourism Planning,* Madrid: WTO.

World Tourism Organization (1980a), *Manila Declaration on World Tourism,* Madrid: WTO.

World Tourism Organization (1980b), *Evaluating Tourist Projects,* Madrid: WTO.

World Tourism Organization (1980c), *Report on Physical Planning and Area Development for Tourism in the Six WTO Regions,* Madrid: WTO.

World Tourism Organization (1981a), *Guidelines for Using National Resources in the Construction and Maintenance of Tourist Plant,* Madrid-WTO.

World Tourism Organization (1981b), *Guidelines for Collection and Presentation of Domestic Tourism Statistics,* Madrid: WTO.

World Tourism Organization (1981d), *Social and Cultural Impact of Tourist Movements,* Madrid: WTO.

10

Community-Based E-Tourism

As per current estimate approximately *2* million people cross an international border each day, compared with only 69,000 in 1950 (French, 2000). Tourism enjoyed exceptional years in 2000 and 2001. World tourism grew by an estimated 7.4 per cent in 2000, its highest growth rate in nearly a decade and almost double the increase of 1999. The fastest developing region in 2000 was East Asia and the Pacific with a growth rate of 14.7 per cent and some 14 million more tourists than 1999. Receipts from international tourism climbed to US $ 476 billion in 2000, an increase of 4.5 per cent over the previous year. Worldwide the average receipt per arrival in 2000 amounted to US $ 680 (WTO, 2001). However, in 2001 international arrivals declined by 0.6 per cent, the first year of negative growth for international tourism since 1982 (WTO, 2002). According to the World Tourism Organisation (WTO), the events of 11 September 2001 determined the results of international tourism in that year. Even so arrivals in Africa and East Asia and the Pacific saw increases of 4.3% and 5.5% respectively. Tourism and information technology and services are the two economic sectors that have experienced the fastest growth and expansion during the transition from an industrial society to a global information society (di Castri, 2002). International tourism is one of the indicators of growing globalisation.

The WTO forecasts that international arrivals are expected to reach over 1.56 billion by the year 2020. The total expected tourist arrivals by region shows that by 2020 the top three receiving regions will be Europe (717 million tourists), East Asia and the Pacific (397 million) and Americas (282 million). East Asia and the Pacific, South Asia, the Middle East and Africa are forecasted to record growth at rates of over 5% per year, compared to the world average of 4.1 per cent.

By 2010, WTO forecasts that the Americas will lose its number two position, behind Europe, to East Asia and the Pacific, which will receive 25% of world arrivals. Tourism offers huge opportunities for developing countries to increase incomes from the growing number of arrivals that land on their shores. However, it has been recognized that many tourism policies developed from central governments without local involvement fail to cater for the sensibilities and aspirations of the communities that tourists visit. The conference on Community Based Ecotourism in Southeast Asia agreed that local communities should have the right to self-determination and to decide whether to accept or not accept the policies that affect their livelihood.

As tourism is essentially a micro-enterprise, tourism lends itself to local entrepreneurial activity, and community-based tourism has emerged as a mechanism for fostering locally based tourism operations, as opposed to those whose financial interests are often located away from the tourist destination. Moreover, as Information and Communication Technologies (ICTs) are beginning to be deployed in rural communities for the purpose of fostering local development, communities are able to implement electronic commerce in support of their CBT operations, and engage in e-CBT.

Furthermore, it will be shown that the Internet is not only a natural partner for tourism, it also a natural partner for the market segment that e-CBT should target. With more than 600 million people on-line by September 2002, and more than 60% of them residing in Europe or North

America, even small and remote communities with an Internet connection can address huge global markets.

e-CBT involves the operation of local tourism activities which are promoted across the internet by a community using a community based telecentre, which provides community access to information and communication technologies. The concept is presented as a method for fostering rural development in developing countries.

Tourism and the Developing World

Tourism is a principal export for developing countries and the least developed countries (LDCs). It is growing rapidly and is the most significant source of foreign exchange alter petroleum (WTO, 2002).

TABLE 1: INTERNATIONAL TOURIST ARRIVALS

	(million)		*Growth rate (%)*	*Market share (%)*	
	2000	*2001**	*2001*/2000*	*2000*	*2001**
World	696.8	692.6	-0.6	100	100
Europe	402.5	399.7	-0.7	57.8	57.7
Americas	128.5	120.8	6.0	18.4	17.4
East Asia and the Pacific	109.2	115.2	5.5	15.7	16.6
Africa	27.2	28.4	4.3	3.9	4.1
Middle East	23.2	22.7	-2.5	3.3	3.3
South Asia	6.1	5.8	-4.5	0.9	0.8

Source: World Tourism Organization (WTO).
* Data as collected by WTO September 2002.

There is a general shift of tourism arrivals towards developing countries. Growth rates of international tourism receipts during the 1990s were, on average, 50% higher in the major developing country destinations than in comparison with the major developed country destinations. Table 1 shows that East Asia and the Pacific and Africa are the only regional locations to increase their arrivals in 2001. By far the largest single developing country international tourism destination is China. The People's Republic accounted for US $10 billion in international tourism receipts in 1996, receiving 22.7 million international visitors, experiencing 19% annual growth rates of receipts since 1980. Together with earnings generated by the Hong Kong Special Administrative Region, China's 1996 receipts surpass US $20 billion. In 2001, China ranked fifth in the world's top tourism destinations, measured both by the number of international arrivals and by international tourism receipts. Yet in terms of Gross National Income per capita, China ranks 108 out of 173 countries in the World Bank's statistical indicators for 2001. China, Thailand and Indonesia together generated 40% of all international tourism receipts accruing to developing countries in 1996.

The World Tourism Organisation says there is a strong economic case for promoting tourism in developing countries, suggesting that affirmative action and pro-poor policies are able to go beyond trickle down and multiplier affects by unlocking opportunities for the poor within tourism (WTO 2002). Success in poverty alleviation through tourism depends, says the WTO, partly on effective community-public-private partnerships that serve to reduce financial leakages and increase economic linkages to the local economy. Financial leakages occur where a disproportionately low percentage of tourism revenues stays in the local market, and they reduce the development impact of tourism. Linkages with the local economy foster revenue retention from tourism activities, and they depend on quality, reliability and competitiveness of local products. WTO suggest various steps that can be taken to increase the benefits to the local economy in tourist destination areas, by:

— facilitating local community access to the tourism market,
— minimising the financial leakages from the local economy,

— maximising the linkages of tourism to the local economy,

— building on and complimenting existing livelihood strategies through employment and small enterprise development,

— ensuring that tourism products contribute to local economic development not just to national revenue generation.

The Ministers and Heads of Delegations of the 49 LDCs met in Gran Canaria, Spain in March 2001 to discuss the contribution that tourism might make to development. They concluded that for a large majority of LDCs, tourism development can be an avenue to increase participation in the global economy, alleviate poverty and achieve socio-economic progress (UNCTAD, 2001). The conference pointed out that in 18 LDCs, tourism is already a prominent economic sector, ranking first, second or third among all export sectors.

In 10 other LDCs, tourism has been a less prominent but growing area of activity demonstrating significant progress over the previous decade. Overall, at least 6 out of 10 LDCs have placed international tourism at the heart of their development strategy, and they expect the sector to spearhead their economic re-specialization. The LDC representatives at the meeting identified international tourism as one of the few economic sectors through which LCDs have managed to increase their participation in the global economy, principally because of the comparative advantages that LDCs enjoy in the provision of tourism services.

They recognised that tourism can be an engine for employment creation, poverty alleviation, reduction of gender equality, and protection of the natural culture and heritage (UN, 2001).

Tourism in Developing Countries

- Tourism is a principal export for 83% of developing countries and it is the principal export for one third of them.
- Developing countries had 292.6 million arrivals in 2000, an increase since 1990 of nearly 95%. The 40 least developed countries had 5.1 million international arrivals in 2000; they achieved an increase of 75% in the decade.
- 80% of the world's poor, those living on less than US $1 per day, live in 12 countries. In 11 of these countries, tourism is significant and growing.
- The developing countries are attracting an increasing share of global international tourist arrivals up from 20% in 1973 to 42% in 2000.
- The developing countries and particularly the LDCs secured a larger increase in the income per international arrival between 1990 and 2000 than did the OECD or the European Union countries. The LDCs secured an increase of 45% between 1990 and 2000 and the developing countries nearly 20%. This compares with 18% for the OECD countries and 7.8% for the EU..
- In 2000, tourism ranked third among the major merchandise export sectors for both developing countries and LDCs. If petroleum industry exports are discounted (and they are significant in only three) tourism is the primary source of foreign exchange in the 49 LDCs. (WTO, 2002)

Community Based Tourism

Community-based tourism is regarded as a tool for natural and cultural resource conservation and community development and it is closely associated with ecotourism, sometimes referred to as community-based ecotourism. It is a community-based practice that provides contributions and incentives for natural and cultural conservation as well as providing opportunities for improved community livelihood. Community-based tourism provides alternative economic opportunities, which are in essence in rural areas. It has the potential to create jobs and generate entrepreneurial opportunities for people from a variety of backgrounds, skills and experiences, including rural communities and especially women. Community-based tourism has been implemented in many developing countries, often in support of wildlife management, environmental protection and/or development for indigenous peoples.

Community based tourism occurs when decisions about tourism activity and development are driven by the host community. It usually involves some form of cultural exchange where tourists meet with local communities and witness aspects of their lifestyle. Eco-tourism also emphasises observation and learning by the tourist, alongside economic and cultural conservation, and the delivery of benefits that ensure long-term sustainability of communities and natural resources (Allcock, 2003).

In Nepal, the Tourism for Rural Poverty Alleviation Programme began in 2001, jointly funded by the United Nations Development Programme (UNDP), the UK Department for International Development (DFID) with advisory services from SNV (Stichting Nederlandse Vrijwilligers) a Dutch development organisation. Operating in six remote locations, the programme employed social mobilisation and tourist awareness programmes in villages to empower local communities to manage their own tourism development. In Vietnam, the International Union for Conservation of Nature and Natural Resources (IUCN) or World Conservation Union, is operating a community based tourism pilot in Sa Pa, a highly visited area with colourful ethnic minorities. Funded mainly by the Ford Foundation, the goal of the project is to assist local stakeholders to achieve an environmentally, culturally and socio-economically sustainable form of tourism, establishing mechanisms that support the active participation of the community in tourism decision-making and implementation. The Nam Ha ecotourism project in Lao PDR uses community-based tourism as a vehicle to integrate environmental and cultural conservation with sustainable socio and economic development.

Working closely with local villagers, limits were set on the number of trekking tourists allowed each year so as riot to overwhelm the communities and to ensure that tourist incomes supplement rather than replace other economic activities. Typically, with community-based tourism, the community runs all of the activities that a tourist engages in; lodging, food, guiding and craft sales. Benefits include; economic growth in rural regions; the distribution of tourism revenue, which can foster improved welfare and equity in the industry; improved resource conservation by local people; and diversification of the regional and national tourism product (Sproule, 1996).

Pro-poor tourism is defined as tourism that generates net benefits for the poor. It maximises the potential for eradicating poverty by developing appropriate strategies in co-operation with all major groups, indigenous and local communities. Benefits may be economic, but they may also be social, environmental or cultural. Pro-poor tourism is not a specific product or sector of tourism, but an approach to the tourism industry.

The core activity is to increase access of the poor to economic benefits. Pro-poor tourism strategies unlock opportunities for the poor; whether for economic gain, other livelihood benefits, or participation in decision-making. Early experience shows that pro-poor tourism strategies do appear able to 'tilt' the industry at the margin, to expand opportunities for the poor and have potentially wide application across the industry. Poverty reduction through pro-poor tourism can therefore be significant at a local or district level. Moreover, the poverty impact may be greater in remote areas, though the tourism itself may be on a limited scale (Roe and Urquhart, 2001). Most examples of community-based in tourism in developing countries qualify as pro-poor tourism as they are designed to foster development at grassroots levels.

Sua Bali: A Community Based Tourism Project

The idea behind "Sua Bali" is to create a reasonably sized holiday resort for western tourists in a Balinese, setting-in such a way that the social and cultural aspects, and the ethnic-religious backgrounds respectively, are taken into account. The name "Sua Bali" means, "getting to know Bali". Sua Bali is a bridge between cultures, which enables people to get to know each other in a better way, something that is threatened by modern tourism. For this reason the holiday resort with six guest houses is situated at the outskirts of the village of Kemenuh and is arranged in the manner of a traditional Balinese farmstead. As a consequence the architecture corresponds to the local type of construction and fits into the surroundings.

Mrs. Ida Ayu Agung Mas, the owner, has involved the population of Kemenuh in the planning and gradual realization of Sua Bali—in numerous individual discussions and in the "Banjar", the village council. This was done in order to make sure that the concept of Sua Bali is truly in line with the traditions and behavioural patterns prevailing in the village of Kemenuh. The staff of Sua Bali predominantly hails from Kemenuh or neighbouring villages. The same goes for construction workers and craftsmen who constructed the guesthouses. Building materials and furniture for Sua Bali were purchased locally. Commodities for the daily needs also come either from the village or from local markets. The village of Kemenuh reaps the benefits of around seventy or eighty per cent of the employment impact and of purchases handled, the rest goes to neighbouring villages.

Each guest pays US $1 extra per night, which Sua Bali gives to the village community. This helps finance various cultural and social tasks or measures to improve the village infrastructure. So far about 900 Sua Bali guests with 5000 overnight stays have contributed around US $3,700 for cultural and infrastructural measures and around US $4,500 for social concerns. Sua Bali is adamant in concentrating its efforts to shape its own tourist programmes in a ways that are distinctive of the country and its lifestyle.

For rural communities, community based tourism holds out a range of attractions:

- Farming and tourism development are often complementary in scope,
- The conversion to services and tourism activities is easier for farmers, even smallholders and poor farmers, than for industry workers, as farmers worldwide have an independent and entrepreneurial capacity and a greater potential for personal initiatives,
- Tourism can enhance human occupation or re-colonise rural spaces that now have easier access to information. In this way, tourism can decrease or stop the rural exodus by providing new economic and job opportunities in rural areas,
- Tourism can bring empowerment and cultural revival to local, isolated and remote populations (di Castri, 2002).

Travel, Tourism and the Internet

The Internet is having a profound impact on the travel and tourism industry. The Internet is restructuring tourism distribution channels and the tourism industry itself

traditional service activity in which, until recently, buyers, sellers and intermediaries were well-defined. Consequently, understanding the relationship between tourism and e-commerce will help in addressing at least three fundamental and broader questions related to the global diffusion of e-commerce:

— how do new ICTs, especially the Internet, affect the trade competitiveness of developing countries,
— how does the old economy combine with the e-commerce in developing countries, and,
— how much of a margin of manoeuvre will the combination of existing practices and emerging opportunities leave to developing country stakeholders to create comparative advantages in global markets?

(UNCTAD, 2000)

Operators and providers of tourism products cannot ignore the Internet if they wish to thrive. Even small and medium sized enterprises, the predominance of which is a common characteristic of the tourism industry can adopt sophisticated technologies through the Internet, and confront their markets with a professional interface that is capable of competing on equal terms with large global corporations. The conventional structure of the tourism industry is dominated by intermediaries that sit between the supplier and the consumer.

Electronic commerce for tourism (e-tourism) can disintermediate and deconstruct the tourism value chain, driving income closer towards the actual providers of tourism experiences. But online payment possibilities, which are fundamental to closing sales, and a lack of local financial and technological infrastructure that is typical of rural and remote locations in developing countries, regularly force e-businesses to establish external subsidiaries and accounts, thereby perpetuating dependence on established intermediary operations. Marketing is a strategic tool for community-based tourism advocacy and sustainability. Marketing can enhance the success of community-based tourism by identifying market segments, defining the products based on the community-based tourism objectives and inputs from market studies, bring the products to a wide audience and help clarify what products are the most viable. The Internet is the ideal technology to handle the information and marketing aspects of community-based pro-poor tourism.

*Jailoo Tourism, the Authentic Way to Experience Kyrgyzstan**

Have you ever slept in a yurt (a Kyrgyz felt tent), drunk fresh milk in the early morning or listened to komuz music on a mountaintop? *Jailoo* (summer pasture in Kyrgyz) Tourism offers you all of these experiences. Jailoo tourism is part of a new approach to developing Kyrgyzstan's tourism industry, a strategy centered on Cultural Tourism. Cultural Tourism emphasizes the interaction and communication of tourists with authentic culture and the everyday life of local people, while encouraging multi-national cooperation and cross-cultural interaction. By taking the tourist into the mountains to spend time in the yurts of Kyrgyz nomads, Jailoo tourism gives the guest a chance to get a taste of Kyrgyz nomadic life.

Jailoo tourism is also focused on community-based tourism, helping local people benefit from the tourism industry while still living in remote villages. Local Kyrgyz nomads learn to offer a unique service to tourists, while gaining extra income during the summer, and participating in the economic development of his country. The nomadic Kyrgyz travel to the Son-Kul pastures in May to spend the summer. Dozens of yurts sprout like mushrooms around the lake. Each Kyrgyz family erects two yurts in preparation of anticipated guests. When tourists visit their encampment, the Kyrgyz empty one yurt and move themselves and their belongings to the second. They usually share all of their possessions with their guests, from dishes and oil-filled lamps, to blankets and mattresses.

Asel Karabakirova, an office assistant at NoviNomad Tourism Company, also a tour guide on the cultural tours, says, "What the locals do for tourists isn't a show. Its their life." The NoviNomad Tourism Company takes great pains to ensure that the vulnerable life style is not endangered by tourism. Tourists are not allowed to pay the nomads directly. The Kyrgyz nomads, in turn, are encouraged to treat the tourists as guests in the traditional code of Silk Road hospitality. Jailoo tourism began with the initiative of Helvetas (www.helvetas.kg or www.tourism.elcat.kg), the Swiss development aid association and founder of NoviNomad Tourism.

Information and Communication Technologies for Development in Developing Countries

Governments and the international and bi-lateral aid agencies are becoming increasingly enthusiastic about the potential for ICTs to alleviate poverty. The United Nations Development Programme (UNDP) has led a global campaign to commemorate the International Day for the Eradication of Poverty, for which the theme in 2001 was the role of ICT in poverty reduction. UNDP has launched the Digital Opportunity Initiative (DOI), a public-private partnership to help developing countries put in place national e-strategies to tackle strategic bottlenecks, facilitate enterprise and community development, and address issues such as connectivity and human capacity. The report of the DOI suggests that experience around the world reveals ample evidence that, used in the right way and for the right purposes, ICT can have a dramatic impact on achieving specific social and economic development goals as well as play a key role in broader national development strategies (UNDP, 2001).

Among the lessons from experience for the role of ICT in development, UNDP includes the following:

— An export focus can produce significant economic benefits.

— It is imperative to use ICT to improve the competitive position of a developing country in the global economy, but this may fail to meet some development goals if it diverts attention from fostering local markets and businesses.

— An explicit focus on using ICT in pursuit of development goals allows countries to achieve a wide diffusion of benefits from ICT and contributes to both broad-based economic growth and specific development goals.

As per report of DOI initiatives that are properly conceived and implemented can have an impact that extends beyond the individual communities they are designed to serve. Model initiatives can be scaled nationally or even regionally, contributing to the critical mass and the threshold levels needed to ignite a virtuous cycle of development (UNDP, 2001).

A common form of providing public access to ICTs in developing countries is the Multipurpose Community Telecentre; also know as information kiosks, information centres or just telecentres. Telecentres are springing up all over the developing world, as grassroots projects driven by communities, non-government organisations or research bodies, or as pilot projects intended by governments as pre-cursors to wider infrastructure projects designed to close the digital divide between better off people in the cities who can more easily get access to the Internet than their poorer compatriots in rural areas. For example, the government of Nepal is implementing a project that will implement 15 pilot rural development telecentres in order to provide communities with shared access to ICTs.

Mechanisms will be developed to ensure that rural communities are able to articulate and prioritise their own information requirements and to implement necessary strategies to meet those requirements. Arising from the pilots, suitable mechanisms and policy interventions will be designed for replicating successes and for achieving a national rollout of rural development telecentres. Similarly, in China, the government is implementing a project for poverty reduction through access to ICTs in the form of telecentre networks, providing demand driven information services to rural communities. The initiative aims to develop an operating cost control model to facilitate management and cost control of village telecentres as well as creating revenue generation alternatives with suggestions and mechanism for attaining self-sustainability.

e-CBT represents a development oriented focus for the deployment of ICTs that is sometimes lacking in interventions that are more concerned with technology than with the benefits it can deliver. e-CBT becomes an explicit focus for using ICT in pursuit of development goals. Moreover, as CBT has a number of potential strengths in terms of development, benefiting a wide section of the community, especially women, e-CBT inherits those strengths and makes it attractive as a development goal to be pursued where the appropriate conditions exist.

Tourism is the one sector where the concept of sustainable development can be better tested, proved or disproved in the field, with a variety of approaches as applied to different environments and cultures.

The three pillars of such development are the modernity of information technology, the tradition of local cultures, and the strength of local participation and empowerment. Access to information technology even in remote places and at low cost, offers unique ways and means to promote the involvement of local populations and to facilitate the establishment, initiatives and activities of small-scale tourism entrepreneurs (di Castri, 2002).

The Target Market for e-CBT

The market for e-CBT is the same as that for CBT, but the introduction of ICTs is particularly suited to the marketing and management of CBT as it is well matched to an identifiable type of consumer. A growing area of consumer research has identified what is known as the neo-consumer. Australian Ross Honeywill, foundation director of the International Centre for Customer Strategy and managing director of the Neo Group coined the term. According to Honeywill, the neo-consumer is an emerging breed of consumer, one that represents only a quarter of the population in developed countries, but which controls half the discretionary spending power of the economy (Honeywill, 2002). The group was identified after consumer research using data from Australia, New Zealand, the US and the UK (Honeywill and Byth, 2001). The neo-consumer market segment possesses the following characteristics that make it relevant to e-CBT:

- travel more often than the average,
- internet savvy, heavy technology users,
- are resilient travellers, for whom travel is an essential lifestyle component.
- spend more on travel than the average,
- independent travellers,
- looking for more experiential tourism,
- don't see themselves as tourists,
- quite likely to use a travel agent, but they want the agent to be their guide or coach,
- want to slay connected 24/7
- not after mass market information,

— seek encounters with the authentic,
— are willing to pay for services that will help them achieve their goals,
— like to research individual experiences,

(Honeywill, 2002)

Neo-consumers are very individualistic, but although they make up 24 per cent of the population in Australia and the USA, they do not fit traditional demographic or slice of life descriptions like Generation X, and Baby Boomers. They can be identified across all age and gender groups by a range of spending, attitudinal, behavioural and psychological characteristics including a desire to be in control of their own lives, a passion for authenticity, an urge for the edge, a desire for change, an appetite for technology and continuous, high-margin consumption (Honeywill and Byth, 2001).

The relationship between neo-consumers and tourism was further characterised at the Pacific Asia Travel Association (PATA) 8th Mekong Region Travel Forum in a keynote address by John Morse, Chairman of Tourism Victoria and former Australian Tourist Commission Managing Director. Morse characterises neo-consumers as follows:

— travel is a "must have" component of their life-style, not a luxury,
— they travel further and more frequently than the average,
— they do not purchase inclusive packages,
— they construct their own itineraries,
— they value independence and choice,
— they are not interested in mass market products or pre-packages itineraries,
— they do not respond to advertising,

— they seek authenticity and uniqueness in their travel experiences, e.g., a street performer would be more interesting than a staged cultural performance,
— they determine their own pace of travel,
— they like to stay in villages,
— they appreciate nature,
— they take time to appreciate the history and culture of their destination,
— they like to visit places that local people appreciate,
— they tend to make travel purchases on the Internet.

Research by the Centre for Consumer Strategy also indicates that:

— neo-consumers are 10 times more likely, than others to travel frequently in the next 12 months,
— they are motivated by cultural experiences,
— they are inexpensive to attract and acquire if you know how to reach and motivate them.
— they will reward someone who creates a partnership of equals, with high margin, high loyalty and high levels of referrals (Honeywill, 2002)

In every part of the world, including the most remote and isolated, tourism operations have been made cheaper and more widely accessible by the new tools of information technology (di Castri, 2002). However, viable alternatives to traditional mass-scale tourism that tends to destroy the environment and displace local people must be found (Urquico, 1998). As a barrier to the negative impacts of mass-tourism, Pauline Sheldon suggests that destinations with highly sought-after natural resources may eventually use IT to restrict their visitors, by choosing from a database visitors with a profile that promises to fit the destination well (Sheldon, 2002). Communities that wish to develop e-CBT need to be mobilised towards both the use of ICTs for their own strategic development and to the requirements for providing satisfying tourism experiences to their target clients. Whilst there is research in each of these areas, there is little (none) into the combined technology and tourism aspects of e-CBT.

The Bai Yang Gou Valley Tourist Region, Xinjinag Province, China

The Bai Yang Gou nature reserve in north Tian Shan Mountains near Urumqi, the capital city of Xinjiang Province in Western China is the home of a nomadic Kazak shepherd community who travel into the surrounding hills during the summer to feed their animals on the lush high summer pastures. During this time they live in yurts, the traditional style of rounded tent and they herd their animals on horseback. The area is one of outstanding natural beauty and the people constitute an ethnic minority with their own traditions and culture. Tourists already visit the Valley, but they are bussed in for an afternoon to witness a few horse riding displays by the Kazaks, then bussed back to the city. Previous attempts to develop tourism based on longer stays have resulted in an abandoned concrete hotel that mars the otherwise pristine location. The community has yet to develop opportunities for mountain trekking, on foot or by horseback, or to provide opportunities for close encounters with their life-style and culture, through for example homestays or escorted tours further into the mountains. Surprisingly, during a visit by the authors in October 2002, the area was well served with telecommunications. A working model for the type of CBT envisaged in Xinjiang exists in the form of an organisation in neighbouring Kyrgyzstan called Novinomad, a Kyrgyz-Swiss joint venture specialising in community based eco-tourism, trekking and horse-riding that was established with the assistance of Helvetas, the Swiss development agency. The research proposes to partner with Urumqi University, arising from an initiative, an e-Commerce Study

Tour to the People's Republic of China, September 26-October 9, 2002, by a group of researchers who came together at a panel called "The New Silk Road" during the 15th Bled Electronic Commerce Conference (Davison et al., 2003). It is anticipated that the Xinjiang Tourism Bureau will also partner with the research team.

Bario, Sarawak, Malaysia

Bario is a remote rural community in the Kelabit Highlands of the Malaysian State of Sarawak, on the island of Borneo. It is the homeland of the Kelabit people, one of the smallest indigenous Sarawakian ethnic minorities. Bario is one of the centres visited by the indigenous Penan tribe, constituting the last remaining nomadic and semi-nomadic peoples living in the rainforest. Bario is also the site of a pioneering international award-winning rural ICT project, e-Bario, which involved the establishment of a development telecentre. This proposal seeks to utilise e-commerce to promote community based pro-poor tourism in Bario in order to raise incomes and to construct a model for doing the same with other rural and remote communities in Asia.

The Kelabit Highlands of Borneo are rich in natural assets; climate, mountains, rainforest, wildlife and local indigenous cultures. Bario, is an isolated farming community accessible only by air. The Bario population has been dwindling and the economic viability of the community is threatened. The new telecentre brings opportunities for local development with ICTs. Bario already enjoys a steady trickle of tourists, but so far the community has done little to promote the area for tourism, although it is eager to do so in order to create jobs, provide enterprise opportunities and raise incomes.

The surrounding mountains provide opportunities for trekking in pristine rainforests and cultural encounters with the indigenous peoples who still live very much to their long-established customs and reside in their traditional community longhouses. The research will partner with University Malaysia Sarawak, which was instrumental in introducing the telecentre, and the Sarawak Tourism Board. An Giang province is located in south Vietnam, in the Mekong Delta region, and shares a 95-km border with Cambodia.

The province is criss-crossed by many rivers and canals, which make a convenient water transport system and tourist attraction. Tri Ton is a centre for the Khmer minority in Vietnam who make up 5% of the population of An Giang Province. Tri Ton District is largely rural, with a small town and many villages that would make attractive locations for CBT. The district enjoys 300,000-400,000 domestic visitors each year who arrive in tour busses from Ho Chi Minh City and visit the two or three principal mass tourist attractions; Soai Lake scenic area; Tuc Dup Hill American war battle location; and Ba Chuc memorial to victims of a Cambodian massacre. These visitors stay for less than a day in the district and they bypass the local cultural attractions of the area that are of interest to foreign visitors; the Khmer villages, temples and the local waterways.

The District People's Committee has a plan to construct a traditional Khmer house for visitors' accommodation in order to entice them to stay longer and to spend more locally. Tri Ton town is well served with communications, with two cyber cafes, each with around 10 computers. All the surrounding villages have telephone access but not computers and the Internet. An Giang Province is the site of an Asian Development Bank project to promote CBT as part of the Greater Mekong Sub-region Tourism Development Project which has the objective to support pro-poor community-based tourism projects in rural areas. The project will ensure that the poor benefit from increased tourism, that current levels of tourism will be effectively managed, cultural traditions and natural habitats preserved, and environmental degradation mitigated. It will develop pilot ecotourism and village-based tourism projects, foster the conservation and improvement of the natural and cultural heritage of selected areas, monitor social impacts, promote the role of women, and establish measures to minimize negative impacts of increased tourism (ADB 2003). However, this project has not included any ICT component that would empower village communities to manage and promote their own CBT projects. The proposal for e-CBT will partner with An Giang University, which is already training village cadres in computer literacy and delivering agricultural information to farmers via the Internet, and with the An Giang Service of Trade and Tourism.

E-commerce technologies will be based on the concept of web services. Web services are dynamic, flexible, interchangeable, network accessible software components that reside on the Internet. Web services encapsulate business processes and data that can be published in a directory, found by a user (human or machine) and combined with other web services to create more complex applications that can be customised at run time for each user (Pollock and Benjamin, 2001). Some of the important features of web services and their applicability to e-CBT are as follows:

— they give customers direct access to the information, data, and functions they need in order to interact with suppliers, without requiring these customers to log onto the supplier's web sit,

— they enable teams of developers to work independently on systems that will interact, because they are working toward a common set of interfaces rather than having to synchronize processing.

Web services solve business and technology problems such as:

- companies that need to respond quickly and reliably to special requests from customers and to special offers from suppliers,
- business processes that need customized tweaks for various situations, customers, suppliers, and changes in the market place,
- business processes that need to interact automatically, across organization and enterprise boundaries.

(Seybold, 2003)

A web services approach to e-CBT allows the assembly and/or construction of a range of software components that will perform the transactions necessary to enable participating communities to promote and sell their CBT products to tourists anywhere on the Internet. Web services are customisable and therefore they can be adapted to the specific and unique requirements of each community, whilst retaining common underlying processes, such as responding to enquiries, offering alternate bookings and pricing, and making reservations and receiving payments. Accordingly, under the proposal, the Information Systems Department of City University of Hong Kong will carry out the following;

- develop a collection of web services capable of effecting the business processes required for each participating community to manage its e-CBT operations,
- provide facilities for their translation and customisation by the participating universities,
- coordinate their packaging and organisation for use by additional communities as they become interested in implementing their own e-CBT operations.

The Department of Information Systems at City University of Hong Kong conducts research that emphasises the practical application of innovative information systems theories, methods and techniques to business and organisational problems within an Asia-Pacific context. Their focus is on action-oriented research that optimises technology within the socio-business environment into which it is introduced. The Department is in the process of forming an area of excellence in e-business, which will expand the industry-academic partnership established by this proposal.

It is already engaged in research into the adoption of e-commerce by Hong Kong's small and medium-sized Travel Agencies, and the development of electronic business practices to assist them. Telecentres will be set up within participating communities with a minimum of one computer with Internet access. Specific designs and implementation will be subject to local conditions and arranged between the communities themselves and the local research partners. Continuing research into the effectiveness of the e-CBT installations will be conducted by all the participating universities in collaboration with each other and with the local tourism authorities.

Summing Up

Both tourism and ICTs represent considerable potential for local development in rural communities in developing countries, bringing unusual and experiential forms of cultural encounters to a market of high-spending, frequent travellers in a manner that is wholly congruent with their lifestyle.

REFERENCES

ADB. Asian Development Bank. Signing for Tourism Project in Vietllam.

Allcock. A, Sustainable Tourism Development in Nepal, Vietnam and Lao PDR, SNV Netherlands Development Organisation, 2003.

Bennett, O., Roe, D. and Ashley, C., Sustainable Tourism and Poverty Elimination Study: A report to the Department for International Development, April 1999.

Davison, R., Vogel, D., Gricar, J., Harris, R. and Sorrentmo, M., Electronic Commerce on the New Silk Road: Rejuvenating a Historical Trade Network, The European Conference on Information Systems June 19-21 Naples, Italy 2003.

di Castri, F., Sheldon, P., Conlin, M., Boniface, P. and Balaji, V., Introduction: Information, Communication and Education for Tourism Development, in Tourism, Biodiversity and Information, di Castri, F. and Balaji, V., (eds.), Backhuys, Leiden, The Netherlands, pp. 423-429, 2002.

di Castri, F., Tourism, Biodiversity and Information, di Castri, F and Balaji, V., (eds.), Backhuys, Leiden, The Netherlands 2002.

French, H. Vanishing Borders: Protecting the Planet in the Age o Globalization Washington, Worldwatch Institute, 2000.

Harris, R.W., Kumar, A., Balaji, V. Sustainable Telecentres? Two Cases from India. ICTs and Development: New Opportunities, Perspectives and Challenges, Ashgate Publishers, forthcoming, 2003.

Heyendael, A., Sustainable Tourism Within the Context of the Ecosystem Approach, in Tourism, Biodiversity and Information, di Castri, F. and Balaji, V., (eds.), Backhuys, Leiden, The Netherlands, pp. 25-44, 2002.

Honeywill, R. and Byth, V. I-Cons: The Essential Guide to Winning and Keeping High-Value Customers, Random House, 2001.

Honeywill, R., Cash in on the Neo Consumer, Traveltrade, June 5 2002, http://www.maryrossitravel.com./whoweare/news/pdf/ traveltrade iun2002.pdf

Honeywill, R., The Global Neighbourhood, The New-Consumer Challenge for Tourism, http://www, customerstrategy.com.au/ The%20New Consumer%20Challenge%20for%20Tourism% 20ATEC"/o20May?'o202002.pdf

Patricia Seybold Group, An Executive's Guide to Web Services: How to Optimize Web Services Investments to Improve Your Customer Experience. www.psgroup.com. http:/www.PS group.com./Vm/Ws/request.asp 2003.

Pollock, A. and Benjamin, L., Shifting Sands: The Tourism Ecosystem in Transformation, DestiCorp Limited, 2001.

Roe, D and Urquhart, P., Pro-Poor Tourism: Harnessing the World's

Largest Industry (or the World's Poor, IED, UK and Khanya, South Africa. 2001.

Sah, J., Social Mobilisation Manual, Based on Syangja Experience. Social Mobilisation Learning Centre, Institute of Animal and Agriculture Sciences, Tribhuvan University, Ranpur Campus, Nepal, 2000.

Sheldon. P., Information Technology Contributions to Biodiversity in Tourism, in Tourism, Biodiversity and Information, di Castri, F. and Balaji, V., (eds.), Backhuys, Leiden. The Netherlands, pp. 449-456, 2002.

Sproule. Keith W. Community-Based Ecotourism Development: Identifying Partners in the Process. The Ecotourism Equation: Measuring the Impacts. Bulletin Series Yale School of Forestry and Environmental Studies, Number 99. New Haven CT: Yale University, 233-250. 1996.

UN. The Third United Nations Conference on the Least Developed Countries. UN General Assembly A/CONF. 191 .BP/4 5 April 2001. Reprinted as the Canary Islands Declaration on Tourism in the Least developed Countries, 2001.

UNCTAD, F-Commerce and Development Report 2001, United Nations, New York and Geneva http://ro.unctad.org/ecomerce/does/edro/en/edro/ptren. pdf.

UNCTAD, E-Commerce and Development Report, 2002, United Nations, New York and Genva, 2002.

UNCTAD, Electronic commerce and tourism: New perspectives and challenges for developing countries, 2000. Expert Meeting on Electronic Commerce and Tourism Geneva, 18-20 September 2000. http://ro/unctad org./ecommerce/does/ecomtour.pdf.

UNCTAD, High-level meeting on Tourism and Development in the Least Developed Countries, Maspalomas Convention and Exhibition Centre, Las Palmas, Gran Canaria 26-29 March 2001. http://ro unctad. org/conference/preconf/tourism.en.htm.

UNDP. Creating a Development Dynamic Final Report of the Digital Opportunity Initiative July 2001. http://www.opt-init.org/framework/DOI-Final-Report.pdf

Urquico, C., Community Based Sustainable Tourism: A Handbook, ASSET. Philippines. 1998

WTO, World Tourism Organization, "Marketing tourism destinations online", p. 4, 1999.

11

Tourism: Continuity and Change

At the down of the 20th century there were far fewer countries than now, and many were administered by a handful of colonial powers. In these developing nations, poverty was then the norm and most tourism was an example of the conspicuous consumption of an elite, with facilities to pamper both the daring explorer and the worldly traveller making the modern version of the Grand Tour. Except or migration, family travel on an international scale was rare, and single women were characteristically well chaperoned—as with the tours of Thomas Cook (Enloe, 1989: 18).

The acceleration of international travel in the early 20th century, for health, business, recreation or religious pilgrimage, led governments to issue passports, require visas, and take a generally more proactive stance toward the protection of their citizens abroad. In 1912, within weeks of the sinking of the *Titanic,* international policies required 24 hour monitoring of wireless communication, ocean liners were fitted with enough life jackets and lifeboats for all passengers, and there were international patrols in iceberg-dense sections of the oceans.

Traveller safety continues to be a major feature of public policies surrounding tourism but the complexity of the task has grown enormously. Problems are most acute in developing nations, where government capacity is limited and tourist numbers are increasing. Such nations disproportionately rely on tourism and are therefore most devastated when other countries discourage tourist travel because of fears (justified or otherwise) over safety. These issues and many more have grown as international tourism arrivals have soared to over 800 million annually. By 2020 that figure is expected to be over 1.6 billion (WTO, 1997). In this chapter, it is possible only to sketch a few policy challenges that the arrival of mass tourism has posed and aggravated for poor nations. However, it is important to stress that, like modernization more generally, the growth in international travel also offers opportunities for many developing societies. In this chapter, five challenges common to developing nations grappling with tourism are explored, obstacles and opportunities involved in meeting these challenges are then discussed in terms of current trends.

The Need for Redistribution

The policy challenges associated with tourism development are common to most nations, but they are intensified in those that are developing. They are characterized not only by poverty, which heightens the gulf between tourists and the average citizen, but also by the more pervasive inability of governments to act on any policy.

Progressive policies may be subject to manipulation or bribery, for example, but governments of developing nations too often lack the power to implement policies of any type. In extreme cases, central governments have little power beyond the capital city and its environs. Indeed, the international rhetoric of privatization and devolution of power must sound quaint when central power is so limited. Consider efforts in Uganda, Kenya or Egypt to protect tourists from rebels, poachers or the regime's religious opponents, even as tourists venture further from the state control of the centre. Poor governments may also lack the capacity to adapt or the flexibility to find appropriate alternative approaches or resist political pressures that may cripple development (Huntington, 1968: 12).

Now, more than 125 nations can be considered developing nations, as measured by low per capita income and a modest or low ranking on such human development criteria as literacy, life expectancy and education. That definition can be refined into degrees and types of impoverishment. Thirty-four nations are the poorest of the poor, with life expectancies ranging from 37 to 60 years (UNDP, 1999), and among these are several members of the former USSR and Yugoslavia, which are currently experiencing economic privation and political decay and might even be regarded as failed states. While per capita income may be the lowest common denominator for categorizing nations, it masks the cruel and often accelerating gap between rich and poor and the redistribution challenge that confronts developed and developing nations.

The crisis is at national as well as international levels. In Indonesia, for example, enormous gaps exist between rich and poor individuals, and between Java and less fortunate regions of the country, but there is no consensus about how this can be remedied. The Hindu island of Bali, for instance, resents the fact that it leads the country in tourism receipts but the money is sent to the Indonesian capital (Richter, 1988). Tourism policies that foster more equitable impacts generally will succeed only if they are designed to reduce disparities and are specifically monitored to ensure competent implementation. This can happen. Groups in Kenya and Madagascar, for instance, try to protect wildlife by giving villagers a stake in employment and income arising from tourism. Scores of such initiatives exist elsewhere, but the conditions that give rise to cooperation and entrepreneurial solutions remain relatively unexamined (Bramwell, 1998).

In 1998, for instance, the World Tourism Organization

sponsored a conference on excellence and sustainability in Poland; a year later, at its Third Global Conference (held in Glasgow), the International Institute for Peace through Tourism focused on 200 'success stories' of how peace, culture and prosperity had been linked through sustainable tourism. At a more general networking level, McLaren (1998: 133-173) has compiled a particularly helpful set of resources for both critics and supporters of tourism to utilize. Much remains to be done. Currently, the tourism sector is best understood as a broad pyramid, the base of which consists of low-skilled, poorly paid employees, usually organized along racial or gender lines, and often denied basic benefits or the right to organize collectively. This is especially true in developing nations.

Countries with high levels of unemployment are not overly concerned with worker conditions, living wages or gender equity (Enloe, 1989: 33-35; McLaren, 1998: 72-73; Richter, 1995: 75-81, 1998a), but lack of attention to these issues in the tourism sector could lead to sabotage of the industry from within and without (Richter, 1982, 1992, 1999a; Richter and Waugh, 1991). In theory, the globalization of the tourist industry could promote the spread of more enlighted policies towards the labour force, but many developing countries are in no position to bargain aggressively with foreign investors.

Moreover, local elites with capital for joint ventures with international partners may be reluctant role models for the industry. The egalitarian cause receives little assistance from the diffuse and transient travelling public, which is unlikely to prioritize basic human rights, let alone working conditions, at their proposed holiday destinations above 'bargains' in package tours, as illustrated by travel to authoritarian Myanmar and China (SLORC'S Burma, 1997). The focus of tourists on their own economic self-interest is captured in a cartoon depicting a couple in a travel office, asking, 'Which country's economic collapse will give us the best bargain for the dollar?' The challenge of redistribution, then, is likely to persist, especially for poor nations. Policymakers need to keep asking: who gets what, when, and how? (Lasswell, 1936). If such questions are not asked, or are ignored, and the labour force in developing nations — in the tourism sector or among the general public — becomes militant, tourism is jeopardized. Long-range risk analysis is needed to assess the extent to which threats are external, and how far they can be affected by internal policy decisions. Much of the implementation will be subject to government regulation, but it will succeed only if governments can muster the political will and capacity to foster equity.

Cultural Challenge of Tourism

Huntington and others consider the clash of civilizations to be the defining political battle of the future, but often the most savage struggles involve culture clashes within nations (Huntington, 1993). Indeed, the second major challenge for policymakers is managing the cultural clashes over tourism in the face of growing hostility to tourism *per se.* Over the last 20 years, criticism of tourism has shifted from the financial costs involved in developing this sector to the cultural costs incurred by societies embracing mass international tourism. The critique is especially germane and strident in developing nations, most of which are socially conservative. According to this view, the mix of traditional citizens and non-traditional travellers can often be a recipe for disaster, and 'differences in cultural behaviour can be so great that mutual understanding is replaced by antipathy' (Archer and Cooper, 1998: 71).

In many respects, the cultural crisis (and others to be discussed) reflects the highly unequal distribution of power and influence. When acknowledging the cultural divide, it is important to identify the 'owners' of a country, to ask who controls the interpretation of its heritage (Richter,

1999b), how its indigenous people and other minority groups are portrayed, and who protects, controls or sells culture to the tourist. Alternatively, cultural features can be considered irrelevant, and the nation marketed instead as a playground of beaches, casinos, and golf courses. In the *Driving Through Malaysia* brochure, for example, tourists are given no hint that they should be interested in anything but their golfing prowess (Anon., 1 997). Perhaps the most striking political reaction to such tourism marketing occurred when nationalist Michael Manley, on gaining power in Jamaica in the early 1980, changed the tourism slogan to 'Jamaica's More than a Beach; it's a Country'. His administration proceeded to alienate the US Reagan administration, which directed its Caribbean Basin Initiative elsewhere. When Manley was later replaced, the tourism slogan became 'Jamaica's Jamaica Again' (Richter, 1989a).

The trivialization of culture is often self-inflicted, as in the Malaysian brochure or Jamaica's post-Manley promotions. It is particularly harmful and controversial when marketing by the National Tourism Organizations (NTOs) is more suggestive than the culture supports. Two examples suffice. During the dictatorship of President Marcos, the NTO of the Philippines advertised 'a fresh peach on every beach', with illustrations to match the copy, and in the 1980s the United States spent taxpayers' dollars instructing potential tourists to 'TRY A VIRGIN ... island'. The territory was not amused, any more than the Caribbean Council of Churches, which challenged the tacky promotion (Richter, 1989a: 78, 1989b). Such advertising is especially distasteful as poor nations continue to struggle with the disease and crime associated with sex tourism generally and child prostitution in particular (Hall, 1992a, 1994: 174-189; Leheny, 1995; Donnelly, 1998).

Increased numbers of culturally oblivious and insensitive tourists have hardened opposition to tourism, particularly among fundamentalist religious groups in such countries as Iran, Egypt, Turkey and Afghanistan, government responses have generally fallen into two policy camps, advocating either control or segregation. In the case of the former, government has limited the number of tourists and their behaviour (Bhutan), insisted on modest dress (Iran), monitored entry to sacred places (India) or has distributed cultural advice intended to minimize the disruption caused by tourists (Sri Lanka) (Richter, 1989a: 163, 177, 102).

The second approach has been to develop enclave tourism, which isolates foreigners from the local population. In many such instances, the staff of the beach resorts and casinos, which are off limits to citizens, are low-paid nationals, as in Malaysian and Egyptian casinos or Maldivian and Indonesian resorts. Indonesia exemplifies how even advice and aid from the so-called developed world — in this case the World Bank — can create oases of culturally alien environments in the midst of traditional society, such as those at Nusa Dua on the island of Bali (Richter, 1988).

Consumption Gap

The consumption gap, which to some extent exists whenever leisured visitors are pampered by poor employees, is exacerbated by the incredible scarcity that exists in poor nations. Unlike tourists, most of whom are from societies where employees may receive up to 5 weeks of paid vacation a year, workers in the tourist sector in developing nations are unlikely ever to be tourists themselves. That makes the 'Paving of Paradise/ to use McLaren's term, or the excessive luxury of tourism resorts, a stimulus to popular resentment (McLaren, 1998).

Golf courses and enormous pools are an insult to more than 1.3 billion people denied access to clean water (UNDP, 1999: 28). In developing nations, infectious disease and gastrointestinal parasites, a direct result of unclean water, kill millions. Those who use such luxury tourist facilities at home and abroad do not seem to care. The Malaysian Sultan Abdul Azaz Shah Golf Club advertises a lifestyle so leisurely and so gracious that thankfully it can be enjoyed only by a select few' (Anon., 1993: 33). In the Public Broadcasting System's *World* television programme, 'Who Pays for Paradise?' (1 June 1978), there was a haunting scene of Gabon women carrying buckets of water on their heads as they walked past a five-star hotel filled with tourists frolicking in a huge pool. More recently, in Kenya a scarce stream was diverted to provide water for tourist resorts (Turco, 1997: 7). In other areas, local people are denied access to now private beaches, or reefs are dynamited to make beaches larger and more sandy. The fishing industry of villages is sacrificed to jet skis and scuba adventures for tourists.

It might be assumed that when tourist facilities are upgraded, host populations will benefit. They do sometimes receive roads, electric power and telecommunications, but scarce foreign exchange is often sacrificed to import luxury items for tourists. Expensive medicines and facilities for wary travellers may consume resources that might otherwise have funded basic immunization programmes and low-tech medical care for tens of thousands; indeed, cost and the location of medical facilities may effectively restrict their use to tourists (Bauer, 1999). As Bushell and Lea have argued, the focus in developing countries needs to shift from travellers' health to more general health care for both the tourist and the host population to prosper (cited in Bauer, 1999: 12).

Terrorism

Terrorism makes tourism a risky strategy to achieve national development. Not so long ago, undemocratic regimes tried to improve their international respectability by attracting tourists, and such attempts have been made by fascist Spain, Marcos-led Philippines and the current regime in Myanmar (Pi-Sunyer, 1979; Richter, 1982, 1999d). The tourism industry has frequently been depressed by war, civil strife and unstable conditions, and tourists have frequently been affected, even to the extent of being caught in the crossfire. However, over the last 20 years tourists have increasingly been targeted by terrorists and used to call attention to the abuses of dictatorial regimes (Richter, 1989a: 9-10, 1992, 1999a). In October 1999, for example, the Myanmar Embassy in Thailand was occupied by a group opposing that brutal regime (Pennington, 1999). The incident was unusual in occurring outside the country at which protests were directed, probably depressing tourism in Myanmar and Thailand. Terrorism is also seen as a way of opposing the perceived cultural costs of tourism, and as a means of sabotaging an industry often presumed to be dominated by outsiders. Although terrorist attacks worldwide peaked several years ago, their salience to the governments affected and the travelling public has grown with media attention. Moreover, tourists are easily isolated targets for attacks designed to protest against tourism or to destabilize fragile regimes dependent on tourism receipts. Tourist lifestyles are different from those of the general population, particularly in developing nations, and so terrorists risk less of a backlash than if they had targeted local businesses or residential neighbourhoods. In addition, the regime can be made to appear impotent and the publicity and impact are worldwide because victims are from a variety of nations.

As a recent development in terrorism against tourists is the way in which they are sometimes targeted because of their nationality. The 1999 murders of eight tourists in the Ugandan forests were ostensibly aimed at US and British policies. Similarly, the NATO bombing of Belgrade and other targets in the spring of 1999 led to fears of protests against tourists from NATO countries in Russia

(Bekker, 1999). Nor are only Westerners targeted. In March 1999, Kurd leaders attempted to derail Turkish tourism by a series of bombing and arson attacks (Anon., 1999). In late December 1999, predominantly Indian tourists were hijacked on a flight from Kathmandu. The prolonged ordeal was designed to pressure India to release political prisoners involved in the Kashmir conflict. The 6-day crisis ended only after a passenger was killed and several prisoners were released.

Sustainability

Undoubtedly, 'Sustainability' is a fashionable topic, but coordinated and consistent efforts to achieve it in the face of soaring tourism are rare indeed. However, some case studies offer hope that the interest in thoughtful development is more than rhetoric (Hawkins and Khan, 1998). More common, however, are examples of policy-makers jettisoning even well-conceived plans and substituting unwise development. Political pressures are particularly hard to resist in developing countries, where seizing the moment to make badly needed profits is more attractive than abstract notions of intergenerational equity. Nations desperate to promote international tourism are not especially susceptible to concepts of tourist carrying capacity, managed growth, or similar environmental niceties (Bramwell, 1998).

Even areas where the main attractions are flora and fauna, and where 'ecotourism' is the buzzword, still allow shortcuts in environmentally sensitive development and permit far too many to visit fragile nesting, hatching or other endangered habitats. Ecotourism can make a virtue of small numbers of tourists, but unfortunately pressures to expand the scale and type of tourism grow with the industry's importance to the economy. In the Galapagos Islands, for example, the once pristine environment now hosts more than 300% of the number of visitors originally allowed (McLaren. 1998: 106).

Another example is Costa Rica, famous for its biodiversity and its commitment to make over 20% of its land mass a series of national parks. For years, growth in tourism was slowed by civil wars in neighbouring Central American nations, and promotion rather than control of tourism was the priority. However, since peace developed in neighbouring states, Costa Rican tourism has skyrocketed and the nation has become seduced by the money that tourism has brought. Lavish beach resorts without sewage systems have been developed and harsh and thoughtless logging practices near national parks threaten mudslides.

The Costa Rican government's problems have been twofold: firstly, they had to develop policies to keep pace with the mushrooming growth in tourism and, secondly, it was necessary to enforce the few existing regulations. However, although the country is politically stable and tourism is well-received, the single-term presidencies required by the constitution make leaders 'lame ducks' almost as soon as they are elected. Political leverage evaporates quickly. In general, most discussions on sustainability focus on natural attractions, but it is also related to the growth, pace and type of tourist and the accompanying infrastructure.

None of these factors can be taken for granted in developing nations. In some, accustomed to a high level of contact with outsiders, trading traditions have led to an entrepreneurial lifestyle that easily accommodates tourism, but elsewhere this is not the case and the potential for conflict can be high.

Fifty years ago, it might have been assumed that former colonial societies would be accustomed to Western visitors and that increasing exposure would lead to a heightened comfort level with international tourism, but this is no longer the case. Because of the rapid increase in tourism, and its expansion to virtually every part of the world, modern tourists are inadequately prepared for visits to areas that seldom if ever saw colonial administrators. As a result, in some countries — notably India, Pakistan, Uganda, Algeria and Guatemala — opposition to tourists in general, and to certain nationalities and religions in particular, has grown. Other governments (for example, Afghanistan, Iran, Iraq and Saudi Arabia) have moved to isolate their people from the allegedly pernicious effects of tourism, especially those emanating from Western women, by restricting or discouraging tourism.

In developing countries too, with highly sophisticated tourism industries, the issue of sustainability is becoming salient, especially as religious conservatives become more influential. As a consequence, some developed countries have discouraged their citizens from travelling to such destinations. At any given time, for example, the US State Department issues advisories on about 40 nations, ranging from simple cautionary statements, to warnings, to 'Don't Go' advisories. These may be based on probable political dangers, but just as often refer to crime and health hazards and, according to some critics, may also reflect political bias.

Even in the absence of tourists, a nation must decide how to allocate scarce resources to nurture and sustain the natural and man-made heritage for its own citizens. Borabadur, Anghor Wat, Dubrovnik, the Amazon and the Galapagos Islands also have a value that should be supported by non-citizens as well. This is why the United Nations Educational, Scientific and Cultural Organization (UNESCO) World Heritage List is critical for reinforcing the political will and helping developing nations to resist development that threatens world treasures (Richter and Richter, 2000). In essence, the allocation of resources to protecting sites, restoring habitats and promoting domestic and international tourism is a political rather than a technical decision.

Similarly, the degree to which national culture is exhibited, modified, of influenced by visitors should not be a function of the advertising budgets of tour operators, the venture capital of investors, or the incapacity of government to know its own needs and those of its citizens. It is a cliche that tourists visit developing nations for sun, sand, sea and sex, and such motivations will continue, and will be facilitated by the Internet's ability to market anything, including child prostitution. But to these 'four Ss' must be added four more: a preoccupation with security, sanitation, safe transport, and the sensible protection of the built and natural heritage.

Senior Tourism

The political and economic importance of huge numbers of senior travellers has been recognized by the United Nations (UN). It declared 1994 the 'Year of the Elderly' and called on countries to recognize that 'Government must draft and implement active policies for training, employment, leisure, and social integration, which take into account the exponential growth in the number of older people' (Senior Tourism brochure, UN, 1999). In addition, a series of conferences on senior tourism focused on this demographic category of people who have money, time and an increasing proclivity for travel — but who also have special requirements in matters of comfort, health and safety (Richter, 1999c). The US senior travel market is illustrative of a trend that will accelerate as 'baby boomers' (those born in the aftermath of the Second World War) retire. Even now, those over 65 form 25% of the population and, more importantly, control 70% of the nation's wealth (Blazey, 1992: 771). They represent an attractive market for developing nations, but they will also be 'high maintenance' travellers, making special demands on impoverished nations for comfort and health, just as early tourists travelled on religious pilgrimage, to shrines or to spas to 'take the waters', the tourist at or near retirement age is increasingly coupling tourism with health or spiritual interests (Hall, 1992b: 141-158). Senior tourism runs the gamut from adventure travel to more sedentary vacations, but increasingly it is older tourists who are eager to move beyond the Grand Tour favoured by earlier generations. Today's seniors may favour precisely those trips that cater to their intellect. Earthwatch, which pairs all ages of tourists with scientists on hundreds of projects, rates its trips by their difficulty rather than by any stereotypical notions about what age or gender can cope. More than half of these trips are in developing nations.

The Elder Hostel movement offers low-frills trips to both developed and developing countries with an emphasis on cultural learning and basic accommodation. Such travel is far less costly for host countries and their guests and more culturally benign than many other types of tourism. Begun in 1975, Elder Hostel now has several hundred thousand participants in scores of countries (Kalinowski and Weiler, 1992:22).

Growth of International Tourism

Several trends complicate the ability of developing nations to handle the problems just discussed, and the first is the sheer growth of international tourism, which will crucially affect developing societies. Over the next two decades, tourism arrivals are estimated to double to over 1.6 billion people (WTO, 1997). Currently, Africa receives only 4% of all international travellers, but as other destinations become saturated, international travel to that continent, and to Asia, Latin America and the Pacific, is expected to soar. Other trends reflect the changing demographic mix of those travelling.

Travel and Disabilities

The third trend is the increasing number of disabled people who are travelling. Their needs are only belatedly receiving attention in developed countries, and are all but ignored in most developing societies. As a participant at the 1985 UN Decade for Women Conference in Nairobi, Kenya, it was sobering to discover that some 100 disabled women had to meet on the University of Nairobi lawn because all the conference buildings were inaccessible. Fifteen years later, the disabled have far more resources, but coverage remains uneven. The passage of the Americans with Disabilities Act in 1990 and the Air Carriers Access Act encouraged and in some cases required accessible facilities for travellers. Although the initial impact was on domestic American tourism, the acts also evoked a response from international cruise lines and tour operators abroad. Indeed, the growing affluence and influence of senior and disabled tourists will encourage developing nations to take their needs into account when promoting new destination areas and attractions. If demographics are not enough to encourage such accessible development, legal initiatives by the disabled, including handicapped students, are likely to affect tour operators and programmes in tourist-generating nations, so that their own operations may require accessibility at the destinations. Among the groups focused on improving travel opportunities are Mobility International, Disabled Peoples International and the Society for the Advancement of Travellers with Handicaps (SATH).

Educational Travel

As a recent phenomenon increasingly students of all ages consider international travel a facet of their education. This partly reflects the expectation that education should be experiential, interactive and participatory. To ensure that student expectations are met, college campuses are reinventing themselves in the face of on-line competition and the challenge of students from everywhere and of all ages (Plummer, 1989). For most universities, the presence of international students and the encouragement of reciprocal educational visits by domestic students makes good economic as well as pedagogical sense. Students who have studied abroad not only are presumed to be better prepared for the 21st century in terms of diversity, language and globalization but they also promote the university overseas. Foreign students are also less likely to be subsidized by the host institution, which makes them worth more financially than a domestic or in-state student. Hosting short-term educational visits allows universities to make use of university facilities during otherwise slow times, e.g. vacations.

Elder Hostel, described earlier, was able to keep its costs down while helping educational institutes make use of facilities during slow times. Service learning is one of the fastest growing forms of educational travel. For more than 30 years, Dutch work camps and some churches have pioneered experiential travel combined with projects in developing nations. Today, the service model is focused more on student expertise than physical effort to assist communities at home and abroad. Some universities require a period of internship or service, but in recent years that interest has expanded to overseas service in developing nations. One of the first to incorporate a service component into its educational programmes abroad was Kansas State University, which in 1990 pioneered international community service programmes. At the time of writing, these extend to 11 developing nations on three continents.

The US Peace Corps has also adopted an internship programme that allows students to explore while working in developing nations, without obliging them to extend their duty abroad. On the non-governmental level, the New York-based Partnership for Service Learning places individuals all over the world.

Students themselves are utilizing university years for travel vacations, overseas study (no longer confined to the junior year of an elite few) and for internships and service-based learning (Eisenberg, 1989; Weiler and Kalinowski, 1990). Are these examples of tourism? They are at least in part, for they expose students, faculty and others to different cultures and traditions. Whether or not students spend money and time in the host society, they can be important assets in national development. They are also valuable to the tourism industry, becoming involved in needs assessments and planning; developing inventories of skills and attractions; teaching hotel and restaurant management and small business development; and engaging in marketing and promotional work.

Information Technology Revolution

The revolution in information technology is reshaping the tourist industry in ways both positive and negative for developing nations, The Internet allows entrepreneurs opportunities to bypass foreign-owned tour companies and to advertise and take reservations directly from groups and individuals. This can be a tremendous advantage for business in a poor nation. However, tourists may be disappointed to find that developing nations lack the computers, fax machines, satellite dishes and cell phone connections required to maintain contact with home and business. At best, such access is uneven, and apt to be located only in the more expensive destination areas. Even among developing regions, great inequalities exist. In all of Africa, for example, there are fewer cell phones than in Thailand (UNDP, 1999: 135). The insecurity that accompanies the globalization of technology was much in evidence in fears that there would be massive computer malfunctions, glitches and power failures when the year 2000 arrived. Such concerns created a virtual depression in some tourist regions — particularly developing countries, which were presumed less prepared for the changeover. The feared breakdowns did not occur, but much of the economic cost did — in the form of decreased travel around the New Year and into the first quarter of 2000.

Political Trends

Global health policies, are threatened by the deregulation of transport, lax sanitation requirements, and the overall reduction in health requirements for travellers (Anon, 1995; Hayden, 1999; Richter, 1999c). Such changes occur as travellers increasingly visit more remote environments, often in regions with substandard health care. This is hazardous not only to the health of tourists, but also to that of the host community and tourist-generating societies (McLaren, 1998: 84-87). Although only a small fraction of international tourism arrivals goes to developing countries, tourism remains for many a major source of foreign exchange. As a consequence, when adequate international health standards are not enforced, poor nations are reluctant to report outbreaks of infectious diseases, or indeed any other threat to tourists.

Negative publicity inevitably leads to reduced tourism receipts, especially if accompanied by the realization that many developing countries are ill-equipped to remedy such problems. Also, the World Health Organization (WHO) has been criticized by the *Lancet* and other medical journals for not doing more to prevent the spread of disease. Member states controlling WHO funding favour the facilitation of tourism over vaccination requirements, health warnings and tough spraying and sanitation regimes for transport. WHO guidelines developed in the 1960s leave nations to cope with diseases such as ebola, the Marburg virus, West Nile fever and even the AIDS epidemic on a country-by-country basis. As a consequence, nations with higher standards are actually violating outdated WHO regulations, which insist on common regulations. Since 1976, over three dozen new infectious diseases have been discovered — mostly in poor countries — and yet WHO has been slow to pressure nations to develop adequate precautions against their spread. Seemingly forgotten are the lessons of 1917/18, when influenza from Fort Riley, Kansas, was responsible for the deaths of 30 million people worldwide (Anon, 1995; Heymann, 1995). Privatization is a mixed blessing. Although it may favour small enterprises, which in other circumstances might have to compete with state-owned facilities, it does nothing to counter the influence of large multinational facilities, which under deregulation and privatization may come to dominate the tourism industry and attract local capital, which could have been invested in smaller, indigenous enterprises (Smith, 1998).

The challenges and trends outlined here are not exhaustive, but they do indicate a daunting policy agenda for developing nations. At the same time, there are grounds for optimism about what tourism can mean for poor nations in the 21st century. In particular, there are numerous ways whereby groups not oriented towards profit and community-based initiatives can reduce the negative effects of tourism and enhance the benefits it brings to developing nations.

One of the first pressure groups to address issues of tourism's negative impacts was the Ecumenical Coalition on Third World Tourism (ECTWT). Formed in the early 1980s, it enlisted the aid of church organizations around the world, developed a useful library and a magazine (*Contours,* which is highly critical of Third World tourism) and sponsored a series of international conferences. It also produced a widely circulated Code of Ethics for Travellers, especially targeted at tourists going to developing nations (de Sousa, 1993). Following the success of ECTWT, other groups were formed: the Tourism Ecumenical Network in Europe; the Center for Responsible Tourism in the USA; Just Tourism in New Zealand; Equations in India; and the Ecumenical Coalition Against Child Prostitution in Asian Tourism (ECPAT), based in the Philippines.

ECPAT, in particular, has been instrumental in publicizing and confronting the growing problem of child prostitution. Once focused specifically on Asian tourism, its concern has now widened to include tourism's links with such exploitation throughout the world. With other organizations, it has documented the international extent of the problem, and the growing use of the internet in its spread. As a result of ECPAT's campaign for stiff penalties against paedophile tourists in both developed and developing countries, some of the former countries have extended their legal jurisdiction to crimes committed against children by their citizens when overseas (McLaren, 1998: 88-89; Patty, 1999) and some developing nations, including the Philippines and Thailand, have sought to try tourists for sex crimes.

The global interconnectedness highlighted and accelerated by the technology revolution has linked professionals in poor countries to the rest of the world in increasingly cheap and effective ways. Moreover, cooperative efforts are being forged to assist poor countries in ways that bypass governments entirely. One such example is the Programme for Monitoring Emerging Diseases (PROMED), which links more than 10,000 doctors in 120 countries by Email. They have been monitoring health conditions throughout the world. Coverage is uneven, particularly in the poórest tropical countries, where outbreaks are most likely to occur, but such responses to health threats are the basis for a future system of health and security surveillance. Such activism has also spurred the WHO to launch WHONET, which links microbiology laboratories to a central database.

Developing countries are also working on strategies to address other problems associated with tourism. In 1996, for example, Costa Rica introduced the Certificate for Sustainable Tourism (CST) to encourage hotels, cruise ships and others involved in tourism to compete with one another to adopt environmentally friendly practices. The achievements of successful companies were rewarded with publicity and other incentives (Richter, 1998a). In its first 2 years, so many hotels and resorts requested evaluation along CST standards that plans were made to include other sectors of the industry. Costa Rica also persuaded all other Central American nations to agree in principle to the future development of similar programmes (Richter, 1998a). At the international level, several branches of the UN now take tourism seriously. These include the WHO, the World Tourism Organization, the World Heritage programmes of the UNESCO, and the United Nations Development Programme. Among their activities is help for developing nations in protecting their environment, their heritage and their health. In one instance, after decades of organizational lethargy, WHO, through WHONET, is accelerating its efforts to detect and prevent the spread of drug-resistant microbes (Pirages and Runci, 2000: 189). However, member nations still need to utilize WHO as an enforcement mechanism for meaningful health regulations — a function that will become increasingly critical as international tourism increases.

One more glaring example is UNESCO's impressive efforts to assist the recovery of Dubrovnik during and after the war in Croatia. When war broke out in 1991, Dubrovnik, already on the list of World Heritage Sites, was reclassified as a Heritage Site in Danger. Even during hostilities, a recovery plan was adapted from an earthquake recovery document compiled 12 years earlier, and repair and restoration plans were under way even before the war ended (Jemo, 1996). Arguably, UNESCO's high-profile involvement prevented the ancient city from being destroyed (Woodward, 1996; Richter and Richter, 2000).

REFERENCES

Anon, (1995) Fortress WHO: breaking the ramparts for health's sake. *Lancet* 28 January, 345(8944), 203-204.

Anon, (2000) Hostages released! *Kansas City Star* 1 January, p. 1.

Archer, B. and Cooper, C. (1998) The positivc and negative impacts of tourism. In: Theobald, W.F. (ed.) *Global Tourism: the Second Decade,* 2nd edn. Butterworth-Heinemann, Oxford, pp. 63-81.

Bauer, I. (1999) The impact of tourism in developing countries on the health of the local host communities. *Journal of Tourism Studies* 10(1), 2-17.

Bekker, V. (1999) 'Are terrorists targeting St Pete? *St Petersburg Times* 17 September, p. 1.

Blazey, M. (1992) Travel and retirement Status. *Annals of Tourism Research* 19(4), 771-783.

Bramwell, B. (1998) Selecting policy instruments for sustainable tourism. In: Theobald, W.F. (ed.) *Global Tourism: the Second Decade,* 2nd edn. Butterworth-Heinemann, Oxford, UK, pp. 361-379.

GIEE (1999) *Safety and Responsibility in Education Abroad.* Workshop Manual, GEE, New York.

CNN (1999b) Busload of US tourists robbed in South African township. *World: News* 12 February, p. 1.

Donnelly, D. (1998) Where have all the children gone? In: McLaren, D. (ed.) *Rethinking Tourism and Ecotourism.* Kumarian Press, West Hartford, Connecticut, pp. 88-89.

Enloe, C. (1989) *Bananas, Beaches and Bases: Making Feminist Sense of International Politics.* University of California Press, Berkeley, California.

Hall, CM. (1992a) Sex tourism in South-East Asia. In: Harrison, D. (ed.) *Tourism in the Less Developed Countries.* Belhaven, London, pp. 64-74.

Hall, C.M. (1992b) Adventure, sport and health tourism. In: Weiler, B. and Hall, C.M. (eds) *Special Interest Tourism.* Belhaven, London, pp. 141-158.

Hall, C.M. (1994) *Tourism and Politics.* John Wiley & Sons, Chichester, UK.

Hawkins, D. and Khan, M. (1998) Ecotourism opportunities for developing countries. In: Theobald, W.F. (ed.) *Global Tourism: the Second Decade.* Butterworth-Heinemann, Oxford, UK, pp. 191-204.

Hayden, T. (1999) Tuberculosis is making a comeback *Newsweek* 8 November, p. 77.

Heymann, D. (1995) Emerging infectious diseases. *World Health* 50(1), 4.

Huntington, S.L. (1968) *Political Order in Changing Societies.* Yale University Press, New Haven, Connecticut.

Lasswell, H. (1936) *Politics: Who Gets What, When and How.* McGraw Hill, New York.

Leheny, D. (1995) A political economy of Asian sex tourism. *Annals of Tourism Research* 22(2); 367-384.

McLaren, D. (1998) *Rethinking Tourism and Ecotravel.* Kumarian Press, West Hartford, Connecticut.

Patty, A. (1999) Australian sex tourists find their laws back home don't take a vacation. *The World Paper* January-February, p. 16.

Pennington, M. (1999) Talks pause with dissidents holding Myanmar Embassy. *Kansas City Star 2* October, p. A17.

Richter, L.K. (1988) Indonesian tourism: the good, the bad and the ugly. *Contours* 14(1), 29-30.

Richter, L.K. (1989a) *The Politics of Tourism in Asia.* University of Hawaii Press, Honolulu.

12

World Tourism Organization (WTO)

> We cannot live only for ourselves. A thousand fibers connect us with our fellow men; and along those fibers, as sympathetic threads, our action run as causes, and they come back to us as effects.
>
> —*Herman Melville*

The World Tourism Organization (WTO/OMT), a specialized agency of the United Nations, is the leading international organization in the field of tourism. It serves as a global forum for tourism policy issues and practical source of tourism know-how.

With its headquarters in Madrid, Spain, the WTO plays a central and decisive role in promoting the development of responsible, sustainable and universally accessible tourism, with the aim of contributing to economic development, international'understanding, peace, prosperity and universal respect for, and observance of, human rights and fundamental freedoms. In pursuing this aim, the Organization pays particular attention to the interests of developing countries in the field of tourism.

The WTO plays a catalytic role in promoting technology transfers and international cooperation, in stimulating and developing public-private sector partnerships and in encouraging the implementation of the Global Code of Ethics for Tourism, with a view to ensuring that member countries, tourist destinations and businesses maximize the positive economic, social and cultural effects of tourism and fully reap its benefits, while minimizing its negative social and environmental impacts.

In 2005, the WTO's membership is comprised of 145 countries, seven territories and more than 300 Affiliate Members representing the private sector, educational institutions, tourism associations and local tourism authorities.

Tourism for Prosperity and Peace

At the start of the new millennium, tourism is firmly established as the number one industry in many countries and the fastest-growing economic sector in terms of foreign exchange earnings and job creation. International tourism is the world's largest export earner and an important factor in the balance of payments of most nations.

As now, tourism has become one of the world's most important sources of employment. It stimulates enormous investment in infrastructure, most of which also helps to improve the living conditions of local people. It provides governments with substantial tax revenues. Most new tourism jobs and business are created in developing countries, helping to equalize economic opportunities and keep rural residents from moving to overcrowded cities.

Intercultural awareness and personal friendships fostered through tourism are a powerful force for improving international understanding and contributing to peace among all the nations of the world.

The WTO recognizes that tourism can have a negative cultural, environmental and social impact if it is not responsibly planned, managed and monitored. The WTO thus encourages governments to play a vital role in tourism, in partnership with the private sector, local authorities and non-governmental organizations.

In its belief that tourism can be effectively used to address the problems of poverty, WTO made a commitment to contribute to the United Nations Millennium Development Goals through a new initiative to develop sustainable tourism as a force for poverty elimination. The programme, known as ST-EP (Sustainable Tourism-Eliminating Poverty), focuses the longstanding work of both organizations on encouraging sustainable tourism with a view to alleviating poverty and was implemented in 2003.

WTO: A Historical Account

The World Tourism Organization had its beginnings as the International Congress of Official Tourist Traffic Associations set up in 1925 in The Hague. It was renamed the International Union of Official Travel Organisations (IUOTO) after World War II and moved to Geneva. IUOTO was a technical, non-governmental organization, whose membership at its peak included 109 National Tourist Organizations (NTOs) and 88 Associate Members, among them private and public groups.

As tourism grew and became an integral part of the fabric of modern life, its international dimension increased and national governments started to play an increasingly important role-their activities covering the whole spectrum from infrastructure to regulations. By the mid-1960s, it became clear that there was a need for more effective tools to keep developments under review and to provide tourism with intergovernmental machinery especially equipped to deal with the movement of persons, tourism policies and tourism's impacts.

In 1967, the members of IUOTO called for its transformation into an intergovernmental body empowered to deal on a worldwide basis with all matters concerning tourism and to cooperate with other competent organizations, particularly those of the United Nations' system, such as the World Health Organization (WHO), UNESCO, and the International Civil Aviation Organization (ICAO).

A resolution to the same effect was passed in December 1969 by the UN General Assembly, which recognized the decisive and central role the transformed IUOTO should play in the field of world tourism in cooperation with the existing machinery within the UN. Following this resolution, the WTO's Statutes were ratified in 1974 by the States whose official tourist organizations were members of IUOTO.

Thus IUOTO became the World Tourism Organization (WTO) and its first General Assembly was held in Madrid in May 1975. The Secretariat was installed in Madrid early the following year at the invitation of the Spanish Government, which provides a building for the Headquarters.

In 1976, WTO became an executing agency of the United Nations Development Programme (UNDP) and in 1977, a formal cooperation agreement was signed with the United Nations itself. In 2003, the WTO was converted into a specialized agency of the United Nations and reaffirmed its leading role in international tourism.

Since its early years, WTO's membership and influence in world tourism have continued to grow. By 2005, its membership included 145 countries, seven territories and some 350 Affiliate Members, representing the private sector, educational institutions, tourism associations and local tourism authorities.

KEY EVENTS

1925 International Congress of Official Tourist Traffic Associations, The Hague, The Netherlands

1934 Creation of International Union of Official Tourist Propaganda Organizations (IUOTPO), The Hague, The Netherlands

1947 IUOTPO is converted to the International Union of Official Travel Organisations (IUOTO)

1969	Intergovernmental Conference in Sofia, Bulgaria and the UN General Assembly, call for creation of intergovernmental organization on tourism
1970	In Mexico, on 27 September (future date of World Tourism Day) IUOTO's Extraordinary General Assembly adopts the Statutes of World Tourism Organization
1975	First General Assembly of the World Tourism Organization is held in Madrid, Spain and WTO is officially launched with Robert Lonati (France) as Secretary-General
1976	WTO Secretariat moves from Geneva to Madrid
1977/1979	WTO General Assembly held in Torremolinos, Spain
1979	"World Tourism Day" created, to be celebrated every year on 27th September
1980	WTO convenes World Tourism Conference in Manila; the Manila Declaration on World Tourism is unanimously adopted
1981	WTO General Assembly held in Rome, Italy
1982	World Tourism Conference convened in Acapulco; Acapulco Document is adopted
1983	WTO General Assembly held in New Delhi, India
1985	Tourism Bill of Rights and Tourist Code adopted at WTO General Assembly, Sofia, Bulgaria
1986	Willibald Pahr (Austria) elected Secretary-General
1987	WTO General Assembly held in Madrid, Spain
1989	WTO General Assembly held in Paris, France
1989	Inter-Parliamentary Conference on Tourism, jointly organized with the Inter-Parliamentary Union, adopts The Hague Declaration on Tourism

1990	Antonio Enríquez Savignac (Mexico) elected Secretary-General
1991	WTO General Assembly held in Buenos Aires, Argentina
1993	WTO General Assembly held in Bâli, Indonesia
1995	WTO General Assembly held in Cairo, Egypt
1996	Francesco Frangialli (France) appointed interim Secretary-General after Antonio Enríquez Savignac's early retirement
1996	Second WTO Forum on Parliaments and Local Authorities: Tourism Policy-Makers, adopts the Bali Declaration on Tourism, Indonesia
1997	WTO General Assembly held in Istanbul, Turkey
1997	Francesco Frangialli (France) elected Secretary-General
1999	WTO General Assembly held in Santiago, Chile
2001	Fourteenth General Assembly held jointly in Seoul, Republic of Korea and Osaka, Japan
2001	Francesco Frangialli (France) re-elected Secretary-General
2003	Transformation of the WTO into a UN specialized agency

Functions of WTO Structure

The bodies of the World Tourism Organization are the:

1. General Assembly: The General Assembly is the principal gathering of the World Tourism Organization. It meets every two years to approve the budget and programme of work and to debate topics of vital importance to the tourism sector. Every four years it elects a Secretary-General. The General Assembly is composed of Full Members and Associate Members. Affiliate Members and representatives of other international organizations participate as observers.

2. *Executive Council:* The Executive Council is WTO's governing board, responsible for ensuring that the Organization carries out its work and adheres to its budget. It meets twice a year and is composed of 29 Members elected by the General Assembly in a ratio of one for every five Full Members. As host country of WTO's Headquarters, Spain has a permanent seat on the Executive Council. Representatives of the Associate Members and Affiliate Members participate in Executive Council meetings as observers.

3. *Regional Commissions:* WTO has six regional commissions-Africa, the Americas, East Asia and the Pacific, Europe, the Middle East and South Asia. The commissions meet at least once a year and are composed of all the Full Members and Associate Members from that region. Affiliate Members from the region participate as observers.

4. *Committees:* Specialized committees of WTO Members advise on management and programme content. These include: the Programme Committee, the Committee on Budget and Finance, the Committee on Statistics and Macroeconomic Analysis of Tourism, the Committee on Market Intelligence and Promotion, the Sustainable Development of Tourism Committee, the Quality Support Committee, the WTO Education Council, the WTO Business Council and the World Committee on Tourism Ethics.

5. *Secretariat:* The Secretariat is led by Secretary-General Francesco Frangialli of France, who supervises about 90 full-time staff at WTO's Madrid Headquarters. He is assisted by the Deputy Secretary-General Dawid de Villiers of South Africa. These officials are responsible for implementing WTO's programme of work and serving the needs of Members. The WTO Business Council is supported

by a full-time Chief Executive Officer at the Madrid Headquarters, a position that is financed by the Spanish Government. The Secretariat also includes a regional support office for Asia-Pacific in Osaka, Japan, financed by the Japanese Government. The official languages of WTO are English, Spanish, French, Russian and Arabic.

Cooperation for Development

Shared Technical Skills

The transfer of tourism knowhow to developing countries is one of the World Tourism Organization's fundamental tasks. As an executing agency of the United Nations Development Programme, WTO contributes decades of experience in tourism to the sustainable development goals of nations throughout the world.

Acting on requests from Member States, WTO secures financing, locates the world's leading experts, and carries out a gamut of development projects-large and small. Long-term projects have included:

- Tourism Master Plan for Pakistan (2001)
- Tourism Master Plans for eight Chinese provinces (2000-2002)
- Development of national parks in Rwanda (1999)
- Tourism development strategy for Moldova (1999-ongoing)
- Integrated development programme for Palestinian Authority (2000)
- Development activities in some 70 countries worth more than US$ 2.5 million (2001-2002)

Projects can also be short and targeted to address an immediate need, for example:

- Tourism legislation in Syria
- Ecotourism plan for Lithuania

- Statistics development in Botswana
- Social impact study for the Maldives
- Management of heritage sites in Ecuador
- Hotel classification for Bolivia
- Women's empowerment plan for Namibia
- Training for quality service in tourism in Peru

Tourism has proven to be a powerful tool in alleviating poverty. It has become the economic mainstay of many of the world's least developed countries (LDCs), providing them with one of the opportunities for development and job creation. A joint programme with UNCTAD called Sustainable Tourism - Eliminating Poverty (STEP) focuses on the twin subjects of sustainable tourism and alleviation of poverty, in order to increase their potential synergies and contribute more strongly to sustainable development in least developed and developing countries. STEP was launched at WSSD in Johannesburg in August 2002.

Regional Activities

Around the World

Direct actions that strengthen and support the efforts of National Tourism Administrations are carried out by WTO's regional representatives.

Each region of the world - Africa, the Americas, East Asia and the Pacific, Europe, the Middle East and South Asia - receives special attention from its regional representative based at the Headquarters of the World Tourism Organization in Madrid.

Regional representatives are WTO's front line of contact with member countries. They are constantly on the go, but regional representatives are much more than travelling ambassadors.

- They meet with the top tourism officials from each

of the countries in their region to analyse problems and offer solutions.

- To create specific development projects, they act as a liaison between tourism authorities and financing sources, especially the United Nations Development Programme.
- They represent WTO at national and regional tourism events.
- They organize national seminars on topics of particular relevance to an individual country.
- They hold regional conferences on problems that are shared by many countries so that Members can exchange experiences and work towards common goals. Recent conferences have been held on the Challenge of Globalization in the Middle East, Human Resource Development in East Asia and the Pacific, the Euro and Tourism in Europe and Quality Standards in the Americas region, Crisis Management in East Asia and the Pacific, etc.
- They help facilitate productive contacts between tourism authorities and other branches of government - often at the presidential level.

All of these activities are designed to help increase the stature of National Tourism Administrations within their own country, while at the same time building awareness of new developments in tourism and improving technical, operational skills.

In a special effort to help boost tourism to sub-Saharan Africa, WTO has developed a specific programme of technical activities for the years 2003 - 2004.

WTO's six Regional Commissions meet at least once a year to discuss the Organization's activities and set priorities for the future. Affiliate Members from the region are encouraged to participate in the meetings and seminars.

Regional Promotion Projects

WTO is in a unique position to carry out special projects that promote tourism to a group of Member States. The Silk Road and the Slave Route are two of these projects, initiated in cooperation with the United Nations Scientific and Cultural Organization (UNESCO).

The Slave Route Project, initiated in 1995 as part of the United Nations' International Year of Tolerance, aims to boost tourism to western African nations. Its immediate goals are to restore monuments, enhance history museums and launch joint information campaigns in selected tourism generating markets, which will motivate foreign visitors to learn about the history of these countries and to discover their roots.

The Silk Road Project, launched in 1994, aims at revitalizing the ancient highways used by Marco Polo through tourism. The Silk Road stretches 12,000 km from Asia to Europe and 22 countries have joined forces for this project: Armenia, Azerbaijan, China, DPR Korea, Egypt, Georgia, Greece, Islamic Republic of Iran, Italy, Israel, Japan, Kazakhstan, Kyrgyzstan, Mongolia, Pakistan, Republic of Korea, Russian Federation, Syrian Arab Republic, Tajikistan, Turkmenistan, Turkey and Uzbekistan. Joint promotional activities include seminars, a brochure and a video.

World Tourism Day

Since 1980, Members of the World Tourism Organization have been celebrating World Tourism Day every year on September 27th. Events include parades, concerts, tourism fairs, seminars, dinners, dances, and free entrance to museums-anything and everything that draws attention to the important role that tourism plays in the local community.

Task Force for Destination Management

To reflect the growing decentralization of tourism administration, WTO formed a task force to focus on issues that are of special concern at the destination level. Some concerns of the task force include: management of congestion at coastal destinations; economic measurement of tourism at the local level; destination marketing for cities; information and communication technologies; human resource development; and risk and crisis management at individual tourism destinations. The Task Force for Destination Management meets periodically and acts as an informal advisory body of WTO, with the aim of encouraging new work in these areas and identifying ongoing WTO projects that are relevant to tourism officials working in destination management.

Business Council

WTO is unique among international intergovernmental organizations in that it is open to membership by the operating sector and promotes various methods of cooperation amongst its Members. Airlines, hotel chains, tour operators, trade associations, consultants, promotion boards and educational institutions make up approximately 350 Members of the WTO Business Council (WTOBC).

WTOBC utilizes a partnership approach to tourism as a method to promote public and private integration and as a model of understanding between the two sectors. To achieve their objectives, WTOBC aids Members in expanding their tourism businesses through industry networking, forming contacts with the necessary government officials strengthening industry-education relationship, and conducting specialized research projects of the private sector.

Currently, the WTOBC is undertaking numerous projects with the hope of creating more public-private partnerships and sustained cooperation amongst tourism industries. These projects include investigations into the factors that affect tourism, methods of managing congestion on sites, assisting small and medium size enterprises, and implementing new technology.

Under the guidance of its Board of Directors, WTOBC continues their research on the above-mentioned Projects accompanied by annual studies, data compilation, research publication and organization of conferences. The Council continues to promote integration between public and private sectors with themes that are of special interest to the business community which include:

- Public-Private Sector Cooperation - Enhancing Tourism Competitiveness
- Marketing Tourism Destinations Online - Strategies for the Information Age
- E-Business for Tourism
- Tourism Taxation - Striking a Fair Deal
- Changes in Leisure Time

Tourism & Technology

The Internet and other computer technologies are revolutionizing the way tourism business is conducted and the way destinations are promoted. WTO's work in the area of new Information Technologies (IT) aims to provide leadership in the field of IT and tourism, as well as helping to bridge the digital divide between the have and have-nots among WTO's membership.

WTO carries out new research and studies of IT in connection with the promotion and development of tourism, such as the publications Marketing Tourism Destinations Online and E-Business for Tourism. It communicates the content of these studies throughout the world in a series of regional seminars.

WTO also operates a Strategic Advisory Board on IT and Tourism that brings together a small number of high-level experts from destinations, private businesses and researchers.

Tourism technology is especially suited to cooperation projects between the public and private sectors. The objective is to keep all Members up-to-date on the constantly changing technologies that will affect the tourism industry in the years to come.

Tourism Education

WTO.HRD

The WTO Human Resource Development Department (WTO.HRD) works to add value to the tourism sector of WTO Member States improving their capacity building and providing direct support in tourism education, training and knowledge. The WTO.HRD coordinates the activities of the WTO Education Council as well as those of the WTO.Themis Foundation with the common goal of achieving the tourism competitiveness and sustainability of WTO Members through excellence in tourism education.

Its mission is to build the knowledge capacity of WTO Members, providing leadership, initiative and coordination in quality tourism education, training and research through public-private partnerships among institutions and WTO Member States. More information

WTO.THEMIS FOUNDATION

Based in Andorra and generously sponsored by its Government, the WTO.Themis Foundation provides the administrative back-up to WTO.HRD to develop and disseminate tourism education, training and knowledge products, thus optimising service to WTO Members.

Its mission is to promote quality and efficiency in

tourism education and training in close coordination with WTO and its Human Resource Development Department (WTO.HRD), facilitating administration and management in implementing its programme of work and enlarging the scope of services to WTO Members.

WTO Education Council

The WTO Education Council (WTO.EdC) is made up of leading tourism education, training and research institutions as well as business schools worldwide that have obtained the WTO.TedQual Certification for at least one of their tourism education programmes. With over 100 members, it forms a chapter of the WTO Affiliate Members, and is well represented in the Board of the Affiliates, their decision-making body. The WTO.EdC is an active agent within WTO and in the development and implementation of the WTO.HRD Programme of Work. More information

The main human resource development products are:

WTO.TedQual: A framework of programmes for quality in tourism education. The WTO.TedQual Certification is granted to training and education institutions by means of a quality audit. The TedQual institutions can request membership in the WTO Education Council (Affiliate Members). There are also TedQual Seminars (Educating the Educators) for Member States and TedQual Consulting on quality issues for education and training centres.

WTO.Practicum: This is a biannual programme for officials from WTO Member States. It is carried out at WTO Headquarters for a period of two weeks and includes GTAT.TPS seminars, workshops, technical visits and working meetings with the responsible staff of the Organization.

WTO.Themis TedQual Practicum: A practicum programme designed especially for officials from WTO

Member States who are proposed by their Governments as liaisons with WTO in matters of education and training.

WTO.GTAT: A set of programmes (General Tourism Achievement Test) designed to improve the performance of teaching and learning in tourism. These include software for examinations and course development and implementation, GTAT Courses to improve specific knowledge and/or prepare for exams, GTAT Diagnosis to ascertain strong and weak points in specific subjects, GTAT Exams and GTAT Certification of Proficiency for students and tourism professionals.

WTO. Sbest Initiative: A framework for a range of WTO Programmes aimed at contributing to excellence in destinations and tourism companies through quality training and education. Programmes include the WTO.Sbest Training, WTO.Sbest Audit and WTO Tourism Labour Market Observatory. Institutions, companies and destinations satisfactorily completing these programmes receive WTO.Sbest Awards. Many of these programmes are executed in coordination with the WTO Destination Management Task Force.

WTO.Tourism Labour Market Observatory: This programme was recently initiated by the WTO Education Council in conjunction with WTO.HRD and the WTO Destination Management Task Force. Its objective is to obtain quantitative and qualitative information on tourism labour markets in key destinations worldwide through panels of employers, workers, consumers and students. This is coordinated through WTO.Sbest tourism destinations and WTO TedQual Centres.

Other products

- WTO.SIS Seminars
- Publications
- WTO.TedProm

- WTO Ulysses Awards for Innovation and the Application of Knowledge in Tourism
- Annual WTO.EdC Conference

Quality and Trade: in search of common denominators, fairness and transparency

This activity follows the previous programme on Quality in Tourism Development. With an increased focus on the economics of tourism, trade and the enterprise it seeks to assist government and private sector Members in determining and pursuing quality-related objectives, standards and measures as a contribution to sustainable development and poverty alleviation.

The following specific areas are covered:

- Trade in tourism services, including access to tourism markets, competition and globalization
- Safety and security, including health issues
- Guidance, harmonization and recognition of quality-related standards.

Reference to standards is present in all these areas. On trade issues, WTO works closely with the United Nations Conference on Trade and Development (UNCTAD) and with the World Trade Organization (WTO-OMC). The aim is to relate tourism policies and strategies to multilateral negotiations according to the General Agreement on Trade in Services (GATS) designed to achieve progressively higher levels of liberalization with a view to promoting economic growth and the development of developing countries. Briefings and debate on trade in tourism are held periodically to help Members carry out comprehensive and informed trade policies.

The inclusion of the safety and security area is explained by it being considered as a fundamental quality factor. The current focus is on preparing a model work plan for tourism destinations based on objective safety and security criteria, a model code of conduct on travel advisories and a revised WTO document *Health Information and Formalities in International Travel*, to be submitted to the 16th session of the General Assembly in 2005 and taking stock of the new *International Health Regulations of the World Health Organization (IHR 2005)*.

Under the chapter of quality standards, the specific aims include guidance to Members undertaking tourism quality programmes, the design of standards based on common denominators and cultural diversity, a hotel classification guidance document, and contributions to the work of the International Organization for Standardization (ISO) on tourism signs and symbols and other tourism related standards.

In relation to each area the Quality and Trade in Tourism department is also engaged in the preparation of "implementation parameters" for the Global Code of Ethics for Tourism. The operation of the Code and the secretariat of the World Committee on Tourism Ethics are now dealt with by Sustainable Development of Tourism department.

Key Publications and Instruments

Tourism in the Least Developed Countries

GATS and tourism

Tourist Safety and Security

Tourism Signs and Symbols

Recommended Measures for Tourism Safety

Health Information and Formalities in International Travel

Creating Tourism Opportunities for the Handicapped

WTO Statement against organized sex tourism

Quality, Hygiene and Safety of Food in the Tourism Sector

Global Code of Ethics for Tourism

Adopted by the WTO General Assembly in 1999 and acknowledged by the United Nations General Assembly in 2001 by a special resolution, the Code sets out a ten-point blueprint for safeguarding the resources upon which tourism depends and ensuring that its economic benefits are equitably shared.

The Code is based on the principles of sustainability that underpin all of WTO's programmes, with special emphasis on involving local communities in planning, managing and monitoring tourism development. It includes nine articles outlining the 'rules of the game' for destinations, governments, tour operators, travel agents, tourism workers and developers, and travelers themselves.

The tenth article involves implementation of the code through the activities of the World Committee on Tourism Ethics.

Sustainable development

Ensuring the sustainable development and management of tourism so that its benefits can be enjoyed for generations to come is the philosophy behind the activities carried out by the Sustainable Tourism Development Section. WTO creates practical instruments that allow tourism managers, in both the public and private sectors, to apply the principles of sustainability to concrete situations. The Section has issued several publications, manuals, inventories and analyses of best practices, which have been widely circulated and organized seminars have been held throughout the world.

Some major projects include:

International Year of Ecotourism—2002

Recognizing the global importance of ecotourism, the United Nations designated the year 2002 as the International

Year of Ecotourism. A World Ecotourism Summit in Quebec, Canada, (May 2002), jointly organized with the United Nations Environment Programme, gathered around 1,200 participants and resulted in the Quebec Declaration on Ecotourism, containing 49 specific guidelines for sustainable ecotourism development and management.

World Summit on Sustainable Development

The World Tourism Organization was actively involved in the preparations for the World Summit on Sustainable Development that took place in Johannesburg on 26 August - 4 September 2002.

Planning for sustainable development of tourism

WTO has published several manuals for tourism planning at the national, regional and local levels. It organizes national seminars on tourism planning for local authorities in developing countries.

Indicators of sustainable tourism

Sustainable tourism indicators are fundamental tools for the planning and monitoring of tourism development. WTO has been involved in this area since 1992, conducting pilot studies, producing a manual and teaching how to use indicators through a series of regional technical workshops in different regions and types of destinations.

Good practices in sustainable development of tourism

Providing successful examples of tourism development and management is an important way of disseminating experiences that can be adapted at other destinations. WTO has published three compilations of good practice cases in sustainable tourism, each of them containing around 50 case studies from more than 30 countries in a structured format.

Key Publications

Sustainable Development of Tourism: Guide for Local Authorities, with three regional supplements (Africa, Americas, Asia & the Pacific)

- A Practical Guide to the Use of Sustainable Tourism Indicators
- Agenda 21 for the Travel and Tourism Industry
- Guidelines for the Development of National Parks and Protected Areas
- Sustainable Development of Tourism - A Compilation of Good Practices
- Sustainable Development of Ecotourism - A Compilation of Good Practices
- Voluntary Initiatives for Sustainable Tourism
- Series of ecotourism market studies

Statistics

Proving the economic impact of tourism with solid facts and figures is the goal of WTO's Section on Statistics and Economic Measurement of Tourism. It helped create the Tourism Satellite Account (TSA) and is now assisting governments implement this accurate system of measuring the demand and supply sides of tourism.

WTO sets international standards for tourism measurement and reporting. Its recommendations on tourism statistics were adopted by the United Nations in 1993, creating a common language of tourism statistics that allows destinations to compare their success with that of their competitors. In 2000, the United Nations approved the Tourism Satellite Account methodology, making tourism the world's first sector to have international standards for measuring its economic impacts in a credible way.

WTO also provides the world's most comprehensive tourism statistics. Member States, private tourism companies, consulting firms, universities and the media all recognize WTO as the world's most comprehensive and reliable source of global tourism statistics and forecasts. Tourism data collected from 190 countries around the world include: arrivals, receipts, overnight stays, mode of transport, length of stay, tourist spending, and origin of visitors.

Tourism Satellite Account

Endorsed by the United Nations Statistical Commission, the Tourism Satellite Account is a joint project of several intergovernmental bodies and industry representatives. It sets a series of global standards and definitions that measure the tourism industry's true contribution in terms of: percentage of GDP, direct tourism jobs and capital investment. In compliance with United Nations recommendations, it runs alongside the national accounts framework. It will provide internationally comparable data developed by a country's own statistical institutions. TSA also puts tourism for the first time on an equal footing with other, less diversified economic sectors. Developing TSA is an opportunity for defining cooperative work between National Tourism Administrations, National Statistical Offices and Central Banks.

Key Publications

- Compendium of Tourism Statistics
- Yearbook of Tourism Statistics
- Tourism Satellite Acount as an ongoing process: past, present and future developments
- Enzo Paci Papers on Measuring the Economic Significance of Tourism, Vol. 1 and 2
- Measuring Visitor Expendituer for Inbound Tourism

Market Intelligence

Assisting governments and tourism professionals in understanding the constantly changing tourism marketplace is the aim of WTO's Section on Market Intelligence and Promotion. Identifying market trends as they are happening; short term and long-term forecasting; analyzing the world's generating markets; conducting research into niche markets; and providing evaluation tools for promotional campaigns are just some of the activities carried out each year.

The annual series of Tourism Market Trends reports provides a timely and comprehensive analysis of tourism results around the world. It enables tourism authorities to compare their performance to other countries of the same region, examining arrivals, receipts and the main factors affecting growth in the previous season.

Special attention is paid to studying tourism products, such as sports, cruises, MICE tourism (meetings, incentives, congresses and exhibitions) and market segments, such as ecotourism, youth or senior tourism. Another important task is the analysis of outbound tourism of both consolidated and emerging markets. Research can be initiated in any specific topics relevant for tourism development. For instance, to increase insight in the evolution of the tourism sector, it was studied how consolidation by means of alliances, mergers and acquisitions in the sub-sectors of accommodation, air transport and distribution is impacting destinations, travel agents, small businesses and the consumer.

To assist Member States with tourism promotion, the Section conducts periodic surveys on tourism budgets and sources of financing. It also provides practical guidance whenever pertinent. For instance, after the September 11th attacks it monitored the subsequent situation of uncertainty, studied lessons learned from past crises and helped Members with strategies to adapt to sudden change in market conditions.

WTO's seven-volume forecast Tourism 2020 Vision on worldwide forecasts is a landmark study based on data gathered from Member States and interviews with over 75 tourism visionaries about the future

of the industry. It predicts that international tourist arrivals will grow by an average of 4.1 per cent annually for the 25-year period 1995-2020. Tourism 2020 Vision includes forecasts of inbound and outbound tourism growth for countries in every region of the world and examines the outlook for several market segments.

Results are disseminated in various ways, such as through presentations and seminars, the WTO website (see the Facts & Figures) and in a broad range of publications, including:

- Tourism Market Trends - five regional volumes and a world volume
- Tourism Highlights
- Tourism 2020 Vision - six regional volumes and a world volume
- Budgets of National Tourism Administrations
- Tourism Generating Markets
- World Tourism Barometer

Communications

Increasing awareness of the importance of tourism, promoting the WTO's work and objectives through effective communication in order to provide transparency of its activities, helping achieve the goals of all sections and keeping you informed about new projects, studies, seminar results and upcoming WTO activities are the primary goals of WTO's Press and Communications Section.

Members receive the WTO News, published quarterly, and the electronic Members' Update, published fortnightly. Non-members are reached through the media. The Press and Communications Section maintains a database of 2,000 key journalists around the world and contacts them regularly through news releases and press conferences.

The entire tourism industry is reached by WTO's website on the Internet and through major international tourism trade fairs where WTO operates an information booth, including:

- FITUR, Madrid
- ITB, Berlin
- MITT, Moscow
- WTM, London

Improving the promotional efforts of Member States through effective media relations, organizing press trips and seminars on media relations and crisis management, are even more goals of WTO's Press and Communications Section. It publishes Shining in the Media Spotlight, a communications manual that includes a directory of major media in the world's top tourism generating markets. The World Conference on Tourism Communications (TOURCOM), to be held in early 2004, will become a regular meeting place of tourism professionals from both, public and private sectors, with the international media.

www.world-tourism.org

Completely renovated in 2001, WTO's popular website on the Internet is available in English, French and Spanish, with a growing section in Russian and - to follow - in Arabic. The attractive homepage offers the latest news from WTO and easy-to-use links to all activities and products. Users have access to basic statistics on world tourism, seminars' programmes, a complete calendar of worldwide tourism events, details on special programmes such as the meetings of the Tourism Recovery Committee, the Silk Road Project, Protection of Children from Sexual Exploitation in Tourism and Sustainable Tourism - Eliminating Poverty (ST-EP).

Publications

One of WTO's most important functions is to serve as a permanent source of information for its Members and the world community. WTO fulfils this task in part through its extensive programme of publications and the new programme of electronic products. The broad span of these products corresponds to the vast sweep both of the Organization's concerns and of the needs of its Members.

Today, WTO has already more than 250 titles available. Every year this list is extended by some 30 to 40 new titles in up to four official languages which are produced by the WTO publications department together with the originating sections. The Publications department runs at WTO headquarters in Madrid a bookshop from which all publications and electronic products can be ordered. Besides, all books and electronic products are displayed in a very detailed form and with excerpts in the WTO Infoshop at www.world-tourism.org/infoshop. Easy purchase and credit card payment options are just some of the comfortable features the shop offers. All products can also be ordered directly from a world-wide network of local distributors.

With the aim of improving the dissemination of our information as much as possible, translation and reproduction rights are also available to editorials that wish to publish WTO publications into other official and non-official languages. Until today WTO publications have been translated into more than 30 different languages.

With its recently launched Depository Library Programme, the WTO publications section encourages libraries to collect all WTO publications and make them available to a wider audience. All libraries which are complying with the requirements for Depositary Libraries are invited to share this initiative and are offered interesting financial conditions.

WTO aims to expand the scope, coverage, and quality of our publications and electronic products, as well as the number of editions available in English, French, Spanish, Russian and other languages. The Secretariat always welcomes feedback about any WTO product. If you would like to be kept informed about new products, you are invited to be registered in our mailing list available at www.world-tourism.org/infoshop under the option "mailing list".

Documentation

With the goal of acting as a true clearing-house, the WTO Documentation Centre endeavours to provide up to date qualitative information on tourism activities and related components on a theme-oriented basis.

The Documentation Centre concentrates its efforts to improve the information linkage networking between itself, WTO Members and other institutional partners, so as to facilitate tourism information access, transfer and exchange worldwide.

With these objectives in mind, the Centre offers online access to a tourism legislation database (LEXTOUR) providing bibliographic and textual data on laws and regulations existing both at the WTO Secretariat and in similar external legislative information systems.

As visible output products, the Centre delivers regular research reports on strategic issues, such as the role, spheres of competence and activities of tourism administrations and tourism investment policies. It also collaborates with other departments within the Secretariat in establishing a permanent tourism taxation monitoring information system.

To consolidate its function as a referral service, a specific database administrated by the Centre disseminates factual data on national and international tourism information holders and brokers (INFODOCTOUR) via the WTO Website. In addition, the Documentation Centre provides an authoritative tool for indexing and retrieving information on tourism and allied fields with the Multilingual Thesaurus on Tourism and Leisure Activities.

Membership of the World Tourism Organization?

WTO has three categories of membership: Full Members, Associate Members and Affiliate Members.

- Full membership is open to all sovereign States.
- Associate membership is open to territories not responsible for their external relations. Membership requires the prior approval of the government which assumes responsibility for their external relations.
- Affiliate membership comprises a wide range of organizations and companies working directly in travel, tourism and related sectors. These may include: airlines and other transport, hotels and restaurants, tour operators and travel agents, banking institutions, insurance companies, travel assistance, publishing groups, etc. Affiliate membership is made up of three groups, the WTO Business Council, the WTO Education Council and the WTO Task Force on Destination Management. Affiliate membership requires endorsement by the government of the state in which the headquarters of the applicant is located.

WTO is the only intergovernmental organization that

offers membership to the operational sector and in this way offers a unique contact point for discussion between government officials and industry leaders. WTO's broad-based Affiliate membership also has its own programme of activities which includes regular meetings and technical seminars on specific study topics.

Appendices

APPENDIX—I

TOURISM ADMINISTRATION RULES OF TIBET AUTONOMOUS REGION

Chapter I: General Provisions

Article 1

The rules is enacted to protect and reasonably develop and utilize the tourism resources, guarantee the legal interest and right of tourists and tourism operators, safeguard the order of the tourism market and promote the tourism to develop healthily.

Article 2

Any organization or individual that develop tourism resources, engage in the tourism operation and tourism activities and carry out tourism administration should observe the rules.

Article 3

The tourism in the rules refers to the industry offering traffic, sightseeing, accommodation, catering, shopping, cultural and recreation services by means of taking advantage of tourism resources and service facilities.

Article 4

In the practice of developing tourism, the principle of opening up, high quality and efficiency should be stuck to.

Article 5

Efforts should be made to enlarge the opening up, encourage and support various economic elements to invest in and develop the tourism resources in various forms. Those who engage in the tourism operation will enjoy the preferential policies of the state and the autonomous region in line with the related regulations.

Article 6

The principle combining strict protection, rational development and sustained utilization of tourism resources should be struck to so as to realize the sustainable development of the tourism.

Article 7

The practice of developing tourism should highlight the regional characters such as snow-capped mountains, grassland, forest, lake, rivers, wetland, wild animals and plants, history and culture and folk customs and ethnic features.

Efforts should be made to develop industrial and agricultural-featured tourist products and enhance the diversification and improvement of the tourist products.

Article 8

The people's government and tourism administrations at various levels should encourage and support the urban citizens, farmers and herdsmen to engage in and participate in tourism operation and offer high quality services and preferential policies to them.

Article 9

The people's government at various levels should enforce guidance to the tourism, and establish a coordinative and efficient mechanism with the related departments to ensure the harmonious development of tourism with related industries.

Article 10

The people's governments at various levels should put the tourism into the national economic and social development plan to make unified planning and ensure necessary investment, enforce the infrastructure building, enlarge the publicity and promotion so as to develop the tourism in an all-round way.

Article 11

The tourism administration of the autonomous region government takes charge of the tourism planning, administration and supervision works of the whole autonomous region.

The tourism administrations of city (prefecture) and county (city and district) people's governments take charge of the tourism planning, administration and supervision of the administrative areas.

The administrations at various levels should do a good work for the administration and service in line with their function definition.

Article 12

The tourism administration of the autonomous region should execute the following responsibilities:

(I) To carry through the tourism laws, regulations and industrial standards, study and map out the long term and annual planning of tourism development and organize the implementation of the plans;

(II) To enforce the tourism administration, foster and develop the tourism market together with the related departments, improve the management and service systems to exert the self-discipline of industrial associations;

(III) To direct the development and utilization of tourism resources, carry out grade assessment to the scenic spots and tourism publicity and important promotion of the region;

(IV) To coordinate the tourism traffic and transport in conjunction with the related departments, coordinate and direct the production and sales of tourism commodities and the implementation of the tourism recreation;

(V) To assess and issue the certificate to the tourism practitioners and map out the tourism service standards;

(VI) To enforce the education of patriotism, legal system and occupational ethic to the tourism practitioners and occupational skill training so as to improve the service quality and the comprehensive quality of the practitioners;

(VII) To compose the standard uniform commentary for the key cultural scenic spots and timely revise the commentary;

(VIII) To supervise and inspect the tourism security and service quality, handle the complaining of the tourists to protect the legal right and interests of the tourists.

Chapter II: Development and protection of tourism resources

Article 13

The tourism administrations at various levels should carry out survey and assessment to the tourism resources in conjunction with the related departments, demonstrate scientifically, map out the tourism development planning and render the planning to the tourism administration of upper level for approval. Upon the planning is approved by the people's government of the same level, the tourism administration should organize the implementation of the planning;

The development planning of tourism should be harmonious with the overall planning of the land utilization, the overall urban planning, the ecological environment building planning, the natural reserve planning, the landscape and well-known scenic spot planning and the cultural relic protection.

Article 14

The practice of newly building, reconstructing and extending the scenic spots and tourism infrastructures should be done in accordance with the tourism development planning and tourism resource development planning of the autonomous region, city (prefecture) and county (city, district).

When examining and approving the tourism application, the related administrations should solicit opinions from the tourism administration.

Article 15

The practice of developing and building tourism programs by taking advantage of forest, water area, natural reserve, cultural relics and historical interests should be done in line with the related laws and regulations of environment protection, cultural relic protection and forest and nature protection.

The cultural relics and natural features of the scenic spots should be protected when developing and building the tourism programs.

Article 16

All units and individuals have the duty to protect the tourism resources and facilities. It is forbidden to quarrying, mining, dig sand, open up the wasteland, hunt and cut woods without approval of the people's government above county level. The laws and regulations should be observed if stipulated otherwise.

It is forbidden to discharge contamination, dump rubbish and discard waste in the scenic spots.

Article 17

The tourism administrations should open tourism routes in junction with the related departments and take part in the standard administration of tourism traffic planning and tourism traffic services.

Chapter III: Tourism operation

Article 18

The operator should obtain the operation qualification and carry out the operation activities by law within the approved operation scope.

Article 19

The tourism operator should offer appropriate services in line with the service standards stipulated by the state and the autonomous region and the agreement with the tourists and guarantee the personal and assets security of tourists. The operators should make real explanation and noticeable warning for the programs that may endanger the personal and assets security and take measures to prevent happening of such dangers.

When the personal and assets security of tourists encounter accidental harms, the tourism operator should immediately adopt rescue measures and report the public security authority, tourism administration or other related department in time.

Article 20

The operators should observe the related laws and

regulations and publicize the service items and price honestly and ensure the service quality.

The tourism operators are not allowed to have such behaviors that harm legal right and interests of tourists as follows:

(I) Not fulfill or not completely fulfill the tourism contract signed with the tourists;

(II) Not offer services in line with the state and industrial standards or offer services not meeting the prices;

(III) To make fa'se publicity to the service scope, content and standards;

(IV) To lure, badger or threaten the tourists to buy goods or accept service consumption that is not agreed in advance;

(V) To sell the counterfeit or goods in inferior quality as the high quality one;

(VI) Other behaviors infringe the legal rights and interests of tourists.

Article 21

The tourism operators should not offer services with the following contents:

(I) Harming the state security and national dignity;

(II) With national, ethnic, religious and sex discrimination;

(III) Propagating pornography and superstition or exaggerating the violence;

(IV) Other contents that the laws and regulations forbid.

Article 21

The tourism operator should not adopt unfair competitive measures in the tourism operation as follows:

(I) Copy the registered trademark, brand and quality certificate signs of other operators;

(II) Use the name of other operators without authorization;

(III) Monopoly prices acting in collaboration with other operators to reap colossal profits and harm the interests of tourists and other operators;

(IV) Sell goods at the price lower than the cost with the purpose of pushing out the competitors;

(V) Entrust non-tourism operators agent or covert agent to engage in tourism businesses;

(VI) Produce and spread fake information that harm the corporate image and credit of other operators;

(VII) Offer fake tourism service information to attract tourists;

(VIII) Other behaviors that upset the market order.

Article 23

The tourism operators operate independently by law and enjoy the following rights:

(I) To refuse the inspection of persons without the certificate of enacting laws;

(II) To refuse the charges, fine and other punishment in breach of provisions of the laws and regulations;

(III) To refuse requirement of offering free service and apportion in other forms;

(IV) To refuse other administrative behaviors that are in breach of the legal procedure;

(V) Other legal rights in the tourism operation.

Article 24

The tourism practitioners who must obtain the vocational qualification in accordance with the state stipulation should obtain the corresponding qualification certificate and take the post with the certificate.

Article 25

The tourism practitioners should not have such behaviors as follows:

(I) To increase or reduce the tourism items or terminate the tourism activities without authorization;

(II) To deceive or mislead the tourists to consume;

(III) To peddle goods to tourists or buy tourists' belongings by force;

(IV) To extort money and things from the tourism operators;

(V) To extort tips or other things explicitly or implicitly from the tourist;

(VI) Other behaviors that the laws and regulations forbid;

Article 26

The tourism practitioners should safeguard the state security and national dignity willingly and explain the scenic spots according to the standards commentary. It is forbidden to have any words or behavior that harms the national interest and dignity.

Article 27

The personality and dignity of the tourism practitioners should be respected and the personal safety is inviolable.

Tourism practitioners have the right to refuse the tourists' irrational requirements that humiliate their personal dignity or infringe the occupational ethic.

Article 28

The guide must meet the following requirements:

(I) Be a citizen of People's Republic of China with firm political position, love the motherland, safeguard the unification of the motherland, fight against the secession, support the socialism system and observe the laws and regulations;

(II) Observe the tourism occupational ethic, serve the tourists heartedly with civil behaviors and standard diction; the service quality should meet the national standards or standards agreed between the travel agency and the tourists;

(III) The guide must obtain the Guide Qualification Certificate issued by the national tourism administration or local guide certificate issued by the tourism administration of the autonomous region.

Chapter IV: Right and responsibility of the tourist

Article 29

The tourist enjoys the following rights by law:

(I) To acquaint with the tourist products and tourism service quality;

(II) To select tourism operators, scenic spots and service mode and tourism goods independently and decide to accept or refuse services out of the contract;

(III) To receive the tourism service with quality meeting the price in line with the contract;

(IV) Personal dignity, folk customs and habit and religious belief of the tourist should be respected;

(V) The personal and asset security is protected by law;

(VI) Other rights stipulated by the laws and regulations.

Article 30

The tourist should fulfill the following responsibilities as follows when engaging in tourism:

(I) Observe the laws and regulations;

(II) Respect the folk customs and habit and religious belief of the visited places;

(III) Respect the personal dignity of the tourism operators and practitioners;

(IV) Protect the tourism resources and ecological environment, cherish the tourism facilities and equipments willingly;

(V) Observe the tourism order and security and sanitation provisions;

(VI) Fulfill the tourism contract or agreement;

(VII) Other responsibilities stipulated in laws and regulations.

Article 31

If the tourist's legal right and interest are infringed or any dispute occurs with the tourism operator, the tourist can settle the problem with the following measures:

(I) Negotiate with the tourism operator;

(II) Complain to the competent tourism administration;

(III) Appeal or complain to the related department or organization;

(IV) Submit the arbitration agreement to arbitration if have;

(V) Bring to the people's court.

Chapter V: Supervision and administration

Article 32

The tourism administration and other administrative department should, within their function scopes, enforce the protection, development and utilization of the tourism resources, and supervision and administration to the tourism project construction, market order, service quality and the ticket price, environment, traffic, security and sanitation of the scenic spots

Article 33

Any unit or individual is not allowed to charge without authorization in addition to paid items stipulated by the state and the autonomous region.

Article 34

The ticket price confirmation and adjustment should be examined and approved strictly in line with the price approval authority scope. The scenic spot is not allowed to raise the ticket price without authorization.

Article 35

The scenic spot management organization should map out the management mechanism to enforce the scenic spot management, safeguard the normal order and maintain the good condition, sanitation and cleanness of the tourism facilities.

Chapter VI: Legal responsibility

Article 36

The tourism administration orders those who break the provision of

Article 28

to correct the mal-behavior; those who refuse to correct the wrong behavior will be cancelled the guide certificate; the travel agency where the guide is employed will be given a disciplinary warning, or be charged to stop operation to rectify the wrong doing; those who commit a crime will be ascertained the criminal responsibility.

Article 37

The tourism administration orders those who break Article 16 (II) to correct the mal-behavior; those who refuse to correct the mal-behavior will be fined 200 yuan to 1000 yuan; those who commit a crime will be ascertained the criminal responsibility.

Article 38

For those tourism practitioners who break Article 25 and Article 26 herein, the tourism administration orders them to correct the mal-behaviors; those who refuse to correct the mal-behavior can be fined 1000 yuan to 20000 yuan and confiscated the illegal earnings if have;

Article 39

For tourists who break provisions of Article 30, the tourism administration can order them to correct the mal-behavior; those who refuse to correct can be fined 100 yuan to 500 yuan.

Article 40

For those tourism operators who break provisions of Article 33, the tourism administration and the price supervision authority order them to correct the mal-behaviors according to their functions; those who refuse to correct the mal-behavior can be ordered to stop operation to rectify and be fined 500 yuan to 2000 yuan for the individual and 10000 yuan to 20000 yuan for the unit; those who have illegal earnings will be confiscated the illegal earnings.

Article 41

Note in unified form printed or supervised by the finance department of the autonomous region will be used for the fine. The confiscated earning should be separated according to the provisions of the state and the autonomous region to turn over to the finance department.

Article 42

The workers of the tourism administration who neglect the duties, abuse the authority or resort to fraudulent practices for personal gains will be given administrative punishment by the unit where he/she works or the upper level; those who commit a crime will be ascertained the criminal responsibility.

Article 43

The person concerned who does not accept the administrative punishment can ask for administrative review or take administrative proceedings.

Article 44

The provisions of the laws and regulations should be observed for those behaviors that break the rules if the laws and regulations stipulate otherwise.

Chapter VII: Supplementary provisions

Article 45

The people's government of the autonomous region is responsible for interpretation of the specific issues arising out of practice.

Article 46

The rules takes effective as of October 1, 2002.

APPENDIX—II

SOUTH ASIAN MEDIA COMMIT TO SUPPORT GOVERNMENTS IN TOURISM DEVELOPMENT

Tourism media from South Asia have responded eagerly to the proposal of the Asian Development Bank (ADB) and Nepal Tourist Board (NTB) to work together in pursuing sustainable development and poverty alleviation through tourism.

This follows a meeting held in the Nepalese capital from 26-27 August, organised by ADB and NTB and supported by the World Tourism Organization, at which press representatives from Bangladesh, Bhutan, India and Nepal met with government officials to evaluate possibilities for closer cooperation in the promotion of tourism, crisis communications and the ongoing fight against poverty.

The main objective of the workshop was to strengthen the relationship between the media and the South Asia Sub-regional Economic Cooperation (SASEC) Programme, to enable the press to make a direct contribution to encouraging tourism in the sub-region, informing travel writers and focusing the media in general on the importance of tourism as an economic activity and the sustainability issues involved.

Much of the discussion was geared to regional cooperation among the four countries, especially between the media and the public and the private sectors.

The workshop was opened by the Nepalese Minister of Foreign Affairs Ramesh Nath Pandey who stressed the need for governments to recognise the importance of the media in tourism development and his country's commitment to pursuing tourism as its main economic activity.

Imtiaz Muqbil, Executive Editor of the Bangkok-based Travel Impact Newswire, said that huge investment plans were already under way in Asia such as the Chinese highway system and India's rapid air-traffic expansion. He predicted a great opportunity for sub-regional development through the new Buddhist circle project, which will connect all the countries.

The four countries are all members of SASEC, one of whose main aims is to reduce the plight of the region's poorer citizens. They account for some 500 million people out of an estimated 900 million poor people in Asia and the Pacific. "South Asia is one of the poorest and most densely populated areas in the world. However, because of the region's unique endowment of resources, it can be transformed into a leading sub region of economic growth," said ADB country director Sultan Hafeez Rahman. "It's good to see that governments and international organizations recognise the importance of our work," commented Rahman Janagir, a journalist from Bangladesh. It was on his initiative that delegates agreed to establish a South Asia Forum of Tourism Journalists (SAFTOJ), to which WTO will act as advisor. Nepal's Assistant Minister for Culture, Tourism and Aviation, Ms Yankila Sherpa, said the "success of (staging) such a demanding event and its outcomes confirm that Nepali tourism is alive and dynamic".

"It is true that there are security problems in remote parts of our country. However, tourism moves on and we ask the media to also highlight this part of reality". Nepal's attractions include the highest mountain in the world, Mt. Everest, and a string of UNESCO world heritage sites that include seven in the Kathmandu valley alone as well as Lumbini, the birthplace of Siddhartha Gautama (Lord Buddha). WTO Chief of Press and Communications Rok Klancnik spoke of the phenomenal expansion of world tourism, while highlighting the vital need for crisis communications, a topic which countries should pay much more attention to, he added.

"Enhancing government - media relationship and increasing capacity in the wide range of tourism communications, including crisis management and the role of the media in poverty alleviation, is at the heart of the TOURCOM Programme, which is itself central to WTO Press and Communications activities."

APPENDIX—III

WTTC'S BLUEPRINT FOR NEW TOURISM CALLS ON GOVERNMENT AND INDUSTRY TO MAKE SIGNIFICANT LONG TERM COMMITMENTS

The World Travel & Tourism Council (WTTC) today revealed its Blueprint for New Tourism, which issues a call to action for both government and the industry to make several long-term commitments to ensure the prosperity of Travel & Tourism - one of the world's largest industries, responsible for 200m jobs and over 10% of global GDP.

The Blueprint for New Tourism contains a new vision for Travel & Tourism and strategies to guide its recovery from a series of unprecedented set backs over the past few years, in the form of terrorism, war, economic slowdown and SARS.

Creation of the Blueprint was approved by the main resolution at the close of the last Global Travel & Tourism summit that took place in May in Vilamoura, Portugal, which was attended by over 500 of the most influential people in the industry.

Jean-Claude Baumgarten, President, said: "There is now a new consciousness amongst governments that they cannot leave the growth of Travel & Tourism to chance. What is needed is a new vision and strategy involving a partnership between all stakeholders - public and private to turn future challenges into opportunities. The Blueprint for New Tourism spells out how that can be achieved."

WTTC's latest projection for the industry is that a quarter of a billion people will work in Travel & Tourism worldwide by the end of the decade, with the prospect of sustainable growth in to the future. This projection is supported by WTTC's latest economic research that indicates consistent growth, at 4.6% pa, over the coming decade.

In order to meet the challenges ahead and achieve the vision, the Blueprint establishes three fundamental conditions:

1. Governments must recognize Travel & Tourism as a top priority
2. Business must balance economics with people, culture and environment
3. All parties must share the pursuit of long-term growth and prosperity

Governments must recognize Travel & Tourism as a top priority

To meet the first condition, governments must:

- Elevate Travel & Tourism as an issue to the top level of policy making
- Create a competitive business environment
- Ensure that quality statistics and data feed into policy and decision-making
- Invest in developing the appropriate human capital
- Liberalise trade, transport, communications and investment
- Build confidence in safety and security
- Promote product diversification that spreads demand
- Plan for sustainable tourism growth, in keeping with cultures and character
- Invest in new technology, such as satellite navigation systems

Business must balance economics with people, culture and environment

To meet the second condition, the industry must:

- Expand markets while protecting natural resources, local heritage and lifestyles
- Develop people to narrow the gap between the 'haves' and 'have-nots'
- Provide traditional tourism products sensitively
- Reduce seasonality and increase yields with imaginative new products
- Improve quality, value and choice
- Agree and implement quality standards at all levels
- Transfer skills and best practice throughout the industry
- Increase the sophistication of information, to make better business decisions
- Communicate more broadly and more effectively

All parties must share the pursuit of long-term growth and prosperity

To meet the third condition, all the main stakeholders must:

- Ally best practice in tourism with government policy
- Prepare sustainable master plans for entire destinations
- Create locally driven processes for continuous stakeholder consultation
- Restructure national tourism boards
- Set environmental policy goals that can be met
- Develop and deploy skills effectively
- Collaborate on information requirements
- Collaborate on security
- Develop confidence on all sides

Jean-Claude Baumgarten concluded: "New Tourism requires a much stronger partnership between the private sector and public authorities. It is geared to delivering commercially successful products – but in a way that ensures benefits for everyone. New Tourism looks beyond short-term considerations. It focuses on benefits not only for people who travel, but also for people in the communities they visit, and for their respective natural, social and cultural environments."

Luis Correia da Silva, Portugal's Secretary of State for Tourism, said: "The strategic importance of Travel & Tourism to our economy can not be underestimated. I am fully supportive of the Blueprint for New Tourism and am delighted to have the opport

APPENDIX—IV

SUSTAINABLE TOURISM

Codes of Conduct

Guidelines for tour operators operating in environmentally-sensitive areas:

1. Make Tourism and Conservation Compatible

Support conservation by developing a positive relationship with organizations and people that play a role in conservation, particularly in the areas that you will visit with your clients.

Encourage your clients to become members in conservation organizations.

Use personal contacts and letters to educate others, and encourage governments and businesses to support projects such as new nature reserves.

Contribute time and money to conservation organizations and projects.

Plan tourism so that it does not conflict with conservation efforts. Obtain permission before visiting nature reserves or other areas where access is restricted. When visiting these areas, be sure that your activities comply with the rules of the park or reserve.

Know the laws and regulations that apply to the import and export of products made from wildlife, and make sure that your clients understand and follow these laws. Encourage your clients to buy products made from wildlife by local people, so long as these products are not made from endangered species and their purchase does not violate the law.

Develop an environmental plan for your daily operations. If you are an operator employing more than 20 people, have a written environmental plan that states your company's commitment to conservation, to using resources in a sustainable way and to the principles itemized in this Code of Conduct. Include specific procedures that your company uses in its daily operations to prevent and minimize detrimental environmental impacts. Make the plan available to your clients.

Use post-trip evaluations to confirm that your tour was environmentally sound. Use feedback from clients as a good way of finding out if your tour met client environmental expectations. In your post-trip evaluations ask your clients whether or not in their view the tour avoided unnecessary negative environmental impacts, and whether the tour operator demonstrated consideration of the natural and cultural environments. As a rule use written post-trip evaluation forms, although oral evaluations are acceptable, especially for smaller operations.

2. Support the Preservation of Wilderness and Biodiversity

Promote maintenance of large, undeveloped areas. The undeveloped regions of the Arctic, for example have a unique value, and are one of the primary reasons why tourists come to the Arctic. This will be undermined by roads, pipelines and other kinds of unsightly large-scale development that fragments the environment.

Support wildlife conservation programs and projects. Make your clients aware of these efforts and ensure that they do not hunt or fish protected or threatened species, enter sensitive wildlife habitat or buy products made from protected species.

3. Use Natural Resources in a Sustainable Way

Where laws permit hunting and fishing, follow all rules and take only what you require. Ensure that your clients obey the laws and regulations and do not contribute to the depletion of local wildlife stocks. Cooperate with community and indigenous hunters' associations.

Make sure that your clients use only appropriate and well-maintained hunting equipment, and that they know how to operate it.

When determining the number of clients that will visit an area, consider the nature and any special vulnerability of the site. In wilderness areas take the site's natural features (wildlife, nesting birds, fragile vegetation, etc.) into account when determining how many clients will be in the area at any given time. Inform other operators in the region of your plans in order to avoid over-visitation of a site.

Use only established trails and campsites where they exist, and avoid creating new ones.

Avoid disturbing wildlife. Instruct your clients on local wildlife and its behavior, and make sure that they view it from an appropriate distance.

4. Minimize Consumption, Waste and Pollution

Your choice of products and the amount that you and your clients consume makes a difference.

Whether you bring supplies with you or buy them, choose biodegradable or recyclable products with minimal packaging.

Compress garbage and take it with you.

Recycle where possible and encourage the communities that you visit to develop recycling programs if they do not have them already. If feasible, provide financial support to encourage the development of these programs, and show your commitment to the communities you and your clients visit.

Limit energy use, including your use of heat and warm water. Keep records of your water and energy consumption, and recycling and waste-reduction efforts.

The transportation you choose for your clients makes a difference. Opt for the means of transport that has the least environmental impact. Minimize the use of fossil fuels and try to use non-motorized transport whenever possible. Where motorized transportation is necessary, choose the technology that causes the least environmental damage and minimal noise (four-stroke instead of two-stroke engines, for example). Do not use motorized transport such as snowmobiles and helicopters unnecessarily; these should only be used to get from one area to another or for seeing specific sites.

Choose accommodations compatible with local traditions and that minimize negative environmental impacts. Choose lodging that has effective waste treatment systems, recycles and disposes of non-recyclable garbage appropriately.

Support efforts to clean up waste and polluted areas by providing money, lobbying governments and businesses, contributing your time and that of your staff, and by encouraging tour clients to support these efforts as well.

Ensure that no evidence of your visit remains behind.

Follow responsible practices for camping and tours, including those that concern waste disposal.

Retain all plastic for proper disposal, and compact all wood products, glass, and metal for a disposal facility. Ensure that any incinerators you use function properly.

5. Respect Local Cultures

Coordinate with the communities that you visit to ensure that you are welcome, and that your visit is not disruptive.

Arrange visits to communities well in advance, and avoid visits that are not pre-arranged.

Reconfirm your visit, preferably 24 hours in advance, and be prepared to pay the community for costs associated with cancelled visits.

Arrange what you and your clients will do during your visit with the community.

Find out what size of group the community prefers for the planned activities. Be sure you have permission to visit to undertake the activities you have planned.

Keep away from sites where people are working, including hunting and fishing sites, unless you have specific agreements with locals.

Be aware of the laws and regulations in the area or waters in which you are operating, and obtain the necessary permits.

Respect the culture and customs of the people whose communities you visit, and make sure that your clients do so as well.

Give all visitors a thorough cultural briefing before visiting local communities. Where possible, hire local lecturers to conduct these briefings. Include information on local customs and traditions, and on appropriate behavior for tourists in the area. Use local "Codes for Visitors" if available.

Ask permission to photograph or videotape.

Ensure that your clients respect religious grounds, churches, cemeteries and other sites with religious or cultural significance, and that they do not remove any artifacts.

6. Respect Historic and Scientific Sites

Respect historic sites and markers, and make sure that your clients do not remove any artifacts. If access to historic or archaeological sites is restricted, obtain permission before visiting. Ensure that your clients behave respectfully. particularly if a site has religious significance.

Respect the work of scientists. Do not enter scientific installations or work sites without making prior arrangements. Do not disturb scientists while they are working, and do not disturb their work sites.

7. Communities Should Benefit from Tourism

Whenever possible, hire local staff and contract with local businesses. Train and hire local people for your operations. Where local people lack the training you require, provide it. Use locally-owned businesses as subcontractors. Develop long-term partnerships with local operators, businesses and suppliers. A local connection most often means a better tourism experience.

Operate in ways that benefit the communities you visit, particularly with respect to supplies. If feasible, buy supplies and services locally. Ask communities what supplies you should bring with you so that your visit and use of supplies does not cause hardship to local people. Encourage your clients to buy locally-made handicrafts and products.

Where possible, choose accommodations owned, built and staffed by local people.

8. Educate Staff

Hire a professional team.

Hire only knowledgeable, environmentally and culturally aware staff, or train your existing staff in these areas. Provide training in how to avoid negative environmental impacts, in safet, and in providing service. Evaluate the performance of your staff, at least annually.

If you are a ship-based tour operator, hire lecturers and conservation-oriented naturalists who will not only talk about wildlife, environmental protection, history, geology and local cultures, but who can guide passengers ashore and who are familiar with safety and local conservation requirements.

9. Make Your Trip an Opportunity to Learn

Provide your clients with information about the environment and conservation. Provide lectures and written materials about the environment, its special characteristics and its global significance. Include information about conservation in general, specific conservation efforts in the areas that you will visit, and specific ways — financial and otherwise — that your clients can support these conservation efforts.

Provide your clients with specific information about the regions they will visit. Include information about climate, wildlife species and habitats, as well as appropriate behavior for these areas.

Ensure that your clients follow the Code of Conduct for Tourists. Enforce the Code in a consistent way. Make sure that clients understand the responsibilities outlined in the Code. Be prepared to use stricter rules when necessary (e.g. when safety is an issue).

10. Follow Safety Rules

Provide local authorities with your itinerary. This is both for safety reasons and to be sure you are complying with local regulations.

Brief all clients and staff on the dangers of wildlife encounters.

Have at least one staff member who is responsible for co-coordinating safety and avoiding dangerous encounters with wildlife.

Source: WWF International Arctic Programme

Glossary

Attendance Building - Marketing and promotional programs designed to increase attendance at conventions, trade shows, meetings, and events.

Attractions - General all-0inclusive term travel industry marketers use to refer to products that have visitor appeal, like museums, historic sites, performing arts institutions, preservation districts, theme parks, entertainment and national sites.

Attractor - A significant tourist attraction, which compels visitation. The primary "must sees" in an area. The top reasons a tourist would choose to visit this area.

AVHRM - Association of Vacation Home Rental Managers.

Bed Tax (Transient Occupancy Tax of TOT) - City or county tax added to the price of a hotel room.

Best Practice(s) - A term used to designate highest quality, excellence, or superior practices in a particular field by a tourism operator.

Blocked - Hotel rooms held without deposit

Booked - Hotel rooms, airline tickets or other travel services held for a specific client.

Booking - Term used to refer to a completed sale by a destination, convention center, facility, hotel or supplier (i.e. convention, meeting, trade show or group business booking).

Business Travel - Travel for commercial, governmental or educational purposes with leisure as a secondary motivation.

Business Travel - Travel for commercial, governmental or educational purposes with leisure as a secondary motivation.

Buyer - A member of the travel trade who reserves room blocks from accommodations or coordinates the development of a travel product.

C of C - Chamber of Commerce

Carrier - Any provider of mass transportation, usually used in reference to an airline.

Chambers of Commerce - Typically, a Chamber of Commerce will specialize in local economic development that can include tourism promotion.

Charter Group - Group travel in which a previously organized group travels together, usually on a custom itinerary.

Commissions - A percent of the total product cost paid to travel agents and other travel product distributors for selling the product to the consumer.

Convention and Visitors Bureau - These organizations are local tourism marketing organizations specializing in developing conventions, meetings, conferences and visitations to a city, county or region.

Conventions and Trade Shows - Major segment of travel industry business. Trade shows differ from conventions in that they have exhibit space that provides product exhibition and sales opportunities for suppliers, as well as information gathering and buying opportunities for customers.

Conversion Study - Research study to analyze whether advertising respondents actually were converted to travelers as a result of advertising and follow-up material.

Co-op Advertising - Advertising funded by two or more destinations and /or suppliers.

Cooperative Marketing - Marketing programs involving two or more participating companies, institutions or organizations.

Cooperative Partner - An independent firm or organization which works with a tourism office by providing cash or in-kind contributions to expand the marketing impact of the tourism office? program.

Country of Residence - Consists of the country where she/he has lived for most of the past year (12 months), or for a shorter period if she/he intends to return within 12 months to live there.

Cover - Each diner at a restaurant.

CTRLA - Car and Truck Rental and Leasing Association.

Cultural tourism - Travel for the purpose of learning about cultures or aspects of cultures (NEAP, 2000).

CVB - Convention and Visitors Bureau.

Destination - A hotel, resort, attraction, city, region, or state.

Destination Marketing - Marketing a city, state, country, area or region to consumers and trade.

Destination Marketing - Marketing a city, state, country, area or region to consumers and trade.

Destination Marketing Organization (DMO) - A company or other entity involved in the business of increasing tourism to a destination or improving its public image. Local tourism marketing organizations, such as convention and visitors bureaus or chambers of commerce.

Discounted Fare - Negotiated air fare for convention, trade show, meeting, group and corporate travel.

Discover America - Theme used by the Travel Industry Association and its marketing partners to market travel within the United States.

Fam Tours - Organized trips for travel agents, tour operators, tour wholesalers or other members of the travel trade for the purpose of educating and ?amiliarizing?them with tourism destinations. By seeing the destinations where they are sending travelers, the travel trade is better prepared to answer customer questions and promote travel to the location. Also called ?ams?or ?amiliarization tours.?

Familiarization Trip - A complimentary or reduced-rate travel program for travel agents, airline or rail employees or other travel buyers, designed to acquaint participants with specific destinations or suppliers and to stimulate the sale of travel. Familiarization tours, also called fam tours, are sometimes offered to journalists as research trips for the purpose of cultivating media coverage of specific travel products.

Feeder Airport/City - An outlying city which feeds travelers to hubs or gateway cities.

FIT (Free Independent Travel) - Individual travel in which a tour operator has previously arranged blocks of rooms at various destinations in advance for use by individual travelers. These travelers travel independently, not in a group, usually by rental car or public transportation.

Foreign Independent Travel or Foreign Individual Travel (FIT) - an international pre-paid unescorted tour that includes several travel elements such as accommodations, rental cars and sightseeing. A FIT operator specialises in preparing FITs documents at the request of retail travel agents. FITs usually receive travel vouchers to present to on-site services as verification of pre-payment.

Frequency - The number of times an advertisement appears during a given campaign.

Fulfillment - Servicing consumers and trade who request information as a result of advertising or promotional programs. Service often includes an 800 number, sales staff and distribution of materials.

Gateway or Gateway City - A major airport, seaport, rail or bus center through which tourists and travelers enter from outside the region.

Geotourism (1998) - Tourism that sustains or enhances the geographic character of the place being visited—its environment, culture, aesthetics, heritage, and the well-being of its residents

GIT (Groups Independent Travel) - Group travel in which individuals purchase a group package in which they will travel with others along a pre-set itinerary.

Gross lettings - This refers to all room lettings, i.e. both paid & complimentary listings are included

Group Rate - Negotiated hotel rate for convention, trade show, meeting, tour or incentive **Head in Beds** - Industry slang referring to the primary marketing objective of accommodations and most destinations - increasing the number of overnight stays.

Group Tour and Group Leader - Group Tour - a travel agent type company which plans motor coach trips. Group Leader: A small, informal group, such as a church group, scout troop, or social group. Usually one person plans the activities for the group. Some travel shows target these planners such as GLAMER.

Hospitality - A general term used in travel & tourism describing the "hospitality industry"; Refers to the general greeting, welcoming, food service, etc

Hospitality Industry - Another term for the travel industry.

Hotel Package - a package offered by a hotel, sometimes consisting of no more than a room and breakfast; sometimes, especially at resort hotels, consisting of (ground) transportation, rooms, meals, sports facilities and other components.

Hub - An airport or city which serves as a central connecting point for aircraft, trains or buses from outlying feeder airports or cities.

Hub and Spoke - Air carriers use of selected cities as ?ubs? or connected points for service on their systems to regional destinations.

Icon - A facility or landmark which is visually synonymous with a destination.

Incentive Tour - A trip offered as a prize, usually by a company to stimulate employee sales or productivity.

Incentive Travel - Travel offered as a reward for top performance and the business that develops, markets and operates these programs.

Inclusive Tour - A tour program that includes a variety of feature for a single rate (airfare, accommodations, sightseeing, performances, etc.)

Inquiry - A request for more information about an attraction or destination.

International Marketing - Marketing a destination, product or service to consumers and the trade outside the of the United States.

Itinerary - A travel schedule provided by a travel agent for his/her customer. A proposed or preliminary itinerary may be rather vague or specific. A final itinerary however provides all details (flight numbers, departure times, reservation confirmation numbers) and describes planned activities.

Joint venture - A form of strategic alliance or co-operative arrangement where ownership is shared and a separate enterprise formed. This may strengthen existing businesses through shared expertise, capital, removal of competition and creation of economies of scale. International tourism joint ventures between foreign organisations and local partners facilitate introduction of foreign products into local markets.

Jungle tourism - Jungle tours have become a major component of green tourism in tropical destinations. A jungle is a subclimax tropical forest consisting of a tangled growth of lianas, trees and scrub which may form an almost impenetrable barrier to the tourist. Jungle tours are a relatively recent phenomenon of Western international tourism.

Key-informant survey - This involves interviewing people who are likely to have some insight into a problem: operating managers; sales staff; managers; suppliers; and consultants.

Keying - A social convention by which social 'reality' is transformed and seen as something else, such as the presentation of a fight as mere horseplay. In tourism, a peculiar, inverted variety of keying is frequently employed: the 'as if' situation in which participants are induced to playfully make believe that presented settings, activities or events are 'real', when as tourists they may be well aware that such occurences are contrived.

Leisure tourist - Leisure tourists, in contrast with business travellers, travel, for pleasure and thus are not under any obligations to frequent specific destinations or facilities. They tend to be price and fashion conscious, concentrate their touristic activities to specific (vacation) times, and are influenced by marketing and publicity. Leisure tourism is heavily influenced by living standards, discretionary income levels and vacation entitlements.

Leisure Travel - Travel for recreational, educational, sightseeing, relaxing and other experiential purposes.

Length of stay - This refers to the period of time which people spend in a destination. Many definitions require that visitors to a destination stay at least 24 hours or overnight, and less than one year, to be considered a tourist. Destination areas often look for means to extend tourists' length of stay in order to increase positive economic impacts.

Market Share - The percentage of business within a market category.

Market Volume - The total number of travelers within a market category.

Maximum room nights - This is calculated based on the total room inventory for all gazetted hotels.

Mission (Sales) - A promotional and sales trip coordinated by a state travel office, conventional and visitors bureau or key industry member to increase product awareness, sales and to enhance image. Target audiences may include tour operators, wholesales, incentive travel planners, travel agents, meeting planners, convention and trade show managers and media. Missions often cover several international or domestic destinations and include private and public sector participants. Mission components can include receptions, entertainment representatives of the destination, presentations and pre-scheduled sales and media calls.

Motorcoach - Deluxe equipment used by most tour operators in group tour programs. Amenities include reclining seats, bathrooms, air conditioning, good lighting and refreshment availability.

Nature tourism - Travel to unspoiled places to experience and enjoy nature.

Net Rate - The rate provided to wholesalers and tour operators that can be marked up to sell to the customer.

No Show - A customer with a reservation at a restaurant, hotel, etc. who fails to show up and does not cancel.

NTA - National Tour Association, comprised of domestic tour operators.

Occupancies - A percentage indicating the number of bed nights sold (compared to number available) in a hotel, resort, motel or destination.

Occupancy rate - A tourism business occupancy rate refers to the number of airline seats or the units of hotel room space sold. This demand is usually measured as a percentage of available seats or space occupied for a given period of time. It is calculated by dividing the number of occupied rooms/ seats by the total number available for sale during the same period.

Outbound - Outbound tourism is defined as tourism involving residents of a country travelling to another country. Outbound tour operators offer package tours abroad. They either operate the tours themselves, or they commission the services of an inbound operator to handle local arrangements at the destination. The country from which the tourists originate is known as the generating market or country.

Package - A fixed price salable travel product that makes it easy for a traveler to buy and enjoy a destination or several destinations. Packages offer a mix of elements like transportation, accommodations, restaurants, entertainment, cultural activities, sightseeing and car rental.

Package Tour - A saleable travel product offering an inclusive price with several travel elements that would otherwise be purchased separately. Usually has a predetermined price, length of time and features but can also offer options for separate purchase.

Paid lettings - This refers to room lettings that are paid for by hotel guests

Person Trip Visit - Every time a person travels more than 100 miles (round-trip) in a day or stays overnight away from their primary domicile, whether for business or leisure purposes.

Pow Wow - The largest international travel marketplace held in the United States, sponsored by the Travel Industry Association of America.

Press Trips - Organized trips for travel writers and broadcasters for the purpose of assisting them in developing stories about tourism destinations. Often, journalists travel independently, though with the assistance of a state? office of tourism of a DMO.

Press/Publicity Release - A news article or feature story written by the subject of the story for delivery and potential placement in the media.

Property - A hotel, motel, inn, lodge or other accommodation facility.

Quality - In tourism, the product is often intangible and quality is not apparent until after it is consumed. Quality has been defined as zero defects or defections, but still may be defined by the customer. The International Organisation for Standardisation defines quality as 'the totality of features and characteristics of a product or service that bear on its ability to satisfy stated or implied needs'. Others believe that quality is 'a combination of outcome and processes, including internal and external conditions, and is obtained when the expectations and needs of customers are met.

Rack Card - the typical tourism brochure sized 4" x 9" and used primarily in tourism racks. Also known as a "teaser."

Rack Rate - The rate accommodations quote to the public. Group rates, convention, trade show, meeting and incentive travel rates are negotiated by the hotel and program organizers.

Reach - The percentage of people within a specific target audience reached by an advertising campaign.

Receptive Operator - Specialists in handling arrangements for incoming visitors at a destination including airport transfers, local sightseeing, restaurants, accommodations, etc. Receptive operators can be a travel agent or tour operator.

Repeat Business - Business that continues to return, thereby generating increased profits.

Reservation Systems (Automation Vendors) - Computerized systems leased to travel agencies offering airline, hotel, car rental and selected tour availability and bookings. Systems are affiliated with major carriers, including American (Sabre), United (Apollo), Eastern (System One), TWA (PARS), and Delta (DATAS II) and feature flight schedules of the sponsoring and other carriers, plus additional travel products.

Resident - a person living in a given country, whether he is a national or not.

Retail Agent - A travel agent.

Retailer - Another term for travel agents who sell travel products directly to consumers.

Room - Double: No guarantee of two beds; Double Double: Two double beds (or two queens or kings); Twin: Two twin beds (or two doubles or queens)

Room Blocks - Several rooms held for a group.

Sales Mission - Where suppliers from one DMO travel together to another state of country for the purpose of collectively promoting travel to their area. Sales missions may include educational seminars for travel agents and tour operators.

Sales Seminar - An educational session in which travel agents, tour operators, tour wholesales or other members of the travel trade congregate to receive briefings about tourism destinations.

Shells - A marketing and sales promotional piece that depicts a destination, accommodation or attraction on the cover and provides space for copy to be added at a later date. Usually shells fit a #10 envelope.

Site Inspection - An assessment tour of a destination or facility by a meeting planner, convention or trade show manager, site selection committee, tour operator, wholesaler or incentive travel manager to see if it meets their needs and requirements prior to selecting a specific site for an event. After site selection, a site inspection may be utilized to make arrangements.

Spouse Programme - Special activities planned for those who accompany an attendee to a convention, trade show or meeting. Note that programs today are not simply for women, but rather for men and women, spouses and friends. Programs must be creatively designed to interest intelligent and curious audiences.

Supplier - Those businesses that provide industry products like accommodations, transportation, car rentals, restaurants and attractions.

Sustainable tourism - this is, according to the World Tourism Organisation, "envisaged as leading to management of all resources in such a way that economic, social and aesthetic needs can be fulfilled with maintaining cultural integrity, essential ecological processes, biological diversity, and life support systems."

Target Audience/Market - A specific demographic, sociographic target at which marketing communications are directed.

Target Rating Points - TRP? are a statistical measurement which allows one to evaluate the relative impact of differing advertising campaigns.

Tariff - Rate of fare quoted and published by a travel

industry supplier (i.e. hotels, tour operators, etc.) Usually an annual tariff is produced in booklet form for use in sales calls at trade shows.

TIA - Travel Industry Association of America.

TOT - Transient Occupancy Tax.

Tour Operator - Develops, markets and operates group travel programs that provide a complete travel experience for one price and includes transportation (airline, rail, motorcoach, and/or ship), accommodations, sightseeing, selected meals and an escort. Tour operators market directly to the consumer, through travel agents and are beginning to be listed on computerized reservation systems.

Tour Wholesaler - An individual or company that sells tour packages and tour product to travel agents. Tour wholesalers usually receive a 20% discount from accommodations, transportation companies and attractions and pass on a 10 to 15% discount to the retail agent.

Tourism - the business of providing and marketing services and facilities for pleasure travellers. Thus, the concept or tourism is of direct concern to governments, carriers, and the lodging, restaurant and entertainment industries and of indirect concern to virtually every industry and business in the world.

Tourism Receipts - Tourism Receipts (TR) measures the total revenue received by Singapore from tourism activity. It includes all payments and prepayments for goods and services made by visitors, transit passengers, air & sea crew and foreign students (staying for one year or less) during their stay in Singapore. Visitors' payments to our national carriers (SIA & Silk Air) for international transport are also included.

Tourist/Visitor/Traveler - Any person who travels either for leisure or business purposes more than 100 miles (round-trip) in a day or who stays overnight away from his/her primary domicile. (ii) Temporary visitor staying at least twenty-four hours in the country visited for a purpose classified as either holiday (recreation, leisure, sport and visit to family, friends or relatives), business, official mission, convention, or health reasons.

Trade Show - a product showcase for a specific industry. Generally it is not open to the public. Differs from a "Consumer Show" in that a trade show targets the professional industry, while a consumer show targets consumers.

Transient Occupancy Tax - TOT or bed tax is a locally set tax on the cost of commercial accommodations and campgrounds.

Travel - Leisure and other travel including travel for business, medical care, education, etc. All tourism is travel, but not all travel is tourism.

Travel Agent - An individual who arranges travel for individuals or groups. Travel agents may be generalists or specialists (cruises, adventure travel, conventions and meetings.) The agents receive a 10 to 15% commission from accommodations, transportation companies and attractions for coordinating the booking of travel. They typically coordinate travel for their customers at the same or lower cost than if the customer booked the travel on his/her own.

Travel Agent - the individual who sells travel services, issues tickets and provides other travel services to the travel services to the traveller sat the retail level.

Travel Product - Refers to any product or service that is bought by or sold to consumers of trade including accommodations, attractions, events, restaurants, transportation, etc.

Travel Seasons - Travel industry business cycles including:
Peak: Primary travel season
Off Peak: Period when business is slowest
Shoulder: Period between peak and off peak periods when business is stronger, but has room for growth.

Travel Trade - The collective term for tour operators, wholesalers and travel agents.

Traveler - Definitions very, but in general a traveler is someone who leaves their own economic trade area, (usually going a distance of a minimum of fifty to one hundred miles) and stays overnight.

Underdevelopment - Within development theory, the concept of underdevelopment suggests that wealthy capitalist countries have held back the development of so-called Third World countries. Tourism in Third World destinations is controlled for the economic benefit of foreign owners, reinforces dependency, lacks involvement of local decision makers, leads to negative sociocultural impacts, and results in the promotion of staged attractions to capture an international tourism market.

Urban recreation - the concept of urban recreation covers recreational activity that takes place in an urban environment in contrast to a rural setting. Participants in such activities are either urban residents themselves, day visitors from rural areas, or tourists. The major activities are shopping, visits to heritage sites, museums, movie theatres, operas, sport and music events, and indoor sports activities.

VFR - Visiting friends and relatives

Visitor - any person visiting a country other than that in which he has his usual place of residence for any reason other than following an occupation remunerated from within the country visited.

Visitor Arrivals - includes all who go through immigration clearance regardless of length of stay. This excludes the following:

a. All Malaysian citizens arriving by land
b. Returning Singapore citizens residing abroad
c. Non-resident air and sea crew (except for sea crew flying in to join ship)
d. All visitors arriving and leaving Singapore on the same ship/vessel and stayed in Singapore for less than 24 hours are not required to complete Disembarkation / Embarkation (D/E) cards, if passenger manifest is submitted
e. All organised tour groups leaving Singapore for Johor Bahru, Batam and Bintan, returning on the same day are not required to complete Disembarkation / Embarkation (D/E) cards, if passenger manifest is submitted
f. Air transit passengers

Visitor Days - Number of Visitor Arrivals x Average Length of Stay

Visitor Expenditure - includes expenditure incurred during a visitor's stay in Singapore, or prepayment by non-package tour visitors (this took effect from 1995). This excludes:

a. international air and sea fare

It is made up of the following components:

a. Shopping
b. Accommodation
c. Entertainment
d. Sightseeing
e. Food & beverage

f. Local transportation

g. Medical/dental treatment

h. Miscellaneous

Visitors Center - Travel information center located at a destination to make it easier for visitors to plan their stay; often operated by a convention and visitors bureau, chamber of commerce or tourism promotion organization.

Visitors Centre - Travel information centre located at a destination to make it easier for visitors to plan their stay; often operated by a convention and visitors bureau, chamber of commerce or tourism promotion organisation.

Vouchers - Forms or coupons provided to a traveler who purchases a tour that indicate that certain tour components have been prepaid. Vouchers are then exchanged for tour components like accommodations, meals, sightseeing, theater tickets, etc. during the actual trip.

Wellness tourism - Wellness tourism is the sum of all the relationships and phenomena resulting from a journey and residence by people whose main motivation is to preserve or promote their health. They stay in a specialized hotel which provides the appropriate professional know-how and individual care. They require a comprehensive service package comprising physical fitness/beauty care, healthy nutrition/diet, relaxation/meditation and mental activity/education. *(Definition developed by the Research Institute for Leisure and Tourism, University of Berne, Switzerland)*

Wholesaler - Develop and markets inclusive tours and individual travel programs to the consumer through travel agents. Wholesalers do not sell directly to the public.

Wine/Culinary tourism - Wine/Culinary tourism is tourism in which the opportunity for wine and/or culinary related experiences contributes significantly to the reason for travel to the destination or to itinerary planning while at the destination. *(Definition used by the Ontario Ministry of Tourism, Culture and Recreation and the Wine Council of Ontario)*

World Tourism Organisation (WTO) - The World Tourism Organisation, a UN-related institution based in Madrid that collects data on tourism and lobbies on behalf of the industry.

World Travel and Tourism Council (WTTC) - The WTTC is made up of chief executives from all sectors of the tourism industry, including accommodation, catering, cruises, entertainment, recreation, transportation and travel-related services. Its central goal is to work with governments to realise the full economic impact of tourism. Its millennium vision is to make tourism a strategic economic and employment priority, to move towards open and competitive markets, to pursue sustainable development, and to eliminate barriers to growth.

Xenophobia - Xenophobia is an irrational fear or contempt of strangers or foreigners. This ancient cultural and political phenomenon is also present in contemporary tourism, mainly manifesting itself in the hostile attitudes of residents towards tourists. Xenophobia should be considered in domestic and international tourism in terms of economic, social and cultural distance, which is accentuated by the type and the number of tourists and the rate of tourism development.

Yield management - The concept of maximising the revenue by raising or lowering prices in respect to demand is known as yield management. The necessary conditions for a successful application of yield management include a fairly fixed capacity, high fixed costs, low variable costs, fluctuations in demand and similarity of inventory capacity. Yield management was popularised with the deregulation of the US airline industry and it is extensively used by this and other tourism sectors.

Yield percentage - To demonstrate the variable effect of both average price rates and occupancy rates, tourism managers develop a comparison focusing upon the yield rates during a given period of time. Managers can increase the yield rate (see yield management) by raising rates when demand is high.

Zoning - Zoning seeks to regulate land uses by separating them based on incompatibility, or allowing like/compatible uses to co-exist. A basic principle of tourism zoning is the conservation of specific environmental features such as wetlands, archaeological and historic sites, important stands of vegetation and unusual geological features. Related to this is the maintenance of visual diversity. Also important is the achievement of successful functional groupings of resort facilities and activities, such as accommodation, commercial and cultural facilities, and recreation facilities in suitable areas. Buffer zones containing mixtures of tourism facilities and less fragile environmental preservation requirements may also be designated.

Select Bibliography

Annapurna Conservation Area Project (ACAP), ACAP Headquarters Ghandruk, Ghandruk Panchayat, Kaski District, Nepal.

Anon, (1993), Congratulations and thanks to the IOC. *Contours* 6(1), 33-34.

Anon, (1999), Kurds plan tourism attack. *Kansas City Star* 16 March, p. A12.

Anon, (2000), Hostages released! *Kansas City Star* 1 January, p. 1.

Archer, B. and Cooper, C., (1998), The positive and negative impacts of tourism. In: Theobald, W.F. (ed.) *Global Tourism: the Second Decade,* 2nd edn. Butterworth-Heinemann, Oxford, pp. 63-81.

Archer, B.H. & Fletcher, J.E., (1990), Tourism: Its economic significance. In M. Quest (ed.), Horwath Book of Tourism (pp. 10-25). London: The MacMillan Press.

Archer, B.H., (1995), The impact of international tourism on the economy of Bermuda. *Journal of Travel Research,* 34 (2), 27-30.

Armington, Stan, (1976), Trekking in the Himalayas, Lonely Planet Publications, Victoria.

Ashley, Caroline, (1998), 'Tourism, communities and national policy: Namibia's experience.' *Development Policy Review* 16 (4): 323-352.

Ashley, Caroline, (2000), *The Impact of Tourism on Rural Livelihoods: Namibia's Experience.* ODI Working Paper no. 128. London, ODI.

Bangs, R., (1993), Clean, green and meant to be seen the ethos of eco-tourism in *Proceedings of the 1993*

World Congress an Adventure Travel and Eco-Tourism Manna. The Adventure Travel Society 97-101.

Barke M. and Newton, M., (1995), Promoting sustainable tourism in an urban context: recent developments in Malaga City, Andalusia, *Journal of Sustainable Tourism* 3(3), 115-134.

Barke, M.J., Towner, and M.T. Newton, eds. (1996), *Tourism in Spain*. Wallingford, Oxford: CAB International.

Barnet, Richard J., and Ronald E. Muller, (1974), *Global Reach: The Power of the Multinational Corporation*. New York: Simon and Schuster.

Barrett, G., (1995), Transport emissions and travel behaviour: a critical review of recent European Union and UK policy initiatives, *Transportation* 22, 295-32.

Barrow, C.J., (1995), Sustainable development: concept, value and practice, *Third World Planning Review* 17(4), 369-386.

Barry, Tom, (1984), *The Other Side of Paradise: Foreign Control in the Caribbean*. New York: Grove Press.

Basu, C.R., (1987), "Human Resource Development," *Indian Journal of Commerce*, Vol. XL (January-June) p. 150-151.

Bauer, I., (1999), The impact of tourism in developing countries on the health of the local host communities. *Journal of Tourism Studies* 10(1), 2-17.

Beaner, Allan, (1975), *Retail Travel Practice*, Beaner and Gardonland Tours Ltd., London.

Beioley, S., (1995), Green tourism—soft or sustainable? *Insights* May. B75-B89.

Bekker, V., (1999), Are terrorists targeting St Pete? *St Petersburg Times* 17 September, p. 1.

Belk. R.W. and Costa. J.A., (1995), International tourism

an assessment and overview. *Journal of Macromarketing* 15(2), 33-48.

Belsky, Jill, (1999) 'Misrepresenting communities: the politics of community-based rural ecotourism in dales Point Manatee, Belize.' *Rural Sociology* 64 (4): 641-666.

Benjamin, Medea, and Andrea Freedman. *Bridging the Global Gap*. Cabin John, MD: Seven Locks Press, 1988.

Bennett, O., Roe, D. and Ashley, C., (1999), Sustainable Tourism and Poverty Elimination Study: A report to the Department for International Development, April http://www.propoortourism.org.uk/dfid_report.pdf

Berger D.J., (1996), The challenge of integrating Maasai tradition with tourism, in M.F. Price (ed.) *People and Tourism in Fragile Environment*. John Wiley & Sons, Chichester, 175-198.

Berger, Thomas R., (1985), *Village Journey: The Report of the Alaska Native Review Commission*. New York: Hill and Wang.

Berle, P., (1990), Two faces of eco-tourism. *Audubon* 92(2), 6.

Bernard, J., (1973), The sociology of community, in J. Reiss Jr and H.I. Wilenskv (eds) *Introduction to Modern Society Series* Scott. Foresman and Co., Glenview.

Berrigan, Tom, (1994), *The Travel Industry Environmental Sourcebook: A Project of the Responsible Tourism Initiative*. Washington, DC: Travel Association of America.

Bezruchka, Stephen, (1974), A Guide to Trekking in Nepal, Sahayogi Prakashan, Kathmandu.

Bhauguan, H.H., (1972), *Public Sector Undertakings*, Vol. 4, No. 1, Feb., 1972.

Bhushan, Y.K., (1964), *Business Organisation and Management*, Sultan Chand and Sons, New Delhi.

Billimoria, R.P. and Singh, N.K., (1985), *Human Resource Development,* Vikas Publishing House, New Delhi.

Black, Maggie, (1995), *In the Twilight Zone: Child Workers in the Hotel, Tourism and Catering Industry* Geneva; International Labor Organisation.

Blake, B. and Bechet, A., (1997), *The New Key to Costa Rica.* Ulysses Press. Berkeley, Calif.

Blake, Beatrice, and Anne Becher, (1997), *The New Key to Costa Rica 13th edition. Berkeley:* Ulysses Press.

Blamey, R.K. and Braithwaite. V.A., (1997), A social values segmentation of the potential ecotourism market, *Journal of Sustainable Tourism* 5(1), 29-45.

Blanchard, F., (1984), Seabird harvest and the importance of education in seabird management on the North Shore if the Gulf of St Lawrence, unpublished PhD thesis, Cornell University, Ithaca, NY.

Blanchard, K., (1994), Culture and seabird conservation: the North Shore of the Gulf of St.Lawrence, Canada in D Nettleship. J. Burger and M.Gochfeld (eds) *Seabirds on Islands Threats. Case Studies and Action Plans,* Birdlife International Conservation, Cambridge, England, 294-310.

Blank, U. and Perkovich, M., (1987), Research on urban tourism destinations, in J.R.B. Ritchie and C.R. Goeldner (eds) *Travel, Tourism and Hospitality Research*, John Wiley & Sons, New York, 165-177.

Blazey, M., (1992), Travel and retirement Status. *Annals of Tourism Research* 19(4), 771-783.

Blunden, G., Cocklin, C. and Davis, P., (1995), Land based production in Northland, Occasional Paper 30, Department of Geography, Auckland University, Auckland. Beo E. (1990) *Ecotourism: The Potentials and Pitfalls* 2 vols. World Wildlife Fund, Washington.

Boissevien, Jeremy, (ed.), (1996), *Coping with Tourists: European Reactions to Mass Tourism.* Oxford Bergham Books.

Boniface, B.G. and Cooper, C.P., (1994), *The Geography of Travel and Tourism,* 2nd edn, Butterworth-Heinemann, Oxford.

Boo, E., (1990), *Ecotourism the Potentials and Pitfalls.* Vol. 2-Country Case Studies World Wildlife Fund. Washington, DC.

Boo, E., (1992b), *The Ecotourism Boom, Planning for Development and Management,* World Wildlife Fund, Washington.

Boo, Elizabeth, (1989), Ecotourism: *The Potentials and Pitfalls. Washington, DC:* World Wildlife Fund.

Booth K., (1990), Recreation—a positive force for island restoration, in D.R. Towns, C.H. Daugherry and I.A.F Atkinson (eds) *Ecological Restoration of New Zealand Islands*, Department of Conservation, Wellington, 278-283.

Bosselman, F.P., (1978), In the Wake of Tourists; Managing Special Places in Eight Countries. *The Conservation Foundation,* Washington, D.C.

Boyle, Godfrey, (1996), "Solar Photovoltaics". In *Renewable Energy: Power for a Sustainable Future*. Ed. Godfrey Boyle. Toronto: The Open University.

Boza, M., (1988), *Costa Rica National Parks,* Editorial Heliconia, Fundacion Neotropic San Jose.

Bramwell, B. and Lane, B., (1993), Sustainable /tourism: an evolving global approach, *Journal of Sustainable Tourism* 1(1), 1-5.

Bramwell, B., (1998), Selecting policy instruments for sustainable tourism. In: Theobald, W.F. (ed.) *Global Tourism: the Second Decade,* 2nd edn. Butterworth-Heinemann, Oxford, UK, pp. 361-379.

Bramwell: B., (1996), in W. Bramwell, I. Henry, G. Jackson, A.G. Prat, G. Richards and J.van der Straaten (eds) *Sustainable Tourism Management: Principles and Practice.* Tilburg University Press. Tilburg, 147-170.

Bramwellm B. Henry: I. Jackson, G., Prat. A.G., Richards, G. and van der Straaten J. (eds), (1996), *Sustainable Tourism Management Principles and Practice*, Tilburg University Press, Tilburg.

Brandon, K., (1996), *Ecotourism and Conservation: A Review of Key Issues*, World Bank Biodiversity Series Paper No. 33, World Bank, Washington.

Brandon, Katrina, (1996), Ecotourism and Conservation: *A Review of Key Issues.* Washington, DC, World Bank.

Brause, Diane, (1996), *Directory of Alternative Travel Resources.* Dexter, OR:Lost Valley Educational Center.

Brent, J.R., and Echtnyer, (1995), "Tourism, Education and Human Resources Development," *Tourism Recreation Research,* Lucknow.

Breslin, P. and Chapin, M., (1984), Conservation Kuna-style, *Grassroots, Development* 8, 26-35.

Briguglio, L. Butler, I.W., Harrison, D. and I cal Hilho, W. (eds.), (1996), *Sustainable Tourism in Islands and Small States. Vol. II: Case Studies, Cassell,* London.

Briguglio, Lino, (1996), *Sustainable Tourism in Islands and Small States.* London: Pinter.

Britton, S. and Clarke, W., (eds), (1987), *Ambiguous alternative: Tourism in Small Developing Countries,* University of the South Pacific, Suva.

Britton, S.G., (1982), "The political economy of tourism in the Third World", *Annals of Tourism Research,* 9(3): 331-358.

Britton. S.G., (1991), Tourism, capital and place: towards a critical geography of tourism, *Environment and Planning D: Society and Space* 9, 451-478.

Brohman, J., (1996), New directions in tourism for Third World development, *Annals of Tourism Research* 23(1), 48-70.

Brohman, John, (1996), 'New directions in tourism for Third World development.' *Annals of Tourism Research* 23 (1): 48-70.

Broken Bud, 1765-D Le Roy, Berkeley, CA 94709; (310) 843-5506. Advocacy for antiprostitution tourism and child trafficking; newsletter.

Butler, R.W., (1981), Tourism and tourism research, in T.L. Burton and E.L. Jackson (eds) *Understanding Recreation and Leisure: Mapping the Past, Charting the Future,* Venture Publishing. State College, 567-595.

Butler, R.W. and Hinch, T. (eds), (1996), *Tourism and Indigenous People,* International Thomson Business Press, London.

Butler, R.W., (1991), Tourism, environment, and sustainable development, *Environmental Conservation* 18(3), 201-209.

Butler, R.W., (1992), Alternative tourism: the thin end of the wedge, in V. Smith and W.Eadington (eds) *Tourism Alternatives: Potentials and Problem in the Development of Tourism,* University of Pennsylvania Press, Philadelphia, 31-46.

Butler, R.W., (1993a), Pre- and post-impact assessment of tourism development, in D.G. Pearce and R.W. Butler (eds) *Tourism Research: Critiques and Challenges,* Routledge, London, 135-155.

Butler, R.W., (1993b), Tourism: an evolutionary process, in G. Nelson, R.W. Butler and G. Wall (eds) *Tourism and Sustainable Development. Monitoring: Planning,*

Managing, University of Waterloo. Heritage Resources Centre, Waterloo, 27-44.

Buxton N., (1997), The Esk Valley Line Partnership, paper to conference on 'Community-Rail Partnerships'. Hudderfield, 8 April 1997.

Buzzworm, (1993), *Earth Journal 1993: Environmental and Almananc and Resource Directory.* Boulder, CO: Buzzwomi Books.

Carncy, Diana, (1999), *Approaches to Sustainable Livelihoods for the Rural Poor.* ODI Poverty Briefing No. 2 (January). London, ODI.

Carr, M.I.L. (n.d.) Ecotourism, National Parks and Land use Planning in Costa Rica—Llanuras of Tortuguero: A Case Study. Unpublished.

Carrere, R., (1995), Loita Maasai endeavour to save sacred forest, *Shainan's Drum 37,* 17.

Carribbean Conference of Churches, PO Box 616 Bridgetown, Barbados, fax (809) 429-2075. The new address of the Ecumenical Coalition on Third World Tourism (ECTWT).

Carriere: J., (1991), The crisis in Costa Rica: an ecological perspective, in D Goodman and M. Redclifts (eds) *Environment and Development in Latin America,* Manchester University Press, Manchester.

Carter, F.W. and Turnock, D., (1993), Problems of the pollution scenario, in *Environmental Problems in Eastern Europe,* Routledge, London, 188-213.

Carter, F.W., (1978), Nature reserves and national parks in Bulgaria, *L'Espace Geographique.* I. 69-72.

Carter, F.W., (1985), Pollution problems in post-war Czechoslovakia, *Transactions of the Institute of British Geographers (New Series),* 10, 174.

Casey, John, (1995), "Here comes the sun." *Civil Engineering.* Vol. 65 No. 54-57.

Chadwick, R.A., (1981), Some Notes on the Geography of Tourism; a comment, *Canadian Geographer,* 25.

Chapin. M., (1990), The silent jungle: ecotourism among the Kuna Indians of Panam *Cultural Survival Quarterly,* 14(1), 42-45.

Charlton, C.A., (1992), *Devon and Cornwall Branch Lines Passenger Survey,* Devon and Cornwall Rail Partnership, Plymouth.

Cheeseman, Ted. No date. *Conservation and the Maasai in Kenya: Trade-off or Lost Mutualism'.'* http:// www. environmentalaction.net/kenya/kenya_policy failure.html.

Chib, S.N., (1989), *Essays on Tourism,* PATA India Chapter, New Delhi Cross Section Publications Pvt. Ltd.

Chopra, Suhita, (1991), *Tourism and Development in India.* London: Ashish Publishing House.

Christaller, W., (1963), Some considerations of tourism location in Europe: the peripheral regions—underdeveloped countries—recreation areas, *Papers, Regional Science Association* 12, 95-105.

Christaller, W., (1996), *Central Places in Southern Germany,* trans. C.W. Baskin, Prentice-Hall, Eaglewood Cliffs. NJ.

Christian Aid, (1995), *Abuse of Innocence: Tourism and Child Prostitution in the Third World.* London: Christian Aid.

Clark, J.R., (1991), 'Carrying capacity and tourism in coastal and marine areas' *Parks* 2(3), pp 13-17.

Clark, W. and Munn, R.F., (eds) (1986), *Ecologically Sustainable Development of the Biosphere,* Cambridge University Press, New York.

Clark. G., Darrall, J., Grove. White, R. Macnaghten. P. and Urry, J., (1994), *Leisure Landscapes—Leisure, Culture and the English Countryside: Challenges and Conflicts,* Council for the Protection of Rural England, London.

Coccossis, H., (1996), Tourism and sustainability: perspectives and implicating, in G.K. Priestley, J.A. Edwards and H. Coccossis (eds) *Sustainable Tourism? European Experience,* CAB International, Wallingford, 1-21.

Cohen, E., (1978), The impact of tourism on the physical environment. *Annals of Tourism Research,* 5(2), 215-237.

Cohen, E., (1987), "Alternative Tourism : A Critique", *Tourism Recreation Research,* 12(2).

Cole, D.N. Petersen, M.E. and Lucas, R.C., (1987), *Managing Wilderness Recreation Use: Common Problems and Potential Solutions,* USDA Forest Service General Technical Report INT-230 Intermountain Forest and Range Experiment Station, Utah.

Colvin, J.G., (1994), Capirona: a model of indigenous ecotourism, *Journal of Sustainable Tourism,* 2(3), 174-177.

Common, M., (1995), *Sustainability and Policy: Limits to Economics.* Sydney- Cambridge University Press.

Commonwealth Department of Tourism (1994), *National Ecotourism Strategy.* Canberra-Australian Government Publishing Service.

Commonwealth of Australia, (1991), *Ecologically Sustainable Development Working Group Final Report: Tourism.* Canberra: Australian Government Publishing Service.

Community Action International Alliance (CAIA), no Maryland Avenue, NE, Suite 304. Washington, DC 20002; (202) 547-2640, fax (202) 547-3136. Organises environmental justice tours of Washington, DC; workshop, publications.

Cook, S., (1996a), Limit of acceptable change committee meeting notes. Curry Country Communications, Gold Beach, Oregon.

Cook, S., (1996b), Draft matrix of limits of acceptable change indicators. Curry County Commissioners, Gold Beach, Oregon.

Cooper, Christopher P., (1994), *Tourism and Hospitality Education.* Guildford, University of Surrey.

Cornwall County Council, (1996), *Transport Polices and Programme: 1997-98 Submission*. Cornwall Country Council, Truto.

Cris, Cooper, (1993), Tourism: Principles and Practice, London.

Croall, J., (1995), *Preserve or Destroy. Tourism and the Environment.* Calouste Gulbenkian Foundation, London.

Crowe, P.L., (1969), The tragedy of the commons revisited, *Science* 166, 1103-1107.

Cullimane, S.L., Cullinane, K.P.B., Fewings, J. and Southwell, J., (1996), Rural traffic management: the Burrator Reservoir experiment, *Transport Policy* 3(4), 213-224.

Cultural Survival, (1993), *State of the World's Indigenous Peoples.* Cambridge: Cultural Survival.

Curry, N. and Pack, C., (1994), Informal county strategies for countryside recreation in England and Wales, *Journal of Environmental Management* 40, 91-101.

Daily G. and Ehrlich, P., (1992), Population, sustainability and the earth's carrying capacity. Bioscience 42(10), 761-771.

Dakov, M., (1976), *Environmental Management in the People's Republic of Bulgaria,* Sofia Press, Sofia.

Dalal Clayton, B., (1992), Modified EIA and indicators of sustainability: first steps towards sustainability analysis, in *Industrial and Third World Environmental Assessment: The Urgent Transition to Sustainability,* 12th Annual Meeting of the International Association for Impact Assessment, 19-22 August. World Bank, Washington 134-146.

Danaher, Kevin, Beyond Safaris, (1991), *A Guide to Building People-on-People Ties with Africa.* Trenton, NJ: Africa World Press.

Daniels, A., (1995), Ahousat band's ecological walk business booms, *Vancouver Sun,* 27 January

Dartmoor National Park Authority, (1994), *Traffic Management Strategy,* Devon County Council and Dartmoor National Park Authority, Bovey Tracey.

Davies E., (1987), Planning in the New Zealand National Parks. *New Zealand Geographer* 43(2), 73-78.

Davison, R., Vogel, D., Gricar, J., Harris, R. and Sorrentmo, M., (2003), Electronic Commerce on the New Silk Road: Rejuvenating a Historical Trade Network, The European Conference on Information Systems June 19-21 Naples, Italy.

Dawson, A.H., (1991), Poland, in Hall, D.R. (ed.) *Tourism and Economic Development in Eastern Europe and the Soviet Union,* Belhaven Press, London and Halstead. New York. 190-202.

Dean Runyan Associates, (1994b), *Travel Industry Employment in Oregon 1991* Oregon Economic Development Department, Tourism Division , Salem.

Deepak, A., Regmi R. and Rimal, N. (1994), *Nepal District Profile A District Wide Socio-Techno-Economic Profile of Nepal.* National Research Associates, Kathmandu.

Deloitte and Touche, (1999), International Institute for Environment and Development (IIED), and Overseas Development Institute (ODI) *Sustainable Tourism and Poverty Elimination Study: A Report to the*

Department for International Development. Unpublished report for Department for International Development, UK.

Devon and Cornwall Rail Partnership, (1996) *Annual Report 1995-1996.* Devon and Cornwall Rail Partnership, Plymouth.

Dex, S., (1985), *The Sexual Division of Labour*, Wheatsheaf Books, Brighton.

Dicken. P., (1994), Global-local tensions: firms and states in the global space economy *Economic Geography* 70(2), 101-128.

Dickens, P., (1996), *Reconstructing Nature: Alienation, Emancipation and the Division of Labour,* Routledge, London.

Dieke, Peter U.C., (1994), 'The political economy of tourism in The Gambia.' *Review of African Political Economy* 62: 611-627.

Din, K.H., (1992), The 'involvement stage' in the evolution of a tourist destination *Tourism and Recreation Research* 17(1), 10-20.

Dixon, J.A. and Sherman, P.B., (1990), *Economics of Protected Areas: A New Look at Benefits and Costs.* London: Earthscan.

DoE, (1995), *Rural England: A Nation Committed to Living Countryside.* Department of the Environment and Ministry of Agriculture. Fisheries and Food. HMSO London.

Donnelly and George (Eds.), (1981), Marketing of Services, American Marketing Association Chicago.

Donnelly, D., (1998), Where have all the children gone? In: McLaren, D. (ed.) *Rethinking Tourism and Ecotourism.* Kumarian Press, West Hartford, Connecticut, pp. 88-89.

Dorst, J. (1977), *Before Nature Dies,* Collins, London.

Dovers, S. and Handmer, J.W., (1993), Contradictions in sustainability, *Environmental Conservation* 20, 217-222.

Drake, S., (1991), Local participation in ecotourism projects, in T. Whelan (ed.) *Nature Tourism Managing for the Environment,* Island Press, Washington, 132-163.

Dredge, D. and Moore, S., (1992), A methodology for integration of tourism in town planning, *Journal of Tourism* 3(1), 8-21.

Driml, S.M., (1991), Research needs for rainforest economics. In N. Goudberg, M. Bonell with D. Benzaken (eds) *Tropical Rainforest Research in Australia.* Townsville: Institute of Tropical Rainforest Studies.

Drummond, L. and Marsden, T.K., (1995), Regulating sustainable development, *Global Environmental Change,* 5(1) 55-63.

Duinker, P.N., (1994), Cumulative effects assessment: what's the big deal? in A.J. Kenned. (ed.) *Cumulative Effects in Canada: from Concept to Practice, Papers from the Fifteenth Symposium held by the Alberta Society of Professional Biologists* April 13-14, Calgary, 159-178.

Dunford, M., (1990), Theories of regulation, *Society and Space* 8, 297-321.

Dyer, R., (1995), *Cury County Receives $225,000 Grant,* News Release (June), Siskiyou National Forest, Grants Pass.

Dymond, S., (1996), Application of the World Tourism Organisation's (1995) indicators of sustainable tourism within the local authority boundaries of New Zealand, unpublished Grad.Dip. Tour, dissertation, Centre for Tourism. University of Otago, Dunedin.

E. (1996), *The Environmental Magazine,* Earth Action Network, P.O. Box, 40901. CT 06881; (203) 854-5559. Covers some environmental travel issues.

Eagles, P., (1992), The travel motivations of Canadian ecotourists, *Journal of Travel Research* 31(2), 3-7.

Eaton, B. and Holding, D., (1996), The evaluation of public transport alternatives to the car in British national parks, *Journal of Transport Geography 4(1), 55-65.*

Eber, Shirley, ed *Beyond the Green Horizon: Principles of Sustainable Tourism.* London: Tourism Concern/ World Wildlife Fund, 1992.

Economist Intelligence Unit. (1991), *Romania: Country Profile 1991-92,* E.I.U. Publications. London.

Ecotourism Society, (1993), *Ecotourism: An Annotated Bibliography for Planners and Managers.* North Bennington, VT. Ecotourism Society.

Edmonton Journal, (1991), Neighbours demand silence from fort, *Edmonton Journal,* 22, August, B2.

Edwards, F. (ed), (1988), *Environmentally Sound Tourism in the Caribbean,* The University of Calgary Press, Calgary.

Eight Northern Indian Pueblos Council, (1996), *8 Northern Indian Pueblos 1996 Visitors Guide,* Eight Northern Indian Pueblos Council, New Mexico.

Eisenberg, G., (1989), Learning vacations. In: *Peterson's Guide,* 6th edn. Peterson Publishers, Princeton, New Jersey, p. ix.

Ekins, P., (1993a), 'Limits to growth' and 'sustainable development' grappling with ecological realities, *Ecological Economics* 8: 269-88.

Ekins, P., (1993b), Making development sustainable in W. Sachs(ed.) (1993) *Global Ecology New Arena of Political Conflict,* Fernwood Publications. Halifax, 91-103.

Elkins, T., (1990), Developments in the German Democratic Republic, *Geography,* 75, 246-249.

Elliott, David, (1996), "Tidal Power". In *Renewable Energy: Power for a Sustainable Future*. Ed. Godfrey Boyle. Toronto: The Open University.

Ellis, J. (1994), Umorrduk Safaris, in *A Talent For Tourism: Stories about Indigenous People in Tourism,* Commonwealth Department of Tourism, Canberra, 31-33.

English Tourist Board, (1991), Countryside Commission and Rural Development Commission. *The Green Light: A Guide to Sustainable Tourism,* English Tourist Board. Countryside Commission and Rural Development Commission, London.

English, E. Philip, (1986), *The Great Escape? An Examination of North-South Tourism.* Ottawa: North-South Institute.

Enloe, C., (1989), *Bananas, Beaches and Bases: Making Feminist Sense of International Politics.* University of California Press, Berkeley, California.

Erbes, R., (1973), International tourism and the economy of developing countries. Paris: Organisation for Economic Cooperation and Development.

Escobar, A., (1995), *Encountering Development: The Making and Unmaking of the Third World,* Princeton University Press, Princeton, NJ.

Euroter, 82, rue Francois Rolland, F 94130 Nogent-sur-Marne, France (321) 4514-6421, fax (331) 439-49144. Publishes principles for developing green tourism in European villages.

Everett, Bob, (1996), "Solar Thermal Energy". In *Renewable Energy: Power for a Sustainable Future*. Ed. Godfrey Boyle. Toronto: The Open University,

Fairchils, H.N., (1928), *The Noble Savage: A Study in*

Romantic Naturalism. Columbia University Press, New York.

Farrell, B. (1986), "Cooperative Tourism and the Coastal Zone", *Coastal Zone Management Journal,* 14(1/2) : 113-130.

Farrell, B.H. and D. Runyan, (1991), Ecology and Tourism, *Annals of Tourism Research* 18(1) : 41-56.

Fennell, D.A. and Eagles, P.F., (1990), 'Ecotourism in Costa Rica: a conceptual framework'. *Journal of Park and Recreation Administration.* 8(1). pp 23-34.

Fennell, D.A. and Eagles, P.F., (1990), Ecotourism in Costa Rica: a conceptual frame work, *Journal of Park and Recreation Administration.* 8(1), 23-34.

FEP, (1996a), *Fort Edmonton Park 1997-1999 Business Plan.* Edmonton Parks and Recreation, Edmonton.

FEP, (1996b), *Criteria for Selection of a New Addition to Fort Edmonton Park* (File Copy) Edmonton Parks and Recreation, Edmonton.

FEP, (1997a), *Statistical Information* (File Copy), Edmonton Parks and Recreation. Edmonton.

FEP, (1997b), *Volunteer Hours Comparisons* (File Copy), Edmonton Parks and Recreation, Edmonton.

Fewings, J., (1995), A rural transport package for Dartmoor *Town and Country Planning* June, 180-182.

Flavin, Christopher and Nicholas Lenssen, (1990), *Beyond the Petroleum Age: Designing a Solar Economy.* World Watch Institute.

Flavin, Christopher, (1996), "Windpower: Small, But Growing Fast." *World Watch,* 35-37.

Foghorn Press, 555 De Haro Street, The Boiler Room #220, San Francisco, CA 94107; (415) 241-9550, fax (415) 241-9648. Outdoor and recreation books.

Forbes, B., (1993), *Tourism Development Plan, 1993-1998,* Brooking-Harbor Chamber of Commerce, Brookings.

Foresta, R.A., (1984), *America's National Parks and Their Keepers,* Resources for the Future, Washington.

Forsberg, P., Harvey, B. and Kelsay, D., (1996), *Curry County: Public Resources from Private Initiative,* Egret Communications, Port Orford, Oregon.

Forster, D.P. and Jozan, P., (1990), Health in Eastern Europe, *The Lancet,* 335,453-460.

Forsyth, Timothy, (1995), 'Tourism and agricultural development in Thailand.' *Annals of Tourism Research* 22 (4): 877-900.

Foster, D.L., (1990), *The Business of Travel Agency Operation and Administration*, McGraw Hill Singapore.

Foster, I.D., (1994), *Introduction to Travel and Tourism*, Macmillan, New York.

France, L., (ed.) (1997), *The Earthscan Reader in Sustainable Tourism,* Earthscan Publications, London.

France, Lesley (Ed), (19970, *The Earthscan Reader in Sustainable Tourism.* London, Earthscan.

Frank, Andre Gunder, (1966-1995), 'The development of underdevelopment.' Reprinted in Stuart Corbridge (Ed.), *Development Studies: A Reader,* pp. 27-37. London, Edward Arnold.

French, H. Vanishing Bordprs, (2000), Protecting the Planet in the Age of Globalisation Washington, Worldwatch Institute.

French, H., (1990), *Green Revolutions: Environmental Reconstruction in Eastern Europe and the Soviet Union.* Worldwatch Institute, Washington DC.

Frenmont, P. (1983), *How to Open and Run a Money Making Travel Agency,* John Wiley and Sons, New York.

Friedman, (1954), *The Public Corporation*, Stevens, London.

Friends of Malac Kahana, PO Box 305, Laie, III 96762; (808) 293 1736, fax (808) 293-2066. Native Hawaiian civic group operates state park; provides training to other native groups to manage parks.

Friends of PRONATURA, 240 East Limberlost Drive, Tucson, AZ 85705; (602) 887-1188, closfree@aol.com. Network of ecological groups working in Mexico.

Friendship Press, (1995), *Having an Excellent Adventure: A Handbook for Responsible Travel—A Guide or Planners and Travelers.* Cincinnati: Friendship Press.

Frissell, S.S. and Stankey, G.H., (1972), Wildernes environmental quality: search for social and ecological harmony. Paper presented at Annual Meeting Society of American Foresters, 4 October, Hot Springs.

Frohlich, M., (1993), Is there a Tourist Culture ? in *Cultural Tourism : International Scientific Symposium.* ICOMOS 10th General Assembly, Sri Lanka, ed. Prematilleka, P.L., 66-69.

Frommer, Arthur. *Arthur Frommer's New World of Travel: A Guide to Alternative Vacations in the Americas and Throughout the World.* New York: Prentice Hall, updated annually.

Fuster, L.D., (1994), *Introduction to Travel and Tourism,* Macmillan, New York.

Gajraj, A.M., (1988), 'A Regional Approach to Environmentally Sound Tourism Development', *Recreation Research,* Vol. 14(2).

Gallie, W.B., (1955-56), Essentially contested concepts, *Proceedings of the Aristotelian Society 56,* 167-198.

Gamble, W.P., (1989), *Tourism and Development in Africa.* London: Murray.

Ganga, Gobind, (1994), *Ecotourism in Guyana: Implications for Sustainable Development.* Georgetown: University of Guyana.

Garland, Alex, (1997), *The Beach.* New York: Riverhead Books, Fiction; a story about young Westerners traveling in Southeast Asia and the never-ending search for the last unspoiled idyll.

Garnham, H.L., (1985), *Maintaining the Spirit of Place,* PDA Publishers, Mesa.

Gascon, C., (1994), *Discover the Lower North Shore: Guide and Directory,* Coaster's Association, St. Paul's River.

Gayle, Dennis J., and Jonathan N. Goodrich, (eds.), (1993), *Tourism Marketing and Management in the Caribbean.* London: Routledge.

Gee Chuck Y., and Makens, Choy, (1989), *The Travel Industry,* Nostrand Reihold, New York.

Gee Y. Chuch, (1990), *Professional Travel Agency Management,* Prentice Hall, U.K.

Gee, Chuck, and Y. Makens, Choy, (1989), *Professional Travel Agency Management,* New York.

Gerald, M. Meier , (1975), *Leading Issues in Economic Development,* Oxford University Press.

Getz, D., (1986), Models in tourism planning towards integration of theory and practice, *Tourism Management* 7(1), 21-32.

Ghimire, Krishna, (19970, *Emerging Mass Tourism in the South.* UNRISD Discussion Paper no. 85. Geneva. UNRISD.

Gibbs, D., (1996), Intégrating sustainable development and economic restructuring, a role for regulation theory, *Geoforum* 27(1), 1-10.

GIEE, (1999), *Safety and Responsibility in Education Abroad.* Workshop Manual, GEE, New York.

Gilbert, D.C., (1989), "Tourism Marketing: Its emergency and establishment, in Cooper C., (Ed.), *Progress in Tourism Recreation and Hospitality Management,* Vol. I, London.

Gill, C., (1992), Balancing tourism and the environment. *Tourism Today,* 34-41.

Gill, R., (1994), Manyallaluk, in *A Talent For Tourism: Stories about Indigenous People in Tourism.* Commonwealth Department of Tourism, Cariberra, 22-21.

Glacken, C., (1967), *Traces on the Rhodian Shore, Nature and Culture in Western Thought from Ancient Times to the End of the Enghteenth Century,* University of California Press, Berkeley.

Global Exchange 2017 Mission Street, San Francisco, CA 94110; (415) 255-7296, fax (415) 255-7698. Reality tours focus on public education about globalisation issues and visit countries like South Africa, haiti, Cuba, Mexico, publications.

Globe 90, (1990), *Tourism Stream: An Action Strategy for Sustainable Development* Environment Canada, Vancouver.

Godwin, N., (1987), *A Complete Guide to Travel Agency,* Albanj, Delmer.

Goe, Y.C., Kevin, B., Dexter, J.L.C., and James, M., (1990), *Professional Travel Agency Management,* Prentice Hall, London.

Golembski, G., (1990), Tourism in the economy of shortage. *Annals of Tourism Research.* 17, 55-68.

Gollin, Jim, and Ron Mader, (1997), *Honduras: Adventures in Nature,* Santa Fe: John Muir Publications.

Gomoiu, M.T., (1991), *Status of the Danube Delta Biosphere Reserve Planning and Management Report 1991 A.* DDBRA, Tulcea.

Gonsalves, Paul, (1987), *Alternative Tourism: An Operations Mannual for Third World Groups.* Bangalore: Equations.

Goodall, B. (1992), Environmental auditing for tourism, in C. Cooper and A.J. Lockwood (eds) *Progress in Tourism and Hospitality Management,* Wiley, Chichester, 60-74.

Goodwin, M. and Painter, J. (1996), Local governance, the crises or Fordism and the changing geographies of regulation, *Transactions of the Institute of British Geographers* 21(4), 635-648.

Goodwin, N., (1987), *A Complete Guide to Travel Agency,* Albanj, Dalmer.

Goodwin.P., Hallet, S., Kenny, F. and Stokes, G., (1991), *Transport: The New Realism.* Transport Studies Unit, University of Oxford, Oxford.

Graefe, A.R. Kuss, F.R. and Vske, J.J., (1900), *Visitor Impact Management,* 2 vols., National Parks and Conservation Association, Washington.

Graham, Scott., (1992), *Handle with Care: A Guide to Responsible Travel in Developing Counties.* Chicago: Noble Press.

Grance, O., (1981), External influence and internal change in the development of geography, in D.R. Stoddart (ed.) *Geography, Ideology and Social Concern,* Blackwell, Oxford, 17-36.

Graphic Arts, *Culture Shock!series* Portland, OR: Graphic Arts Center Publishing, various years.

Gratton, C. and Straaten, J. Van der, (1994), The environmental impact of tourism in Europe, in C.P. Cooper and A. Lockwood (eds) *Progress in Tourism, Recreation and Hospitality Management, Vol 5* John Wiley Chichester, 201-219.

Gray, Matthew, (1998), 'Economic reform, privatisation and tourism in Egypt.' *Middle Eastern Studies* 34 (2): 91-112.

Great Barrier Reef Marine Park Authority, (1993), *Annual Report* 1992-1993. Townsville. Great Barrier Reef Marine Park Authority.

Greenpeace, (1992), *Impacts of Tourism Development in Pacific Islands.* San Francisco: Greenpeace Pacific Campaign.

Greenwood, D.J., (1989)m Culture by the pound: and anthropological perspective and tourism as cultural commodification, in V.L. Smith (ed.) *Hosts and Guests. The Anthropology of Tourism.* University of Pennsylvania Press, Philadelphia, 171-186.

Gregory A., (1983), *The Travel Agent: Dealer in Dreams,* 4th Ed., The Prentice Hall, London.

Grekin, J. and Milne, S., (1996), Toward sustainable tourism development the case of Pond Inlet. NWT, in R.W. Butler and T. Hinch (eds.) *Tourism and Native Peoples,* Toutledge, London 76-106.

Grotta, (1992), Daniel, and Sally Wiener Grotta. *The Green Travel Sourcebook: A Guide for the Physically Active, the Intellectually Curious, or the Socially Aware.* New York: Wiley.

Grubb, Michael J. and Niels I. Meyer, (1993), "Wind Energy: Resources, Systems, and Regional Strategies". In *Renewable Energy: Sources for Fuels and Electricity.* Ed. Thomas B. Johansson, et al. Washington D.C.: Island Press.

Gunn, C, (1994), *Tourism Plcnning Basics, Concepts, Gases,* Taylor & Francis, Washington.

Gunn, C., (1988b), *Vacationscape: Designing Tourist Regions,* 2nd edn, Van Nostrand Reinhold, New York.

Gurung, C.P. and De Coursey, M., (1994), The Annapurna Conservation Area Project: a pioneering example of sustainable tourism? in F. Cater and G. Lowman (eds.) *Ecotourism. A Sustainable Option?* John Wiley & Sons, New York, 177-194.

Gurung, Harka, (1980), Vignettes of Nepal, Sajha Prakashan, Kathmandu.

Hall, C., (1985), *Costa Rica: a Geographical Interpretation in Historical Perspective, Dcllplain Latin American Studies, No. 17,* Westview Press, Boulder, Colorado.

Hall, C.M. and Johnston, M. (eds), (1995), *Polar Tourism: Tourism in the Arctic and Antarctic Regions,* John Wiley, Chichester.

Hall, C.M. and Wouters, M.M., (1994), Managing nature tourism in the sub-Antarctic islands, *Annals of Tourism Research* 21, *355-374.*

Hall, C.M. Mitchell, L. and Keelan N., (1992), Maori cultural heritage and tourism in New Zealand, *Jornal of Cultural Geography 12(2), 115-128.*

Hall, C.M., (1992a), *Wasteland to World Heritage: Preserving Australia's Wilderness,* Mellboutne University Press, Carlton.

Hall, C.M., (1992b), Adventure, sport and health tourism. In: Weiler, B. and Hall, C.M. (eds) *Special Interest Tourism.* Belhaven, London, pp. 141-158.

Hall, C.M., (1992b), *Hallmark Events, Impacts, Management and Planning,* Belhaven Press. London.

Hall, C.M., (1994), *Tourism and Politics.* John Wiley & Sons, Chichester, UK.

Hall, C.M., (1995), *Introduction to Tourism in Australian Impacts, Planning and Development,* 2nd edn., Longman Australia, Soputh Melbourne.

Hall, C.M., (1996), Tourism and the Maon of Aotearoa, New Zealand, in R. Butler and J. Hinch (eds). *Tourism and Indigenous Peoples.* International Thomson Business. Press. London, 155-175.

Hall, C.M., (1997), *Tourism in the Pacific Rim: Development, Impacts and Markets,* 2nd edn, Addision Wesley Longman, South Melbourne.

Hall, CM., (1992a), Sex tourism in South-East Asia. In: Harrison, D. (ed.) *Tourism in the Less Developed Countries.* Belhaven, London, pp. 64-74.

Hall, D.R. (ed.), (1991b), *Tourism and Economic Development in Eastern Europe,* Belhaven Press, London and Halstead, New York.

Hall, D.R., (1990a), Eastern Europe opens its doors. *Geographical Magazine.* 62, 10-15.

Hall, D.R., (1990b), Stalinism and tourism: a study of Albania and North Korea. *Annals of Tourism Research,* 17, 36-54.

Hall, D.R., (1990c), The changing face of tourism in Eastern Europe. *Town and Country Planning.* 59,348-351.

Hall, D.R., (1992b), Czech mates no more? *Town and Country Planning,* 61, 250-251.

Hall, D.R., (1992c), Skills transfer for appropriate development. *Town and Country Planning.* 61. 87-89.

Hall, D.R., (1993a), *Albania into the Twenty-first Century,* Pinter, London.

Hall, D.R., (1993b), Impacts of economic and political transition on the transport geography of Central and Eastern Europe, *Journal of Transport Geography,* 1, 20-35.

Hall, D.R., (1993c), Transport implications of tourism development, in Hall. D.R. (ed.) *Transport and Economic Development in the New Central and Eastern Europe,* Belhaven Press, London, 206-225.

Hall, D.R., (1995), Tourism change in Central and Eastern Europe in A. Montanari and A.M. Willians (eds) *European Tourism: Regions, Spaces and Restructuring, John Wiley, Chichester,* 221-243.

Hall, Michael, and Stephen Page, (eds.), (1996), *Tourism and the Pacific: Issues and Cases.* London: Thomas Business Press.

Hall. D.R. (ed.), (1991), *Tourism and Economic Development in Eastern Europe and the Soviet Union,* Belhaven Press, London.

Halliday, J. and Chehak, G., (1996), *Native Peoples of the Northwest,* Sasquatch Books, Seattle.

Hampton, Mark, (1998), 'Backpacker tourism and economic development.' *Annals of Tourism Research* 25 (3): 639-660.

Hanmer, Lucia, John Healey, and Felix Naschold. (2000), *Will Growth Halve Global Poverty By 2015?* ODI Poverty Briefing 8 (July. London: ODI).

Hansen, N., (1992), Competition, trust and reciprocity in the development of innovative regional milicux, *Papers in Regional Science 7* 1(2), 95-105.

Hardin, G., (1969), The tragedy of the commons. *Science* 162, 1243-1248.

Harman, W.W., (1993), Rethinking the central institutions of modern society: society and business, *Futures* 25 (December), 1063-1071.

Harris, R.W., Kumar, A., Balaji, V., (2003), Sustainable Telecentres? Two Cases from India. ICTs and Development: New Opportunities, Perspectives and Challenges, Ashgate Publishers, forthcoming.

Harris, W.W., (1974), Three parks: an analysis of the origins and evolution of the national parks, movement, unpublished MA thesis, Department of Geography, University of Canterbury, Christchurch, New Zealand.

Harrison, D. and Price, M.F., (1996), Fragile environments, fragile communities: An introduction, in M.F. Price (ed.) *People and Tourism in Fragile Environments.* John Wiley & Sons, Chichester, 1-18.

Harrison, David, (ed.), (1992), *Tourism and the Less Developed Countries.* New York: Halstead Press.

Harrison, L.C.; and Husbands, W., (1996), *Practicing Responsible Tourism: International Case Studies in Tourism. Planning. Policy and Development.* John Wiley & Sons, Inc.

Hart, A.J., (1992), Planning for tourism in Christchurch in comparative study, unpublished MA thesis,

Department of Geography, University of Canterbury, New Zealand.

Harvey, B and Kelsay, D., (1994-96), *Various Progress Reports—Cury Country Sustainable Nature-Based Tourism Project*. Egret Communications, Port Oxford, Oregon.

Hawkins, D. and Khan, M., (1998), Ecotourism opportunities for developing countries. In: Theobald, W.F. (ed.) *Global Tourism: the Second Decade*. Butterworth-Heinemann, Oxford, UK, pp. 191-204.

Hayden, T., (1999), Tuberculosis is making a comeback *Newsweek* 8 November, p. 77.

Hayes, John L., (1976), Trekking North of Kathmandu, Peter Purna Banks Avalok, Kathmandu.

Hays, S.P., (1957), *The Response to Indusrialism, 1885-1914, University of Chicago Press, Chicago.*

Hays, S.P., (1959), *Conservation and the Gopel of Efficiency: The Progressive Conservation Movement 1890-1920.* Harward University Press, Cambridge, Mass.

Healy, R.G., (1996), Tourism, Ecotourism and Sustainable Development, unpublished mimeo, Duke University, Raleigh, NC.

Hendee, J.C. Stankey, G.H, and Lucas, R.C., (1978), *Wilderness Management,* Miscellaneous Publications No. 1365 USDA Forest Service, Washington.

Hewison, R., (1987), *The Heritage Industry: Britain in a Climate of Decline,* Muthuen, London, 160.

Heyendael, A., (2002), Sustainable Tourism Within the Context of the Ecosystem Approach, in Tourism, Biodiversity and Information, di Castri, F. and Balaji, V., (eds.), Backhuys, Leiden, The Netherlands, pp. 25-44.

Heymann, D., (1995), Emerging infectious diseases. *World Health* 50(1), 4.

Hill, C., (1990), The paradox of tourism in Costa Rica, *Cultural Survival Quarterly* 14(1) 14-19.

Hinch, T.D. and Butler, R.W., (1996), Indigenous tourism a common ground for discussion in R. Butler and T. Hinch (eds) *Tourism and Indigenous Peoples,* International Thomson Business Press. London, 3-19.

Hinrichsen, D. and Enyedi, G., (eds), (1990), *State of the Hungarian Environment,* Statistical Publishing House, Budapest.

HMGN: (1994), Ministry of Tourism and Civil Aviation Department of Tourism, *Nepal Tourism Statistics 1993*, Rising Sun Printers, Kathmandu.

Hoffman, M.S. (ed.), (1991), *The World Almanac and Book of Facts 1992,* Pharos Books, New York.

Holing, Dwight, (1991), *Earthtrips: A Guide to Nature Travel on a Fragile Planet.* Los Angeles: Conservation International and Living Planet Press.

Holloway, C.K., (1990), *The Business of Tourism,* Pitman, London.

Holloway, J.C., and Robinson C. (1995), Marketing For Tourism, Pitman, London.

Honey, M., (1994), Paying the price of ecotourism, *Americas* 46(6), 40-47.

Honeywill, R. and Byth, V. I-Cons, (2001), The Essential Guide to Winning and Keeping High-Value Customers, Random House.

Honeywill, R., (2002), Cash in on the Neo Consumer, Traveltrade, June 5 http://www.maryrossitravel.com./whoweare/news/pdf/traveltrade iun2002.pdf.

Honour, H., (1975), *The New Golden Land: European Images of America from the Discoverers to the Present Times,* Pantheon Books, New York.

Honour, H., (1981), *Romanticism,* Penguin Press, Harmondsworth.

Hooks, bell, (1992), *Black Looks. Race and Representation,* Boston: South End Press.

House of Commons Environment Committee, (1995), *The Environmental Impact of Leisure Activities,* HMSO, London.

Houseal, B., MacFarland, C, Archibold, G. and Chiari. A., (1985), Indigenous cultures and protected areas in Central America, *Cultural Survival Quarterly,* 9(1), 10-20.

Howard, C., (1993), Costa Rica 'selling out' to foreigners, *San Franciso Chronicle* 9 August, A10.

Howe, J., (1982), Kindling self-determination among the Kuna, *Cultural Survival Quarterly* 6(3), 15-17.

Hubbs Clay, (ed.) *Alternative Travel Directory.* Amherst. Transitions Abroad Publishing, annually.

Hudson, R. and Willims, A.M., (1994), *Dividend Britian,* Wiley, Chichester.

Hudson, R., (1995), Towards sustainable industrial production: but in what sense sustainable? in M.Taylor (ed.) *Envirìonmental Change: Industry, Power and Policy:* Avebury, Aldershot, 37-56.

Hughes, G., (1991), Are the costs of cleaning up Eastern Europe exaggerated? Economic reform and the environment, *Oxford Review of Economic Policy,* 7(4), 12-24.

Hull, J.S., (1996), Using the Internet to promote a sustainable tourism industry: a case study of the flower North Shore of Quebec. Paper presented at the International Geographical Union. The Hague, Netherlands, August 1996.

Human Rights Watch, (1995), *Burma: Entrenchment or Reform: Human Rights Development and the Need for Continued Pressure.* Washington, DC: Human Rights Watch/Asia Watch.

Hunter, C.J., (1995), On the need to re-conceptualise sustainable tourism development. *Journal of Sustainable Tourism 3* (3), 155-65.

Hunter, Colin, (1995), *Tourism and the Environment: A Sustainable Relationship?* London: Routledge.

Huntington, S.L., (1968), *Political Order in Changing Societies.* Yale University Press, New Haven, Connecticut.

Huntington, S.L., (1993), The clash of civilisations. *Foreign Affairs* 12(3), 22-49.

Hutchinson, J., (1994), The practice of partnership in local economic development, *Local Government Studies* 20(3), 335-344.

Inkpen, Gary, (1994), *Information Technology for Travel and Tourism.* London: Pitman Publishing.

Inskeep, E., (1991), *Tourism Planning: An Integrated and Sustainable Development Approach,* Van Nostrand Reinhold, New York.

Inskeep, E., (1991), *Tourism Planning: An Integrated and Sustainable Development Approach* Van Nostrand Reinhold, New York.

Inter-Hemispheric Education Resource Center. *Inside.* Albuquerque, NM: Inter-Hemispheric Resource Center, n.d.

Interlock Media/Environmental Media Unit, 607 Boylston Street 401 Boston, MA 02116; (617) 236-4471, fax (617) 236-4429, intlock@ix.netcom.com. International and training films and videos on Indigenous rights, environmental movements, domestic and Third World.

International Bicycle Fund, 4887 Columbia Drive South, Seattle, WA 98108-1919; (206) 628-9314; intlbike@scn.org. Promotes bicycle transport, economic development, international understanding, and safety education, newsletter, links with other auto-free and bicycling organisations around the world.

International Union for the Conservation of Nature (IUCN), (1990), *1990 United Nations List of National Parks and Protected Areas,* IUCN, Gland.

Ise, L., (1961), *Our National Park Policy A Critical History,* Published for Resources for the Future by The Johns Hopkins Press, Baltimore, Md.

Iwersen-Sioltsidis, Susanne, and Albrecht Iwersen, (1996), 'Tourism and developing countries.' *Intereconomics* 31 (6): 301-306.

Jackson, C., (1994), Gender analysis and environmentatlism, in M. Redelift and T. Benton (eds) *Social Theory and the Global Environment,* Routledge, London. 113-149.

Jackson, I., (1990), Tourism and sustainable development in the Caribbean, in Cox, J. and Embree, C. (eds) *Sustainable Development in the Caribbean,* Institute for Research on Public Policy, Halifax. 127-138.

Jackson, P. and Thrift, N., (1995), Geographics of consumption, in D.Miller (ed.) *Acknowledging Consumption,* Routledge, London, 204-237.

Jackson, P., (1995), Changing geographics of consumption, *Environment and Planning* A-27, 1875-1876.

Jacob, M., (1994), Toward a methodological critique of sustainable development, *Journal of Developing Areas* 28, 237-252.

Jafari, J., (1989), Soft Tourism, *Tourism Management,* 9(1) : 82-84.

Jaimes, Annette, (ed.), (1992), *The State of Native America.* Boston: South End Press.

Jamal, T.B. and Getz. D., (1995), Collaboration theory and

community tourism planning. Annals of Tourism Research *22(1), 186-204.*

Jamiesan. W. (ed.), (1990), *Maintaining and Enhancing the Sense of Place for Small Communities and Regions,* University of Calgary, Calgary.

Jansen-Verbeke, M., (1986), Inner city tourism: resources, tourists, and promoters *Annals of Tourism Research* 13(1), 79-100.

Jefferson, Allan, and Leonard Lickorish, (1991), *Marketing Tourism: A Practical Guide.* Essex: Longman Group.

Jefferson, T., (1861), *Notes on the State of Virginia,* Harper & Row, New York.

Jemo, I., (1996), *Experiences in the Postwar Reconstruction of the Historical Core of Dubrovnik.* Paper prepared for International Conference on Settlement Revitalisation in Postwar Reconstruction, Zagreb, April 26-27.

Jenner, P. and Smith, C., (1992), *The Tourism Industry and the Environment,* E.I.U. Publications. London.

Jessop, B. Peck, J. and Tickell, A., (1996), Retooling the machine, economic crisis, state restructuring, and urban politics. Paper presented to the Annual Meeting of the Association of American Geographers, 9-13 April, Charlotte.

John Muir Publications PO, Box 613, Santa Fe, NM 87504; (505) 982-4078. "Adventures in Nature" travel guide series.

Johnston, C.R., (ed.), (1990), Breaking out of the tourist trap. *Cultural Survival Quarterly* 14(1 & 2).

Johnston, R.J., (1991), *Geopgraphy and Geographers: Anglo-American Human Geography Since* 1945, 6th edn., Edward Arnold, London.

Jones, G., (1991), Le Development touiristique de la zone Vicux-fort/Blanc-Sablon en Basse-Cote-Nord du Golfe

St Laurent, unpublished Master's thesis. Universite du Quebec a Rimousski, Rimounski, Quebec.

Kincaid, Jamaica, (1988), *A Small Place,* New York: PLUME/ Penguin Books,

King Mahendra Trust for Nature Conservation (KMTNC) (1994a), Annapurna Conservation *Area Project: Conservation for Development,* (KMTNC), Kathmandu.

Kinnaird, Vivian, and Derek Hall, (eds.), (1994), *Tourism: A Gender Analysis.* New York; Wiley.

Kirkby, S.J., (1995), Introduction, in J.Kirkby, P.O.keefe, and I.Timberlake (eds) *The Earthscan Reader in Sustainable Development,* Earthscan Publications, London.

Kleinhenz, C. and Hallitzky, E., (1991), *Costs and Benefits of the Sumava National Park. Management Plan for the WWF,* University of Passau. Passau.

Kotler, P., (1980), *Marketing Management: Analysis, Planning, Implementation and Control*, Englewood Cliffs, Prentice Hall.

Kotler, P., (2000), Tourism marketing, London.

KPMG Consulting, (1995), *Technology and Tourism Marketing in Canada,* Canadian Tourism Commission, Ottawa.

Kramer, P., (1094), *Native Sites in Western Canada, Altitude Publishing, Canmore.*

Krawetz, N.M. MacDonald, W.R. and Nichols, P., (1987), *A Fraework for Effective Monitoring,* Canadian Environmental Assessment Research Council, Ottawa.

Kretchmann, J. and Eagles, P. (1990), An analysis of the motives of ecotourists in comparison to the general Canadian Population, *Society and Leisure* 13(2): 499-507.

Krotz, Larry, (1996), *Tourists: How Our Fastest Growing Industry is Changing the World.* New York: Faber and Faber.

Laarman, J.G. and Perdue, R., (1989), Science tourism in Costa Rica, *Annals of Tourism Research* 16, 205-215.

Lang, R., (1988), Planning for integrated development, in F.W. Dykernan (ed.) *Integrated Rural Planning and Development,* Mount Allison University, Sackville, 81-104.

Larsen, K. (1993), Around Manaslu, *Buzzworm: The Environmental Journal* 5, 60-64.

Lasswell, H., (1936), *Politics: Who Gets What, When and How.* McGraw Hill, New York.

Lavery, P., (ed.), (1971), *Recreational Geography,* David and Charles, London.

Law, C.M., (1993), *Urbane Tourism Attracting Visitors to Large Cities,* Mansell, London.

Lawson, F., and M. Baud-Bovy (1977), *Tourism and Recreation Development,* London: Architectural Press.

Lea, John, (1988), *Tourism and Development in the Third World.* London: Routledge,

Leheny, D., (1995), A political economy of Asian sex tourism. *Annals of Tourism Research* 22(2), 367-384.

Leininger, A., (1993), *Algunos aspectos de la geograia touristica y su application en Costa Rica, Escuela de Ciensias Geograficas.* Universidad National Costa Rica, Heredia, unpublished.

Leiper, N., (1990), Tourist attraction systems, *Annals of Tourism Research* 17(3), 367-384.

Lemons, J. and Brown, D.A., (1995), *Sustainable Development, Science, Ethics and Public Policy,* Kluwer Academic Publishers, London.

Lew, A.A and van Otten, G.A., (eds), (1998), *Tourism and Gaming on American Indian Lands,* Cognizant Communications Corporations, New York.

Lew, A.A and Yu, L., (eds), (1995), *Tourism in China. Geographic, Political and Economics Perspective,* Westview Press, Boulder, Colorado.

Lewand, Alan A., and Lawrence Yu, (eds.), (1995), *Tourism in China.* Boulder, CO. Westview Press.

Lime, D.W. and Stankey, G.H., (1971), Carrying capacity: maintaining, outdoor recreation quality, in *Forest Recreation Symposium Proceedings,* Northeast Forest Experimental Station, Upper Darby, 174-184.

Lindberg, K., (1991), *Policies for Maximising Nature Tourism's Ecological and Economic Benefits,* World Resources Institute, Washington.

Lindberg, Kreg, and Donald Hawkins, (eds.), (1993), *Ecotourism: A Guide for Planners and Managers.* North Bennington, VT:'Ecotourism Society.

Lipietz, A., (1992), *Towards a New Economic Order: Postfordism, Ecology and Democracy,* Polity Press, Cambridge.

Liu, Juanita, (1991), *Pacific Islands Ecotourism: A Public Policy and Planning Guide.* Honolulu: Pacific Business Center Program, University of Hawaii.

Long, V.H., (1990), Tourism development, conservation and anthropology, *Practicing Anthropology* 14(2), 14-17.

Loomis, J.B.; and Walsh, R.G., (1996), *Recreation Economic Decisions: Comparing Benefits and Costs* (2nd Edition) Venture Publishing, Inc. State College Pennsylvania.

Lowenthal, D., (1958), *George Perkins Marsh: Versatile Vermonter,* Columbia University Press, New York.

Lowndes, V., Nanton, P., McCabe, A. and Skelcher, C., (1997), Networks, partnerships and urban regeneration, *Local Economy* 11(4), 333-342.

Lowyck, E., Van Langenhove, L. and Bollaert, L., (1992), Typologies of tourist roles, in P.Johnson and T.Barry (eds), *Choice and Demand in Tourism,* Mansell, London. 13-32.

Lozawa, Tomoya, (1980), Trekking in the Himalayas, Yama-Kei, Publishers, Tokyo.

Lujan, C.C., (1993), A sociological view of tourism in an American Indian community maintaining cultural integrity at Taos Pueblo, *American Indian Culture and Research Journal* 17(3), 101-120.

Lumsden, L. (1992), The Peak District National Park: The Upper Derwent, *Marketing for Tourism: Case Study Assignments,* Macmillan, London.

Lundberg, D.E., Stavenga, M.H. & Krishnamoorthy, M., (1995), *Tourism Economics.* New York: John Wiley & Sons, Inc.

MacCannell D., (1976), *The Tourist: A New Theory of the Leisure Class;* Schoken Books, New York.

MacCannell, Dean, (1989), *The Tourist: A New Theory of the Leisure Class.* New York: Shocken Books.

Madeley, John, (1999) *Big Business. Poor People: The Impact of Transnational Corporations on the World's Poor.* London, Zed Books.

Mader, Ron, (1997), *Mexico: Adventures in Nature.* Santa Fe: John Muir Publications.

Maderey, John, (1995), *Foreign Exploits, Transnationals and Tourism.* London. Catholic Institute for International Relations.

Mathieson, A and Wall, G., (1982), *Tourism: Economic, Physical and Social Impacts,* Longman, Harlow.

Matley, I.M., (1976), *The Geography of International*

Tourism, Resource Paper 76-1, Association of American Geographers, Washington.

Matthews, W.H., (1975), Objective and subjective judgement in environmental impact analysis, *Environment Conservation* 2, 121-131.

Mattson, V.E., (1985), *Frederick Jackson Turner: A Reference Guide* G.K. Hall, Boston.

Maxwell, Simon, (1999), *The Meaning And Measurement Of Poverty.* ODI Poverty Briefing 3 (February). London, ODI.

McAfee, Kathy, (1991), *Storm Signals: Structural Adjustment and Development Alternatives in the Caribbean.* Boston. South End Press.

McCool, S.F. and Stankey, G.H., (1992), Managing for the sustainable use of protected wildlands: the limits of acceptable change framework. Paper presented at IVth World Congress on National Parks and Protected Areas, Caracas, Venezuela, February 10-21.

McDonald, Neil, (1990), *The Caribbean, Making Our Own Choices.* Oxford: Oxfam.

McHugh, E., (1996), Time travelling, in *The Australian Magazine, Territory Tapestry: Special Promotion for the Australian Magazine*, 23-24 November, 35-36.

McIntosh, Robert Woodrow, and Charles R. Goeldner, (1995), *Tourism: Principles, Practices and Philosophics.* New York: Wiley,

McKercher, B., (1993b), The unrecognised threat to tourism: can tourism survive sustainability? *Tourism Management* 14(2), 131-136.

McLaren, D., (1998), *Rethinking Tourism and Ecotravel.* Kumarian Press, West Hartford, Connecticut.

McIntyre, G., (1993), *Sustainable Tourism Development:*

Guide for Local Planners, World Tourism Organisation, Madrid.

Meadows, D.H., Meadows, D.L. Randers, J. and Behrens, W.W., (1972), *Limits to Growth,* Universal Books, New York.

Medlik, R., (1988), 'What is Tourism? Teaching Tourism into the 1990s. Published in the Proceedings of International Conference. *Tourism Educators,* July, 1988, University of Surry, Guildford, U.K.

Mieczkowski, Zbigniew, (1995), *Environmental Issues of Tourism and Recreation.* Lanham, MD. University Press of America.

Milne, S. and Pohlmann, C. (forthcoming) The evolving hotel industry: evidence from Montreal, in K. Debbage and D. laonnides (eds) *The Economic Geography of Tourism*, Routledge, London.

Milne, S. and Wenzel, G., (1991), Tourism and economic development in the Baffin Region of Canada's Northwest Territories, unpublished paper, McGill University, Montreal.

Milne, S., (1997), Tourism, dependency and South Pacific microstates, beyond the vicious cycle? in D.G. Lockhart and D. Drakakis-Smith (eds) *Island Tourism: Trends and Prospects,* Pinter, London 281-301.

Mings, R.C., (1978), Tourism Industry Development : at the Cross roads, *Tourist Review* 33(3) : 2-9.

Ministere des Transports du Quebec, (1988), *Statistiques de transports maritime* Government du Qucbec, Quebec.

Ministry of Tourism, (1992), *Tourism Sustainability,* Discussion Paper Ministry of Tourismm Wellington.

Ministry of Tourism, (1993), *The Resourcement Management Act-A Guide for the Tourism Industry,* Ministry of Tourism, Wellington.

Mitchell, L., (1969), Recreational geography evolution and research needs, *professional Geography* (21(2), 117-119.

Mohnder, (2003), "Tour operator industry in India: An Analysis of operational Dimensions" In Tourism Development Journal Vol.-1, No. 1.

Montanari, A. and Williams, A.M., (1995), *European Tourism: Regions Spaces and Restructuring,* Wiley, Chichester.

Montanari, Amanda, and Allen M. Williams, (eds.), (1995), *European Tourism: Regions, Spaces and Restructuring.* New York. Wiley.

Mora Castellane, E., (1996), *EI securestro de una nacion, Ambien-Tico* (March 1996, Revista mensual del proyecto 'Actualidad Ambiental en Costa Rica', Escuela de Ciencias Ambientales, Universidad Nacional de Costa Rica, No. 38, 9-11.

Mowforth, M. and Charlton, C.A., (1996), *Valuing Rural Branch Lines: A Methodology for Investigation and Guide for Potential Researchers.* Devon and Cornwall Rail Partnership, Plymouth.

Mulchand, S., (1993), Northern exposure, *Asia Travel Trade,* September, 26-27.

Munt, Ian, and Figbert Higino, (1993-1997), 'Belize: ecotourism gone awry.' Reprinted in Lesley France (Ed.), *The Earthscan Reader in Sustainable Tourism,* pp. 98-101. London, Earthscan.

Murphy, P.E., (1985), *Tourism: a community approach,* Methuen. London.

Mutchell, England Murphy, P. (1991) Geography and tourism, *Annals of Tourism Research* 18, 57-70.

Myers, N. and Gaia Ltd staff, (1984), *Gaia: An Atlas of Planet Management,* Anchor/Doubleday, New York.

Nadler L., (1980), "Defining the field—is it HRD or O.D.

or.......". *Training and Development Journal*, published by ASTC 34, No. 12, p. 66.

Naisbitt, John, (1994), *Global Paradox.* New York: Avon Books.

Narthan, H., (1991), Heritage centre owners to offer creditors. Times Calumn, 6, April.

Nash, Dennis, (1996), *The Anthropology of Tourism.* Oxford: Pergamon Press.

Nash, R. (ed.), (1968), *The American Environment: Readings in the History of Conservation,* Addison-Wesley Publishing, Reading, Mass.

Nash, R., (1963), The American wilderness in historical perspective, *Journal of Forest History* 6(4), 2-13.

Nath, B., Hens, I and Devuyst, D, (eds), (1996), *Sustainable Development*VUB University Press, Brussels.

Nelson J.G. and Butler, R.W., (1975), Recreation nd the environment, in I.R. Manners and M.W. Mikesell (eds) *Perspectives an Environment* association of American Geographers, Washington, 290-310.

Nelson, J.G., (1973), Canada's national parks—past, present and future, *Candadian Geographical Journal* 86(3), 68-89.

Nicholson- Lord, D., (1994), Hitting- and obliterating- the trail, *World Press Review* January, 48.

Nicholson, M.H., (1962), *Mountain Gloom and Mountain Glory,* Norton, New York.

Pannell Kerr Forster Management Consultants, (1990), *Fort Edmonton Park: Opportunities for a Major Tourist Attraction,* Pannell Kerr Forster Management Consultants, Edmonton.

Pareek, V. and T.V. Rao, (1981), *Designing and Managing Human Resources Systems.* Oxford Publications, New Delhi.

Parks Canada, (1999), *Parks Canada—Guiding Principles*

and Operating Policies. Ministry of Supply and Services, Ottawa.

Partners for Livable Places, (1981), *Tourism and Communities: Process, Problems, and Solutions,* Washington, DC: Partners for Livable Places.

Pattullo, Polly, (1996), *Last Resorts: The Cost of Tourism in the Caribbean.* London: Cassell.

Patty, A., (1999), Australian sex tourists find their laws back home don't take a vacation. *The World Paper* January-February, p. 16.

Pearce, D. (1981), *Tourist Development,* London: Longman.

Pearce, D., (1989), *Tourism Development (Second Edition), John Wiley, New York.*

Pearce, D., Barbier, E, and Markandy, A., (1987), *Sustainable Development and Cost-Benefit Analysis,* London Environmental Economics Centre, Paper 88-01.

Pearce, D., Markandya, A. and Barbier, E., (1989), *Blueprint for a Green Economy.* London: Earthscan Publications.

Pearce, D.G., (1979), Towards a geography of tourism, *Annals of Tourism Research* 6(3), 243-272.

Pearce, D.G., (1991), *Tourism Today: A Geographical Analysis.* Longman, Harlow.

Pearce, D.G., (1992), *Tourism Organisations,* Longman, Harlow.

Pearce, D.G., (1995), Planning for tourism in the 1990s: An integrated, dynamic multiscale approach, in R. Butler and D.g, Pearce (eds) *Change in Tourism: People, Places and Processes, Routledge, London, 229-244.*

Pearce, P.L., (1991), Analysing tourist attractions, *Journal of Tourism Studies* 2(1), 46-55

Pearce, P.L., (1993), Fundamentals of tourist motivation, in D.G. POearce and R.W. Butler (eds) *Tourism*

Research: Critiques and Challenges, Routledge, London 118-189.

Pearce, P.L., (1995), From cultural shock and culture arrogance for culture exchange, ideas towards sustainable socio-cultural tourism, *Journal of Sustainable Tourism* 3(3), 143-154.

Pelton, R.Y., Aral, C. and Dulles, W., (1998), *Fielding's The World's Most Dangerous Places,* 3rd edn. Fielding, Inc., Redondo Beach, California.

Pennington, M., (1999), Talks pause with dissidents holding Myanmar Embassy. *Kansas City Star 2* October, p. A17.

Peppet, D., (1984), *The Roots of Modern Environmentalism* Croom Helm, London.

Perkins, H., Devlin, P., Simmons, D. and Batty, R., (1993), Recreation and tourism, in A.Memon and H. Perkins (eds) *Environmental Planning in New Zealand,* Dunmore Press, Palmerston North, 169-192.

Perrottet, T., (1996), Grace & fervour, *The Weekend Australian, The Weekend Review: Travel,* 14-15 December, 16.

Pigram, J., (1990), Sustainable tourism: Policy considerations. *Journal of Tourism Studies.*

Pigram, J.J., (1990), Sustainable tourism: policy considerations, *Journal of Tourism Studies,* 1(2), 2-9.

Pilarski, Michael, (1997), *Friends of Trees Guide to Hawaii.* Bellingham, WA: Friends of the Trees.

Pilgrim, J., (1983), *Outdoor Recreation Resource Management.* Croom Helm, Kent.

Pinchot, G., (1968), Ends and means, in R. Nash (ed.) *The American Environment: Readings in the History of Conservation,* Addison-Wesley, Reading, Mass., 59-64.

Pirages, D. and Runci, P., (2000), Ecological interdependence and the spread of infectious disease. In: Cusimano, M.K. (ed.) *Beyond Sovereignty*. Bedford/St Martin's Press, New York, pp. 176-194.

Pizam, A. and Knowles, T., (1994), The European hotel industry, in C.P. Cooper and A. Lockwood (eds) *Progress in Tourism, Recreation and Hospitality Management, Vol, 5* John Wiley, Chichester, 135-152.

Pleumarom, A., (1999), "Tourism, globalisation and sustainable development" in Third World Network Dossier for CSD 7, Third World Network, Malaysia.

Plummer, J.T., (1989), Changing values. *The Futurist* 23(1), 8-13.

Pollock, A. and Benjamin, L., (2001), Shifting Sands: The Tourism Ecosystem in Transformation, DestiCorp Limited.

Poon, A., (1990), Flexible specialisation and small size: the case of Caribbean tourism, *World Development* 18(1), 109-123.

Poon, Auliana, (1993), *Tourism, Technology and Competitive Strategies.* Wallingford, Oxford: CAB International.

Potter, R.B.; Lloyd-Evans, S., (1997/98), "Sun, fun & a rum deal: perspectives on development in the Commonwealth Caribbean" *Focus,* v. 44, no. 4, pp. 19-26.

Potvin, J.R., (1991), *Indicators of Ecologically Sustainable Development, Synthesized Workshop Proceedings,* Canadian Environmental Advisory Council, Ottawa.

Powell, J.M., (1976), *Conservation and Resource Managements in Australia* 1788-1914, *Guardian. Improvers and Profit: An Introductory Strategy,* Oxford University Press, Melbourne.

Poynter, J.M., (1993), *Tour design, marketing and management*, Prentice Hall, New York.

Poynter, M.J., (1993), *Tour Design, Marketing and Management.* The Prentice Hall, London.

Prentice, Richard, (1993), *Tourism and Heritage Attractions.* London: Routledge.

Price, M.F., (ed.), (1996), *People and Tourism in Fragile Environment,* John Wiley & Sons, Chichester.

Pridham, G., (1996), *Tourism Policy in Mediterranean Europe: Towards Sustainable Development?* Occasional Paper 15, University of Bristol, Centre of Mediterranean Studies, Bristol.

Priestley, G.K., Edwards, J.A. and Coccossis, H., (1996), *Sustainable Tourism? European Experiences,* CAB International, Wallingford.

Priestly, Gerda K.J. Arwel Edwards, and Harry Coccossis, (eds.), (1996), *Sustainable Development? A European Experience.* Wallingford, Oxford: CAB International.

Prior, D., (1996), 'Working the network': local authority strategy in the reticulated local state. *Local Government Studies* 22(2), 92-104.

Rames, K.T., (1995), *Structural Adjustment, World Trade and Third World Tourism: An Introduction to the Issues.* Bangkok: ECTWT.

Ramsar, (1992), New opportunities for cooperation in Europe, *Ramsar Newsletter,* 13. 2-7.

Rao, T.V. and Pereira, (1986), *Recent Experiences in Human Resource Development,* Oxford Publications, New Delhi.

RDC, (1997), *The Economic Impact of Recreation and Tourism in the English Countryside. Rural Development Commission and Countryside Commission, London.*

Redclift, M. and Benton, T., (1994), *Social Theory and the Global Environment,* Routledge, London.

Redclift, M., (1987), Sustainable Development and the

market a framework for analysis *Futures* 20(6), 638.

Reed, D., (1990), *The European Bank for Reconstruction and Development: an Environmental Opportunity,* World Wide Fund for Nature, Washington.

Reed, Ralph Thomas, (1952), *American Express: Its Origin and Growth.* New York: Newcomen Society in North America.

Rees, W.E. and Wackernagel. M., (1994), Ecological footprints and appropriated carrying capacity: measuring the natural requirements of the human economy, in A-M. Jansson, M. Hammer. C. Folke and R. Contanza (eds) *Investing in Natural Capital*, Island Press, Washington.

Relph, E., (1976), *Place and Placelessness,* Pion, London.

Renshaw M., (1989), Tour Operations in Collaghan (Eds.), *Travel and Tourism,* Business Education Publishers, Durham.

Richter, L.K., (1988), Indonesian tourism: the good, the bad and the ugly. *Contours* 14(1), 29-30.

Rovinski, Y., (1991), Private reserves, parks and ecotourism in Costa Rica, in Whelan. T. (ed.) *Nature Tourism: Managing for the 'Environment,* Island Press, Washington, 39-57.

Ruitenbeek, H.J., (1991), *Indicators of Ecologically Sustainable Development: Towards New Fundamentals.* Canadian Environmental Advisory Council, Ottawa.

Runte, A., (1974), Yosemite Valley Railroad highway of history, *National Parks and Conversation Magazine: The Environmental Journal,* 48 (December), 4-9.

Runte, A., (1979), *National Parks: The American Experience,* University of Nebraska Press, Lincoln.

Rural Development Commission (RDC), (1992), *Harvesting*

the Benefits from Visitors to the Countryside, Rural Development Commission, London.

Russell, B., (1946), *A History of Western Philosophy,* Counterpoint Unwin Paperbacks, London.

Ryel, R. and Grasse, T., (1991), Marketing ecotourism: attracting the elusive ecotourist, in T. Whelan (ed.) *Nature Tourism,* Island Press, Washington, 164-186.

Sachs, W., (ed.), (1993), *Global Ecology: A New Arena of Political Conflict.* Fernwood Publications, Halifax, NovaScotia.

Sadler, B., (1986), Commentary, II, in *Proceedings of the Workshop On Cumulative Environmental Effects: A Binational Perspective,* the Canadian Environmental Assessment Research Council and the US National Research Council Board on Basic Biology, Ottawa, 71-75.

Sah, J., (2000), Social Mobilisation Manual, Based on Syangja Experience. Social Mobilisation Learning Centre, Institute of Animal and Agriculture Sciences, Tribhuvan University, Ranpur Campus, Nepal.

Sahabat Alam Malaysia (Friends of the Earth Malaysia), 19 Kelawai Road, 10230 Penang, Malaysia, 04-376-930. Works on tourism issues.

Sax, J.L., (1976), America's national parks: their principles, purposes and prospects: *Natural History* 85(8), 57-88.

Sayet; A and Waler. R., (1992), *The New Social Economy,* Blackwell, Oxford.

Schaller, D.T., (1996), *Indigenous Ecotourism and Sustainable Development: The Case of Rio Blanco, Ecuador,* http://...www.geog.umn.edu/-schaller/ Rioblanco Summary htnol.

Schneider, D.M., Godschalk, D.R. and Axler, N., (1978), *The Carrying Capacity Concepts as a Planning*

Tool, Planning Advisory Service Report No. 338, American Planning Association, Chicago.

Scottish Tourist Board, (1994), *Tourism and the Environment*, Scottish Tourist Board, Edinburgh.

Sen, Amartya, (1981); *Poverty and Famines: An Essay on Entitlement and Deprivation.* Oxford. Clarendon Press.

Seth, P.N., (1997), *Successful Tourism Management,* Vol. II Sterling Publication (P) Ltd., New Delhi.

Shackely, M., (1994), The land of Lo, Nepal/Tibet: the first eight months of tourism, *Tourism Management* 15; 17-26.

Shah, Kishore, and Vasanti Gupta, (2000), *Tourism, the Poor and Other Stakeholders: Experience in Asia.* London, ODI.

Shankland, R., (1970), *Steve Mather of the National Parks,,* 3rd end, Alfred A. Knopf, New York.

Shaw, D.J.B., (1991), The Soviet Union, in Hall, D.R. (ed.) *Tourism and economic development in Eastern Europe and the Soviet Union,* Belhaven Press, London and Halstead, New York, 119-141.

Shelby, B. and Heberlein, T.A., (1984), A conceptual framework for carrying capacity determination, *Leisure Sciences* 6(4), 433-451.

Sheldon, P., (2002), Information Technology Contributions to Biodiversity in Tourism, in Tourism, Biodiversity and Information, di Castri, F. and Balaji, V., (eds.), Backhuys, Leiden. The Netherlands, pp. 449-456.

Sheldon, P.J., (1989), Tour Wholesaling, in Witt S., and Moutinho L., (Eds.) *Tourism, Marketing and Management Handbook*, Prentice Hall, U.K.

Sheldon, Pauline, (1997), *Tourism Information Systems.* Wallingford, Oxford: CAB International.

Sierra Club Adventure Travel Guides, Sierra Club Books,

730 Polk Street, San Francisco, CA 94109; (805) 965-3452. For "Adventuring In...."travel guide series.

Simon, F.L. (1995), Tourism development in transition economies: the Cuba case. *The Columbia Journal of World Business.* , v. 30 (Spring 1995) p. 26-40.

Simpson, Pally, and Geoffrey Wall, (1999), 'Consequences of resort development: a comparative study.' *Tourism Management* 20: 283-296.

Sinclair, M. Thea, (1998), 'Tourism and economic development: a survey.' *The Journal of Development Studies* 34 (5): 1-51.

Sindiga, Isaac, (1996), "Domestic tourism in Kenya.' *Annals of Tourism Research 23* (I): 19-31.

Singh, Shalini, (1997), "Developing Human Resources for the Tourism Industry in India." *Journal of Travel and Tourism,* IITTM Vol. 1, No. I, Gwalior.

Singh, Tej Vir, H. Leon Theuns, and Frank M. Co. (1989), *Towards Appropriate Tourism: The Case of Developing Countries.* New York: Peter Lang.

Smith, S.L., (1989), *Tourism Analyses,* Longman, Harlow.

Smith, S.L.J., (1988), Defining Tourism, a supply side view, *Annals of Tourism Research,* 15 (2), Pergamon, London.

Smith, Stephen L. J., (1995), *Tourism Analysis. A Handbook.* Essex: Longman Scientific & Technical.

Smith, V. (ed.), (1977), *Hosts and Guests: The Anthropology of Tourism,* University of Pennsylvania Press, Philadelphia.

Smith, V., (1989), Eskime tourism micro-models and marginal men, in V.I., Smith (ed.) *Hosts and Guests: The Anthropology of Tourism,* 2nd edn., University of Pennsylvania Press, Philadelphia, 55-82.

Smith. V., (1996), The Inuit as hosts: heritage and wilderness tourism in Nunavut, in M.F. Price (ed.) *People and*

Tourism in Fragile Environments, John Wiley, Chichester, 33-50.

Sofield, T., (1991), Sustainable ethnic tourism in the South Pacific: some principles, *Journal of Tourism Studies,* 2. 56-72.

Sofield, T.H.B., (1996), Anuha Island Resort, Solomon Islands: a case study of failure in R. Butler and T. Hinch (eds) *Tourism and Indigenous Peoples:* International Thomson Business Press, London, 176-202.

Sooacmalelagi, L., Hunter, S. and Brown. S., (1996), Alternate tourism development in Western Samoa. Paper presented at 3rd Pacific Indigenous Business Conference 11-13 December 1996 Oxford Koala Hotel, Sydney.

Springate, C, (1991), Where eagles dare. *Green Magazine,* 3(3), 26-29.

Sproule, Keith W., (1996), Community-Based Ecotourism Development: Identifying Partners in the Process. The Ecotourism Equation: Measuring the Impacts. Bulletin Series Yale School of Forestry and Environmental Studies, Number 99. New Haven CT: Yale University, 233-250.

Stabler, M.J., (ed.), (1997), *Tourism and Sustainability, Principles to Practice,* CAB International Wallingford.

Stanfield, C.A. and Rickert, J.E., (1970), The recreational business district, *Journal of Leisure Research* 2(3), 213-225.

Stankey, G.H. McCool, S.F, and Stokes, G.L., (1984), Limits of acceptable change: a new framework for managing the Bob Marshall Wilderness Complex, *Western Wildlands* 103(3), 33-37.

Stoffle, R.W. Last, C, and Evans, M., (1979), Reservation

based tourism: implications of tourism attitudes for Native American economic development. *Human Organisation 38(3)* 300-306.

Stratford, A.H., (1993), *Air Transport Economics in the Supersonic Era,* The Macmillan.

Suresh, K.T., (ed), (1994), *Tourism Issues in Public Domain.* Bangalore: Equations.

Syratt G., (1995), Manual of Travel Agency Practice, Butterworth, Oxford.

Taylot, G. (1995), The community approach: does it really work: *Tourism Management* 16(7), 487-489.

Thompson, J., (1991), East Europe's dark dawn. *National Geographic,* 179(5), 37-69.

Timothy, Dallen J., and Geoffrey Wall, (1997), "Selling to tourists: Indonesian street vendors.' *Annals of Tourism Research* 24 (2): 322-340.

Turnock, D., (1979), Water management resources in Romania, *GeoJournal,* 3,609-622.

Wet Tropics Management Authority, (1995), *Draft Wet Tropics Plan* WTMA, Cairns.

Wheeller, Brain, (1992), "Is progressive tourism appropriate?" *Tourism Management* 13(1) : 104-105.

Wheeller, Brian, (1991/1997), "Tourism's troubled times: responsible tourism is not the answer.' Reprinted in Lesley France (Ed.), *The Earthscan Reader in Sustainable Tourism,* pp. 61-67. London, Earthscan.

Wilkinson, P.P., (1989), "Strategies for future development in island microstates", *Annuals of Tourism Research* 16(2) : 156-177.

Williams, P., (1990), "Tourism Technology and Environment", *Journal of Travel Research,* Vol. XXIX, No.2, pp. 55-56.

Index